The Primate Zoonoses

This book offers an accessible and up-to-date reference on primate zoonoses. Recent years have witnessed a rise in human diseases zoonotically transferred from wild primates, with outbreaks such as Ebola and concerns regarding newly emerging infections. The authors go beyond simply providing an inventory of diseases, helping readers to understand how and why they are transmitted. Important consideration is given to the contemporary cultural and ecological factors involved.

Loretta A. Cormier is Associate Professor in the Department of Anthropology at the University of Alabama, USA.

Pauline E. Jolly is Professor in the Department of Epidemiology (School of Public Health) at the University of Alabama, USA.

The Primate Zoonoses
Culture Change and Emerging Diseases

Loretta A. Cormier and Pauline E. Jolly

LONDON AND NEW YORK

First published 2018 by Routledge

2 Park Square, Milton Park, Abingdon, Oxfordshire OX14 4RN
52 Vanderbilt Avenue, New York, NY 10017

Routledge is an imprint of the Taylor & Francis Group, an informa business

First issued in paperback 2020

British Library Cataloguing-in-Publication Data
A catalogue record for this book is available from the British Library

Library of Congress Cataloging-in-Publication Data
A catalog record has been requested for this book

ISBN: 978-1-138-21950-2 (hbk)
ISBN: 978-0-367-60732-6 (pbk)

Typeset in Times New Roman
by Apex CoVantage, LLC

Contents

Tables vi
Preface vii

1 The ecological context 1

2 Viruses 21

3 Protozoa 55

4 Bacteria 83

5 Helminths 105

6 Concluding remarks 109

References 112
Index 133

Tables

2.1 DNA Viruses 25
2.2 RNA Viruses 45
3.1 Enteric Protozoa 61
3.2 Vector-Borne Protozoa 73
4.1 Bacteria 99
5.1 Helminths 107

Preface

This Routledge *Focus* short form book addresses emerging primate zoonoses in the context of culture change. Primate zoonoses are increasingly becoming a global concern. Many parasites of wild primates can be readily passed to humans due to our close biological relationship with nonhuman primates. A number of recent and emerging diseases have wrought this out including chikungunya, Zika, HIV/SIV, and *Plasmodium knowlesi* malaria. Wild primates are also implicated in the spread of the Ebola virus. Although the natural host is believed to be bats, humans have been infected after contact with African great apes, which presumably contracted it originally from bats or another host species.

An important aim of the book is to describe the cultural and ecological contexts in which the sharing of parasites occurs. For example, SIV is an ancient disease in several wild primate species, and the hunting of bushmeat has been implicated in its transmission to humans. However, the culture history of human ancestors using wild primates as food has been documented as early as *Homo erectus* in the archaeological record. It is important to understand the contemporary and ecological factors such as deforestation, development, and globalization that have created conditions that facilitated the AIDS pandemic. An additional concern is that when a parasite enters into a new population, the parasite may evolve and become more virulent. Both Zika and chikungunya are wild primate viruses that were first documented in humans in the mid-20th century, both with mild symptoms in humans. But as they have spread more widely in the human population, they have become more neurotoxic, as in the tragic cases of infants infected *in utero* being born with microcephaly and other neurological issues.

The main focus of the book is the spread of parasites from wild primates to humans. Nonhuman primates have long been used as experimental models in research, testing of vaccines and antibiotics for human diseases, because many are often susceptible. But here, the primary concern is with those parasites that have spread in natural contexts. Where applicable, mention is given to research centers or zoos where captive primates have unintentionally been infected with human parasites. For example, there are cases of African primates in U.S. zoos that have tested seropositive for the vector-borne American *Trypanosoma*, presumably due to being housed in outdoor environments. Attention is also given to the acquisition of human parasites by wild primates, which is becoming more common in nature preserves with ecotourism. Ironically, the preserves that were intended to protect wild primates can increase their potential for exposure to novel human parasites. Such anthroponoses in wild primates can have potentially devastating effects on endangered wild primate populations.

The first part of this book addresses the ecological context for wild primate zoonoses, including a discussion of emerging infectious disease, modes of transmission, and cross-infection. Also addressed are anthropogenic contexts that have altered host-parasite relationships and facilitated parasite sharing. The remainder of the book addresses four broad categories of parasites: viruses, protozoa, bacteria, and helminths. For each category, the parasites known to be shared by humans and wild primates are discussed.

1 The ecological context

Emerging infectious disease

Nonhuman primates contribute substantially to emerging infectious diseases in humans. Of the approximately 75% of emerging pathogens that are also zoonotic, nearly 25% are found in nonhuman primates (Cleaveland et al. 2007; Taylor et al. 2001). Both the major taxa of the organisms (viruses, bacteria, protozoa, and helminths) and their mode of transmission play important roles in the potential for a given parasite to become an emerging infection in humans. According to Taylor et al. (2001), although virtually all of the helminths (parasitic worms) can be considered potentially zoonotic, they are far less likely to be the source of an emerging infection than viruses or protozoa are. More narrowly, considering helminth cross-transmission among human and nonhuman primates, the literature review for this book identified numerous studies demonstrating broad susceptibility among species in the order Primates to each other's helminths. However, they are rarely the source of emerging infections. Two notable exceptions are the lymphatic filariasis and the larvae (cercariae) of schistosomiasis, which are both vector-borne. All vector-borne parasites have a higher risk of becoming emerging infectious disease than parasites transmitted through other means have (Taylor et al. 2001). The ecological context is also of paramount importance in understanding under what conditions any given parasite may potentially be spread among species.

Zoonoses and anthroponoses

The World Health Organization (WHO) defines a zoonosis as any disease or infection that is naturally transmissible from vertebrate animals to humans (WHO 2016a). The phrase "naturally transmitted" excludes infections that are intentionally induced in laboratory settings. In the past, humans have also been the subject of experimental infection with animal pathogens. One example involves studies in the 1960s when over 200 prisoners were inoculated with various strains of wild primate malarias to determine if infections could be established in humans (Coatney 1968; Cormier 2011). Many species of wild primates have been used as models in the study of human diseases, particularly Rhesus macaques, chimpanzees, owl monkeys, and squirrel monkeys. However, acquisition under experimental conditions should not technically be considered cases of zoonotic or anthroponotic disease, although such studies can provide information about potential susceptibility.

A gray area exists when considering parasite exchange among captive nonhuman primates. In the literature, the phrase "natural transmission" or "natural infection" is sometimes applied to situations where human and nonhuman primates have been exposed to and acquired each other's parasites, such as in zoos and in primate research centers. Describing such infections as natural is problematic and can be misleading, for although the infections were not acquired through experimental induction of parasites, they are also not natural settings. One example is the protozoa *Trypanosoma cruzi*, the agent of Chagas disease. The protozoa is indigenous to the Neotropics, but can also survive in the southernmost areas of the United States. In southern U.S. zoos, Asian and African species of primates have been found to harbor the parasite (see Chapter 3), but the parasite does not exist in their natural habitats. Primate sanctuaries with semi-captive primates also represent a gray area. These facilities often take in rescued orphans or former pets that would not be able to survive independently in the wild. Although they have access to natural habitat, they are also often in frequent contact with humans. In some contexts, even primates in wildlife preserves that sponsor ecotourism may not be in entirely natural conditions for they may become well habituated to humans.

Anthroponoses are infectious diseases of humans that can be naturally transmitted to animals. In the broadest sense, the term "primate zoonosis" can elide the distinction between anthroponosis and zoonosis. Because humans *are* primates, the primate zoonoses are those diseases that may cross between members of the taxonomic order Primates. In many cases among primate species, the barrier preventing an infectious agent in a host species from cross-infecting a novel species may not be due as much to biological differences as to ecological differences that prevent two primate species from coming into contact. For our purposes here, the primary focus is on wild primate diseases that cross over into human populations.

The term "pathogen" is often used to describe an infectious agent, but some caution should be used, for not all infectious agents cause pathogenic symptoms in their hosts. In Nunn and Altizer's (2006:3) work on primate infectious disease, they prefer the broad term "parasite," defined as any organism that lives on and draws nutrients from a host, including both microparasites and macroparasites, drawing on the distinction made by Anderson and May (1991). Microparasites have direct reproduction within a host and include viruses, bacteria, fungi, and protozoa. Macroparasites are those that do not have direct reproduction within the host and include helminths (e.g., parasitic worms) and arthropods (e.g., ticks and mites).

A parasite may infect several different types of hosts, differentiated below (Hubálek and Rudolf 2010; Salfeder et al. 1992; Soloman et al. 2015). Broadly, the term "host" refers to any species that has been detected to harbor a parasite. A reservoir is one or more species that serve as the natural, long-term host of a parasite, and ensures the persistence of the parasite. Some parasites, such as those involved in vector-borne diseases, have both a primary (definitive) and secondary (intermediate) host. The host in which a parasite completes sexual maturity is the primary host, while other stages of the life cycle occur in the secondary host. For example, among the plasmodia that cause malaria, mosquitoes are the primary host while a variety of vertebrates serve as secondary hosts. An amplifying host is a species that harbors the parasite in sufficient concentrations such that it is able to propagate the parasite. In contrast, a dead-end host is one that may be infected, but is not able to transmit the parasite to others. Accidental hosts are those in which the parasite is not usually found; such hosts may be dead-end hosts or could potentially become amplifying hosts.

Due to long-term host and parasite co-evolution, infections may be relatively benign among members of the reservoir population. Parasites that are virulent enough to kill their hosts are less likely to spread than those whose hosts can survive to continue to propagate the organism. However, in vector-borne diseases, parasites may continue to be quite virulent in human reservoirs, who serve as secondary hosts. McNeill (1976) has argued that in vector-borne diseases, in the triad of the host-vector-parasite, "benignness" can only be accomplished in the relationship between the parasite and the vector or the parasite and the secondary host, but not both. Further, given that vectors are short-lived, it is more likely that benignness would involve in the vector-parasite relationship than in the human-parasite relationship. Ewald (1994) proposed the *adaptive severity hypothesis* to explain the persistence of virulence in vector-borne diseases. He argues that in non-vector-borne diseases, the host has to be well enough to move and spread the disease. But in vector-borne diseases, it is not necessary for the secondary host to be well enough to be mobile, for the vector itself is mobile and is able to spread the parasite. Moreover, virulence is associated with higher parasite densities, which means that vectors can be more readily infected. Thus, virulence in the secondary host may benefit the parasite. Incapacitated secondary hosts are also easy targets for the vector.

Spillover, spillback, and spread

Parasite amplification in a host population is necessary for the parasite to achieve sufficient densities to be effectively transmitted. Reservoir hosts are amplification hosts, but amplification may also occur in spillover infections. In spillover infections, a parasite of a reservoir population comes in contact with a novel host population (Weaver 2005). Spillover infections may result in high levels of virulence, and secondary spillovers are also possible.

Cleaveland et al. (2007) make an important distinction between "samplers" and "spreaders" in spillover events. Samplers are involved in situations where spillover occurs in a localized population, while spreaders are involved in pandemic disease, such as in the case of HIV and Ebola viruses.

In the case of pandemic HIV, most scholars attribute its origin to a host switch from chimpanzees to humans (see Chapter 2). Its propagation in the human population from samples in rural sub-Saharan Africa to spreaders in urban cities in Africa and then globally are due to a number of social and cultural factors (Mayer et al. 2008; Reid 2009). These include the development and urbanization of Africa, which increased communication and travel between rural and urban areas. Medical technology also played a role in the early spread of HIV through the reuse of contaminated needles and blood transfusions. Intravenous drug users also became spreaders due to needle sharing. Human sexual behaviors contributed to the spread of HIV for individuals who had contact with multiple partners, particularly homosexual men and sex workers and their clients. And critical to the spread of HIV was globalization with its consequent ease of international travel, which spread the virus worldwide. More recent emerging diseases may have similar potential. Two examples are Zika and chikungunya viruses. Both were first isolated in the mid-20th century in both African wild primates and human populations (see Chapter 2), but they resulted in relatively benign illnesses that did not spread widely. In recent years, global epidemics have occurred with both of these viruses, which have diversified with potential for neurotoxicity in humans.

The spread of Ebola shares many characteristics with HIV since it may be transmitted through blood and body fluids, but it may involve a longer infection chain (from bats to apes to humans), similar to the Hendra virus in bats, horses, and humans. Quammen (2012) describes a case study of a Hendra virus outbreak in a horse stable in eastern Australia (Quammen 2012). Fruit bats, which are the reservoir, had been roosting in fig trees in a horse pasture, and a horse likely was exposed to the virus by eating grass contaminated with bat urine, feces, or saliva. The virus then spilled over into other horses at the stables, manifesting in virulent infection, with half a dozen horses dying within 12 hours. The horses became effective amplifying agents, and the virus had a secondary spillover into three men who were caretakers of the horses, one of whom died.

This case study of the Hendra virus is relevant to understanding the transmission of Ebola virus in humans. The reservoir for the Ebola virus remains unknown but is suspected to be in fruit bats (Cárdenas and Basler 2013). The virus is virulent in chimpanzees and gorillas, and there are documented cases of humans acquiring the virus from great apes (see Chapter 2). One might argue that Ebola is not a true primate zoonosis, because the known primate amplifiers were not the reservoir hosts. However, if some humans acquire Ebola directly from wild primates, arguably it qualifies as a primate zoonosis, for in these cases, the end of the infection chain is from wild primate to human. Thus, it is not necessary for a primate to be the natural reservoir for a primate zoonotic infection to occur.

Modes of transmission

Zoonotic parasites are transmitted to humans through three key routes: direct contact, indirect contact, or shared vectors (Taylor et al. 2001). Direct contact involves contact with blood or body fluids. Such direct contact typically occurs in hunting contexts through exposure to blood and body fluids but may also occur through bites and scratches from animals. Pet-keeping also provides a context for exposure to blood and body fluids, but due to close contact may also include inhalation. Indirect contact most often occurs with exposure to contact with animals feces, particularly those that are waterborne, but may also include contact with fomites or distant consumption of bushmeat. Vector-borne zoonotic diseases involve agents that transmit parasites between animals and humans. The primary vectors responsible are arthropods, but gastropod vectors and helminth parasites are involved in schistosomiasis. After infection, some parasites may also be transmitted vertically from mother to child during pregnancy or childbirth.

Direct contact and indirect contact

Hunting activities are the primary means through which humans have direct contact with nonhuman primates. Potential for parasite transfer occurs when hunters are exposed to blood, body fluids, or other body tissues through handling bushmeat. Hunters also risk being bitten or scratched by frightened or wounded animals. Individuals involved in the butchering of bushmeat are at even greater risk through accidental cuts. Once a parasite spills over into the human population, human-to-human contact may continue through routes including sexual contact, blood donation, organ transfer, or other exposure to body fluids, depending on the particular parasite involved.

Primate pet-keeping poses risks for parasite transmission. Direct exposure may occur from bites and scratches from pets, but close contact may also pose risk of transmission of parasites in air-borne droplets. Occupational exposure is another context where direct contact occurs with nonhuman primates, including workers in zoos, primate sanctuaries, and primate research centers. Laboratory workers who handle nonhuman primate blood products are at risk for accidental exposure and also for bites and injuries when they handle animals. Laboratory and zoo workers are also responsible for maintaining the hygiene of the animals kept and come into contact with feces, urine, and other body fluids when cleaning cages.

An additional means of direct contact with potential to spread parasites is xenotransplantation. The World Health Organization defines animal-to-human xenotransplantation as

> living cells, tissues, or organs of animal origin and have human body fluids, cells, tissues or organs that have *ex vivo* with these living, xenogeneic materials, has the potential to constitute an alternative to the material of human origin and bridge the shortfall in human material for transplantation.
>
> (WHO 2016b)

A number of such procedures have used nonhuman primates. Keith Reemtsma made one of the first attempts involving transplantation of chimpanzee kidneys into patients with renal failure (Reemtsma et al. 1964). Reemtsma performed 13 of these transplants and most failed within 4–8 weeks due to either rejection or infection; however, one patient survived 9 months (Cooper et al. 2015). In 1984, an infant, "Baby Fae," made international headlines when she received a baboon heart transplant, but she survived only 20 days after the procedure (Bailey et al. 1985). In 1992, a baboon-to-human liver transplant was attempted, but the patient survived only 70 days (Starzl et al. 1993). A baboon-to-human bone marrow transplant was attempted in 1995 in an AIDS patient (Ildstad 1996). Although it failed to engraft, the patient did show temporary improvement after the procedure (Fricker 1996). As of March 2016, over 120,000 people in the U.S. were awaiting organ donation (HRSA 2016). Despite failures, potential still exists for procedures to be modified in the future. However, this raises ethical considerations, for it would require a mass breeding program of wild primates to meet the needs. Additionally, there is increasing concern, particularly for nonhuman primates, that known or unknown parasites may be spread.

The most significant way that parasites can be transmitted indirectly between humans and animals is through water-borne infections (Cotruvo et al. 2004). Here, parasites are typically transmitted through the fecal-oral route, but transmission may also involve exposure to urine or animal carcasses through parasites in the soil. Risk is highest in rural areas, where sanitation may be poor and humans and nonhuman primates share the same water sources. Human infections may arise from utilizing contaminated water for drinking, food preparation, or bathing. Keeping pets in the household may involve direct exposure to primate species. When raised near primate habitats, livestock may also be a source of infection for primates. Indirect contact may also occur through exposure to fomites, which are any objects contaminated with parasites that remain infectious for a period of time. A wide range of objects can carry fomites, including skin cells, clothing and bedding, eating utensils, and furniture surfaces.

Vector-borne transmission

Vector-borne parasites have the most complicated ecologies, for transmission involves the triad of the vector (primary host), animal host (secondary host), and the parasite. Vector-borne parasites also present some of the most serious challenges in controlling zoonotic disease due to the mobility of the vector. Mosquitoes are responsible for most of the vector-borne diseases; most others are caused by other arthropods. Vector-borne parasites that share human and wild primate hosts include viruses, protozoa, and helminths.

Of the approximately 49 genera and over 3,000 species of known mosquitoes, only a few are important in parasite transmission between humans and wild primates. *Aedes* species are most important for the transmission of viral diseases such as dengue, chikungunya, yellow fever, and Zika. *Anopheles* species are most important for the transmission of malarial diseases.

Two key cycles, sylvatic and urban, have been described for vector-borne infections, but a variety of intermediate stages may also come into play (e.g., Harper 2011; Higgs and Beaty 2005; Weaver 2005). The sylvatic or jungle cycle is enzootic with parasites circulating between mosquitoes and a single or multiple reservoir host species. In the strictest sense, the sylvatic cycles only involves infection of wild animals. However, humans may become accidental hosts of sylvatic parasites when they enter forest zones for a variety of activities, such as hunting game or extracting forest resources. Depending on the parasite, human beings may become dead-end hosts and transmit the infection no further, or if a competent host, they can potentially transfer the infection to other people.

In the urban or domestic cycle, spillover from the enzootic cycle occurs and humans become a source of parasite amplification. In densely populated cities with multiple susceptible human beings available, widespread epidemic disease may occur, with the potential for humans to become a new reservoir host. Today, with the increasing availability and ease of international travel, parasite transfer may move beyond the boundaries of the sylvatic and urban cycles in a localized area and spread globally.

The relationship between the urban and sylvatic cycle may involve several species of mosquito that are adapted to different ecological niches and have different feeding preferences.

Bridge vectors are those that acquire a parasite from an infected wild animal and subsequently transmit the agent to the human host (Go et al. 2014). Bridge vectors are important in maintaining the sylvatic cycle, for they may allow transmission of parasites vertically in the forest canopy, where it can continue among arboreal primates with forest-adapted mosquito species. In such cases, even though an urban epidemic may be contained, the parasites can persist in the interepidemic periods in forest monkeys with potential for new epidemics to emerge. This is perhaps the greatest challenge for public health. Vector-control measures such as insecticide-treated mosquito nets, local pesticide spraying, house screening, and removal of stagnant water in human domestic areas can be effective in the short-term, but the potential remains for re-emergence if the parasites are maintained in wild forest species in interepidemic periods.

The relationship between the sylvatic and urban cycles in primate parasite transmission is typically typically leads to long-term endemic (enzootic) cycles with accidental spillover into urban areas, for this is the node in the cycle that is most important to human health. However, spillover may occur from human populations into wild primates and other animals. Yellow fever and some forms of malaria (*P. malariae*, *P. simium*) were introduced by humans into the wild primate populations, likely around the time of colonization, and the diseases subsequently became endemic in wild primate populations, establishing a new enzootic cycle among wild primates (see Chapter 2). Similarly, when Asian dengue was introduced to Africa, spillover occurred into wild primate populations into a new enzootic cycle. However, there is no evidence that dengue has become enzootic in New World primates, despite its presence in an urban cycle in Latin America (see Chapter 2). The urban cycle can also be maintained in dormancy by overwintering of some species of mosquitoes. Overwintering involves hibernation of mosquitoes and other insects under colder conditions (Leather et al. 1995).

The nonhuman primates

Overview of nonhuman primates

Today, there are approximately 500 recognized species and 79 genera of living primates, with many more differentiated subspecies located in South and Central America, Africa, and Asia (Estrada et al. 2017). Classifications have changed over time, particularly with the development of molecular genetics, so that in some cases groups designated as subspecies are reclassified as separate species, and in others, subspecies are merged into a single genus. Reclassification has also occurred over time at the level of the genus and family and at even higher levels. For example, in the past, humans and the great apes were separated into families of hominids and pongids. Today, hominids include both the great apes and humans, with the term "hominin" now referring specifically to early and modern humans.

Colloquially, primates are divided into four categories: humans, monkeys, apes, and prosimians. Two taxonomic conventions exist for dividing the two suborders of primates, which differ in where the tarsiers are placed. The tarsiers are similar to the prosimians in terms of their behavioral ecology, but are evolutionarily more closely related to monkeys, apes, and humans. In gradistic classification, the tarsiers are grouped with the suborder "Prosimii" with the lemurs and lorises; all other primates are grouped under "Anthropoidea." In cladistic classification, the tarsiers are grouped in the suborder "Haplorrhini" with monkeys, apes, and humans, while the suborder "Strepsirrhini" only contains the lemurs and lorises. The terms strepsirrhine and haplorrhine refer specifically to nose morphology (wet versus dry rhinarium), which is one of the features that separate the lemurs and lorises from the other primates.

Among wild primates, a number of factors influence their susceptibility to disease. In Nunn and Altizer's (2006) book *Infectious Diseases in Primates*, the authors explore the relationship between primate socioecology and the risk of acquiring infectious diseases. Group size, group composition, population density, mating patterns, social status, habitat use, extent of range, and multi-species associations may all affect the patterns of infectious disease within primate groups. For example, larger-sized groups tend to have less risk per individual for exposure to vectors than do smaller-sized groups. Primate groups that form multi-species associations have greater risk of exposure to novel parasites. These patterns of parasite transmission affect not only the health of primate species but also affect which primate species pose greater risks to humans.

Problems with surveillance

Accurate epidemiological surveillance for the presence of infectious disease in human populations can often be challenging, but the difficulties are even greater when attempting to make assessments in nonhuman primate populations. One major problem is access. Wild primates must be first located, and then sometimes captured for blood samples to be taken. Even among hunter-gatherers that utilize wild primates for food, locating game in the forest may be an all-day enterprise that may not be successful (Cormier 2003). The method of location and capture introduces a number of different types of bias into a study. One is that the primate community's behavioral and ecological characteristics influence which types of primates are able to be obtained for study. These include variables such as habitat and range, species size and group size, population density, and a number of other characteristics that influence which animals can be located and captured and which are more difficult to find.

Differing primate species occupy different types of environmental zones and ecological niches (Strier 2011; Fleagle 1999). Species that occupy savannah and grassland habitats are easier to locate than are dense forest species. In the literature review for this book, grivets (*Chlorocebus*) and baboons (*Papio* spp.) are notably overrepresented in studies. Although all primates make some use of both terrestrial and arboreal habitats, terrestrial species are easier to locate than arboreal species are. Among arboreal species, different levels of the forest canopy are utilized, including the understory, canopy, and emergent layers. Those primates who tend to occupy the understory or subcanopy are easier to locate than those who occupy the highest emergent layers of the forest. Within the forest, species may prefer primary forest, secondary forest, or disturbed forest. Those species that occupy dense, undisturbed primary forest are more difficult to locate than those that prefer peripheral areas.

Individual size and group size also affect the ability to locate a given species. Larger-bodied primates are easier to visualize in the forest than smaller-bodied primates are. Group size varies among species. For example, among New World primates, it is not uncommon for squirrel monkeys to live in groups of 100 individuals, but tamarins and marmosets typically are composed of an adult female, two adult males, and two immature twins. Clearly, it is easier to locate animals that have larger group size than those that have smaller group size. Other important factors are range and population density. Some species occupy broad ranges and others have more narrowed territory that they typically utilize. Population density affects ability to locate animals. Rarer endangered species are more difficult to locate than those that are more abundant. Speed of movement may also have an effect. Slow-moving howler monkeys are easier to capture than rapidly moving capuchins are. Howler monkeys also make loud vocalizations to advertise territory, which can make them easier to locate.

In Africa, researchers often make use of the bushmeat market for surveillance of wild primate parasites. Such contexts of opportunistic sampling contain similar types of bias. The primates that are most likely to be hunted are not representative of all primates, nor are they necessarily the ones most likely to spread an infection, particularly if it is vector-borne. In South

America, health assessments of primates are often conducted in primate relocation programs, such as when natural habitats are flooded for dams. Otherwise, the highly arboreal New World primates must be located and trapped, anesthetized, or killed for assessment. In recent years, advances in molecular genetics have led to developments in testing for parasites in fecal samples that do not require the capture or killing of animals to document seropositivity. However, some of the problems still remain, for animals still have to be located to be able to collect feces, and such collection is more difficult among animals that occupy higher levels of the canopy or denser areas of the forest.

Another challenge in studies among wild primates involves determining pathogenicity and host competence. Although it is sometimes possible to isolate a parasite in a species, oftentimes the indicators used are seropositivy and seroprevalence, which measure the existence of antibodies to a parasite within an individual (seropositive) or across a sample group (seroprevalence). Such measures are limited in understanding pathogenicity in a species, except that it is clear that the individuals tested were able to survive the infection. High levels of seroprevalence in a population may suggest a potential reservoir population. In some cases, blood or other samples are taken from animals when their carcasses are found, which may indicate that the parasite contributed to death. Wolfe et al. (2005) has used the term "viral chatter" to describe the presence of large numbers in a sample that are seropositive, which would also be relevant to other types of parasites. They argue that such chatter can be important sentinels in signaling an increased presence of a parasite, which could lead to a human-adapted parasite emerging and spreading among human populations.

Research among captive animals in zoos and laboratories provide better evidence of the pathogenicity of a parasite, for the course of a clinical disease can be observed and documented. However, when a parasite is acquired outside of experimental inoculation, it can be difficult to determine the source. A facility may contain multiple enclosures containing primates of many different species, but because they are in relatively close proximity, parasites can be transmitted from one group to another through tracking feces when cleaning cages or by vectors that have access to multiple species.

Anthropogenic contexts

Deforestation and development

Development and deforestation not only endanger many of the world's wild primate species, but also create contexts that foster the exchange of parasites. The effect of human beings on the environment has resulted in massive changes in the landscape due to both a growing population size and a wide variety of cultural innovations that have allowed humans to modify the landscape more effectively to meet their needs. Major land use changes include deforestation and forest fragmentation, agriculture (crops and livestock), resource extraction (logging and mining), and infrastructure development (roadways, railways, dams). Such changes may foster parasite exchange by bringing wild primates directly into closer proximity to humans, but also may change the ecological relationships among hosts, parasites, and vectors in a variety of ways.

Inseparable from landscape changes is the effect of explosive increases in the human population. The current world population is approximately 7.3 billion people, with an average of one birth every 8 seconds and one death every 11 seconds (U.S. Census Bureau 2016). Advances in medical technology have both decreased infant mortality rates and increased human life expectancies, which contribute to population growth. From a long-term evolutionary perspective, it is difficult to determine precisely human population numbers at different points in history. A rough estimate by Livi-Bacci (2012) suggests that the human population was around 1 million in the Paleolithic Age, 10 million in the Neolithic Age, 100 million in the Bronze Age, 1 billion during the Industrial Revolution, and will be a projected 10 billion by the mid-21st century. That can be contrasted with the estimated 300,000 remaining chimpanzees (*Pan troglodytes*) (Butynski 2003).

Population changes affect the ways that diseases are transmitted among human populations and between animals and humans. In the Paleolithic Age, prior to the emergence of agriculture and the associated rise in population, the likelihood for epidemic outbreak was smaller. This was true not only because humans were not living in close association with the animals they were later to domesticate, but also because of lower population densities. A local spillover from animals into humans was unlikely to spread far, because hunting-and-gathering populations lived in small, widely dispersed groups (Kurpiers et al. 2016).

Forest fragmentation, in some cases, may pose a greater risk than clear-cutting the forest. Wolfe et al. (2005) have described some of the effects and consequences of behaviors that fragment the forest. Logging may involve the selection and extraction of high-value timber. Both roads that are built to access forest products and the patchy removal of trees can fragment the forest. Here the potential for parasite exchange is higher than in clear-cutting, for there is greater contact between humans and forest animals. For groups that hunt wildlife, building of roads gives a greater number of access points to animals and can make hunting more efficient. Another consequence of roads is that while they are beneficial in providing people living in remote areas better access to health care facilities, they also increase the potential for a localized pathogen to spread broadly when introduced to a larger human community.

Loss of biodiversity

Human modification of the landscape affects parasite transmission in complex ways, involving both the loss of animals' habitats and the loss of species biodiversity that may affect hosts, parasites, and vectors. Such changes include changes in the environmental niche to which species are adapted, changes in the composition of species in a niche and in the spatial distribution of species, and possible environmental contamination.

In theory, loss of biodiversity could be assumed to reduce the transmission of zoonotic infections through reducing the population of reservoir hosts. By this logic, if there were fewer wild animals, there would be fewer diseases that could cross over into humans. However, the evidence suggests that loss of biodiversity tends to increase risk. In a metanalysis of the literature, Gottdenker et al. (2014) found that land use changes increased pathogen transmission, particularly for zoonotic infections, in 56.9% of the studies reviewed, while they decreased pathogen transmission in only 10.4% of the studies.

Keesing et al. (2010) described a number of ways that loss of biodiversity increases risk to humans (in terms of both disease transmission and emergence), including parasite prevalence, host range, and host switching. Loss of biodiversity can affect prevalence rates of parasites. Decreased diversity and lowered population densities of reservoir hosts means that there are fewer animals available to infect, increasing the levels of parasite load across the population. Here, humans coming into contact with any given animal are more likely to encounter an infected animal (and are also more likely to encounter an animal with a high parasite load). In addition, loss of natural reservoir may facilitate host switching.

Loss of biodiversity may also affect the host range of the parasite. When a parasite has a wide natural host range, it may include species that are less competent hosts and are less likely to be able to transmit the parasite. Here, loss of biodiversity may selectively reduce less competent hosts and increase more competent hosts. Keesing et al. (2010) provide several examples of this process occurring with West Nile virus and U.S. bird species. But they raise the critical question of *why* more competent hosts should be differentially affected by loss of biodiversity.

By analogy, they point to patterns in resiliency and adaptability in plants. Weedy plants tend to become more abundant when biodiversity declines, but also tend to be more competent hosts than less weedy plants. This may have a relationship to the theory of r/K selection (MacArthur and Wilson

1967). Strictly speaking, the theory suggests that parental investment differs in rapidly reproducing species (r-selected) versus slowly reproducing species (K-selected). But as applied here, r/K selection suggests that rapidly reproducing, short-lived species may invest less in immune defenses than slowly reproducing, long-lived species. For vertebrate animals, the evidence is less clear, although several studies have demonstrated differences in immune response among closely related bird species and mice species that differ in reproduction rates and life span (e.g., Martin et al. 2006; Martin et al. 2007; Lee et al. 2008). However, these differences in immune response do not point to a clear difference in overall immunocompetence.

The focus has been on trade-offs between immune investment and reproductive investment, but it may very well be that other dimensions of the life histories of hosts may play an important role in understanding why hosts who are less immune competent tend to be more resilient to habitat destruction than those who are more immune competent.

Among bats, some evidence exists to support the life history hypothesis. In a study of 15 species of bats in central and western Africa, viral richness was higher in bats that lived in more fragmented forest, but the study also found increased viral richness in larger-bodied bats (Maganga et al. 2014). Thus, life history traits may not simply be a matter of r versus K selection. Bats are believed to be the reservoir host for both Ebola and Marburg viruses (see Chapter 2), with wild primates serving as an intermediate amplifying host whereby the virus can be transmitted to humans through contact with blood, body fluids, and/or tissues. Thus, in the fragmented forest, changes in the host-parasite relationship among viruses and bats likely influence the probability that wild primates are also affected in the fragmented forest, and ultimately, change the risk for human infection

Bushmeat, pet trade, and pet-keeping

Bushmeat hunting is one of the most important means through which wild primate parasites are transmitted to humans. Bushmeat consumption is widespread among indigenous hunters in both the Neotropics and the Afrotropics, but the epidemiological risks for transmission of infectious agents differ in these two regions. Of the estimated five million tons of bushmeat consumed annually in the two regions, Africa accounts for 98% (Fa et al. 2002). In large part, this is due to the relatively low population density of indigenous Amazonians. In Brazil, they comprise only about 0.4% of the population (Le Tourneau 2015). In addition, there is not the same type of commercial market for bushmeat in Amazonia that is found in Africa. The threat to wildlife from bushmeat hunting is also much more serious in the Congo Basin, where mammals must produce approximately 93% of their body mass to balance the current extraction rate compared with only 4% for the Amazon Basin (Fa et al. 2002). However, that should not serve to minimize other threats to Amazonian monkeys from deforestation and development or to suggest that Amazonian hunters are not at risk for monkey parasite transmission. In the Asian tropics, rural and traditional peoples often depend on hunting wild animals for food security (Lee et al. 2014), and both Asian apes and monkeys are hunted (Corlett 2007).

Wild primates are one of the most important sources of bushmeat. In Amazonia, a review of literature identified 49 indigenous groups who hunt wild primates for food (Cormier 2006). In western and central Africa, 76% of bushmeat species hunted were mammals, and primates constituted the largest group of mammals representing 35% of mammalian species (Kurpiers et al. 2016). Bushmeat activities include hunting, transporting, butchering, and consuming wild animals, all of which offer opportunity for exposure to wild primate parasites. Butchering, which is most likely to be done by women, poses the greatest risk, while more distant consumption poses the least risk (Kilonzo et al. 2013; Wolfe et al. 2005). In Cameroon, among HIV-1 positive persons, 55% reported butchering wild primates (LeBreton et al. 2007). Animals that are sick may also be more readily captured, increasing the likelihood of zoonotic transmission (Kilonzo et al. 2013).

Bushmeat hunting now extends beyond subsistence activities of local hunters. Toledo et al. (2012) describe the illegal wildlife trade as the second-largest black market worldwide, second only to narcotics trafficking. The bushmeat trade is a multi-billion dollar industry and is difficult to stem because it is a key contributor to local economies in the developing world (Brashares et al. 2004). It has been estimated that five tons of bushmeat *per week* is smuggled from Africa into Paris through the Charles de Gaulle airport for the European luxury market, which includes nonhuman primates (Chaber et al. 2010).

Local pet-keeping of wild primates is often linked to bushmeat hunting. When wild primates are hunted for food, orphaned infants and juveniles may be returned to the household and kept as pets. In other cases, wild primates are intentionally hunted and captured to be sold for profit in the pet trade. In both cases, opportunities for parasite exchange are ample. In the fieldwork experience of one of this book's authors (Cormier 2003) among the Awa-Guaja of the Brazilian Amazon, many households had more pet monkeys than human members. Infant and juvenile monkeys clung to the heads of women throughout the day and were sometimes breastfed. Children played with pet monkeys and often received bites and scratches. As the monkeys grew older, they became more aggressive and were tied up in the household where they defecated on the dirt floors of huts. In this context, the possibility of parasite transfer could occur through body fluids, fecal material, air-borne pathogens, and shared vectors.

On the other hand, the risk of exposure to wild primate parasites may be diminished to a degree with pets due to their age. The young age of primates that are typically captured as pets may mean that they have had less time for exposure to parasites than adults. That seems to be the case with SIVsmm (progenitor of HIV-2, see Chapter 2) and sooty mangabeys (*Cercocebus atys*) kept as pets in Liberia and Sierra Leone. Marx et al. (1991) found only 1 positive out of 25 in Liberia and Chen et al. (1996) found only 4/91 positive in Liberia and Sierra Leone, which was significantly lower than the rate found in one feral troop (4/10), as well as rates found in bushmeat.

Pets may also be responsible for spillover from human populations into wild populations. This could potentially occur with the Zika virus, which has recently entered into human populations in the Neotropics. To date, Zika has only been isolated in two species of monkeys: marmosets (*Callithrix jacchus*) and capuchins (*Sapajus libidinosus*) (Favoretto et al. 2016). One capuchin was in a coastal screening area for wild animals and the others were being kept as pets and so likely acquired the virus from humans. The marmosets were co-habitating with humans, but also moving freely back and forth in the forest, which provides a ready means for the virus to spread more widely in wild primate populations.

One example and cautionary tale of how environmental changes can affect the relationship between humans and wild primates involves *Plasmodium knowlesi*. The first known case of *Plasmodium knowlesi* naturally transmitted from a monkey to a human occurred in 1965 in a civilian army employee who spent five nights surveying the forest in the Pahang region of Peninsular Malaysia (Chin et al. 1965). In response, a large NIH study was carried out to investigate the possibility of monkey-to-human *P. knowlesi* transmission (Warren et al. 1970). Over 1,000 blood samples were taken from villagers living adjacent to the forest in the area near where the worker had been infected. *None* of the blood samples were found to contain *P. knowlesi*. According to the study, at that time the villagers were involved in rice cultivation and living near the forest along the Pahang River, and the forest was otherwise largely undeveloped with few roads. It was concluded that humans are not naturally infected with *P. knowlesi* unless they enter into a cycle of transmission of nonhuman primate malaria in the jungle.

Forty years later the situation changed, with epidemic outbreaks of *P. knowlesi* in human populations in Indonesia and Malaysia. Specifically in the Pahang, five patients who were hospitalized for malaria in 2004–2005 all tested positive for *P. knowlesi* (Cox-Singh et al. 2008). Today, Malaysia has one of the highest rates of deforestation in the world (Hansen et al. 2013).

The vector for human *P. knowlesi* in the Pahang region has been established to be *An. cracens*, which was not known to the area when extensive surveys were carried out in the 1980s and 1990s (Jiram et al. 2012). According to Jiram et al., *An. cracens* is simio-anthrophilic, but demonstrates a preference for humans and a preference for fruit orchards over the forest in the region. The long-tailed macaque (*Macaca fascicularis*) is indigenous to the area and also a natural host of *Plasmodium knowlesi* (Coatney et al. 1971). The long-tailed macaque is also a notorious crop raider, including of fruit groves, in Malaysia and other areas where they are native (Lee and Priston 2005). In this case, the evidence seems to suggest that deforestation altered the behavior of both the macaques and their mosquito vectors. Loss of habitat and forest resources brought the macaques into closer proximity to humans, where they take advantage of village fruit groves. With the macaques came their mosquito vectors, which although once not known in human areas began demonstrating a preference for fruit groves over forests and a preference for humans over macaques. This is a change that has occurred in the last 40 years and had led to the emergence of a new form of human malaria.

Anthroponoses and primate conservation

Anthroponotic disease may pose a greater risk to wild primates than zoonotic disease poses to humanity, particularly for endangered species with limited habitat ranges. Today, 60% of all primate species are threatened with extinction and 75% have declining populations (Estrada et al. 2017). Ironically, efforts to provide safe havens in reserves may exacerbate the problem, for they are often associated with ecotourism or at least contact with human researchers or park caretakers through direct contact, shared water sources, or contact with fomites (e.g., Köndgen et al. 2008; Schaumburg, Mugisha et al. 2012). In addition, domesticated animals associated with humans have the potential to have contact with primate populations.

A number of studies have documented increased intestinal parasites (bacteria, protozoa, helminths) among primates living in close contact with humans and/or domesticated animals compared with those with less human contact. Bublitz et al. (2015) compared gastrointestinal parasite load between Madagascar lemurs living in an intact forest area with those in a disturbed area with frequent exposure to tourism and other human activities. None of the lemurs in the intact forest was found to harbor pathogenic bacteria, but those in the disturbed area were positive for enterotoxigenic *E. coli*, *Shigella* spp., *Salmonella enterica*, *Vibrio cholorae*, and *Yersinia* spp., which were also present in local people, livestock, and rodents.

Several examples from Old World monkeys and apes show similar findings. *Cryptosporidium* and *Giardia* sp. were found among red colobus monkeys (*Piliocolobus tephrosceles*) and red-tailed guenons (*Cercopithecus ascanius*) monkeys in a highly disturbed area of the Kibale National Park in Uganda, but none in the undisturbed forest (Salzer et al. 2007). Ghandour et al. (1995) found that in Saudi Arabia, zoonotic intestinal parasite concentration was higher among *Papio hamadryas* living in areas with maximum human contact (36–58.5%) versus 9.5% in areas of minimum human contact. In Kenya, the Tana River red colobus (*Procolobus rufomitratus*) and mangabey (*Cercocebus galeritus*) intestinal parasite loads were higher among monkeys in disturbed and fragmented forest than elsewhere (Mbora and McPeek 2009; Mbora et al. 2009). Nizeyi et al. (1999) compared gorillas in human-habituated areas with non-human-habituated areas and found that 73% of the cases of *Cryptosporidium* infection were found in human-habituated areas. The habituated area is a site of ecotourism, but local cattle are also allowed to graze at the periphery of the park, which are another potential source of infection. The nematode *Capillaria hepatica* has also been found in habituated mountain gorillas in Rwanda (Graczyk et al. 1999).

Among New World monkeys, *Giardia* sp. infection among howler monkeys (*Alouatta caraya*) in Argentina was significantly higher at a rural site where livestock was present than in the remote forest (Kowalewski et al. 2011). In Peru, saddleback and moustached tamarins (*Saguinus fuscicollis* and *S. mystax*) that were in close proximity to humans did not show evidence of human helminths. However, they had increased loads of a common wild primate helminth (*Prosthenorchis elegans*) than a forest group had, presumably due to alterations in their habitat (Wenz et al. 2010). Similarly, among indri (*Indri indri*) in Madagascar, groups in closer contact with humans had decreased leukocyte counts, a higher diversity of parasites, and an increased load of lice than did indri living in undisturbed areas (Junge et al. 2011). The latter two studies suggest that habitat disturbance itself may increase the susceptibility of wild primates to parasitic disease, even if the parasites are not acquired from humans.

Human-associated bacteria that have become drug resistant may also be transmitted to primates. Schaumburg, Mugisha et al. (2012) found high rates of drug-resistant *Staphylococcus aureus* in two chimpanzee sanctuaries in Zambia and Uganda. Sanctuaries often house orphans that would be unable to survive in the wild and remain in sanctuaries for the remainder of their lives. They found *S. aureus* in 58% of the chimpanzees; of those, 45% were human-related with some degree of drug resistance. The authors express the concern that any attempts to reintroduce these chimpanzees into the wild would expose forest-living primates to these new strains.

Viruses typically associated with humans may also have devastating effects on primates.

Polio outbreaks have been documented in wild chimpanzees on several occasions. In 1964, a disease consistent with polio resulted in paralysis of seven chimpanzees in Beni, Zaire, after workers plowed an area in their habitat for a papaya plantation (Kortland 1996). In 1966, a disease with symptoms consistent with polio resulted in the death of six chimpanzees and permanent paralysis in six others in the Gombe National Park in Tanzania (Wallis and Lee 1999). In 1988, an outbreak of disease consistent in symptomology with measles among mountain gorillas (*Gorilla beringei*) in Rwanda resulted in the deaths of six gorillas and illness in 27 others (Ferber 2000).

Warfare and conflict are well known to affect patterns of disease transmission among humans, but they may also affect disease ecology among wild primates. Such situations can lead to increased bushmeat hunting and human encroachment into wild primate habitats, leading to increased potential for parasites to be shared. In the Democratic Republic of Congo, two wars occurred between 1996 and 2003 with over five million human fatalities and millions of others displaced (Nackoney et al. 2014). The region is home to three endangered great apes: *Pan troglodytes schweinfurthii*, *Gorilla beringei grauer*, and *Pan paniscus*. Yamagiwa (2003) describes a loss of 50% of the endangered eastern lowland gorilla (*Gorilla beringei graueri*) population in the Kahuzi-Biega National Park in the Democratic Republic of Congo over a four-year period related to warfare at the fall of the Mobutu regime. A number of interrelated factors contributed to the crisis. The normal park protection services broke down, a large number of refugees entered the area, and the desperate and starving people invaded the park to hunt bushmeat. Nellemann et al. (2010) have described a similar situation in the Virunga National Park with the local gorilla population. Fleeing refugees entered the park and set up camps and militias entered the park to extract charcoal, endangering gorilla habitats. Park rangers attempted to intervene to prevent the smuggling of charcoal out of the park and in retaliation, over 190 rangers were killed. In 2007, soldiers killed ten gorillas in retaliation. Such conditions also set up conditions for the spread of parasites between humans and wild primates.

Unfortunately, we do not know the extent of the damage from anthroponotic infections to wild primate populations. As humans continue to encroach into wild primate habitats, it can be anticipated that the problem of both zoonotic and anthroponotic parasite transfer will only worsen. In the following chapters, a review is provided of specific parasites, their disease potential, and the wild primate species implicated.

Note

1 Some researchers make a distinction between amplifying and competent hosts, with the former being able to concentrate the parasite and the latter being able to both concentrate and transmit the virus. In Clements's (2012) *The Biology of Mosquitoes*, amplifying and competent hosts are treated as synonyms, as are dead-end and incompetent hosts.

2 Viruses

DNA viruses

Adenoviridae: Mastadenovirus

Over 100 different adenoviruses have been identified in vertebrates, but all human adenoviruses belong to the genus *Mastadenovirus*, which includes the mammalian adenoviruses (Rhee and Barouch 2015; Robinson et al. 2013). The human adenoviruses are divided into species (A to G) with approximately 60 types within those groups (Robinson et al. 2013). The human species are typically designated in the literature as HAdV-A (human adenovirus A), HAdV-B, etc.

Human adenoviruses are transmitted through the fecal-oral route or through inhalation of respiratory droplets and are very common, with most individuals demonstrating evidence of prior infection by the age of ten (Rhee and Barouch 2015). Infections are typically subclinical, mild, or self-limiting and can result in a variety of symptoms depending on the type, including respiratory tract infection, urinary tract infection, gastroenteritis, and conjunctivitis (Rhee and Barouch 2015). However, human adenovirus is considered an emerging opportunistic pathogen in immunocompromised and vulnerable individuals, including neonates, HIV-infected persons, and those receiving organ transplants, in whom it can result in a disseminated life-threatening disease (Lion 2014; Rhee and Barouch 2015).

Both Old World and New World primates are infected with a variety of adenoviruses, unrelated to the human species (Wevers et al. 2011). However, a number of recent studies have found evidence of human adenoviruses in wild African great apes. The studies have demonstrated evidence of previous infection with human adenoviruses in a number of widely dispersed locations in Africa. Evidence of all the human adenoviruses except HAdV-G have been found in African great apes. The geographic and species diversity suggests the possibility that human adenoviruses originated in the great apes, although it is possible that the presence of human adenoviruses in the great apes is the result of a host switch from humans. The evidence suggests that the adenovirus species currently classified as "human" may be better designated as hominid (African great ape and human) rather than hominin (human). In addition, evidence exists for genetic recombination of HAdV-B among wild gorillas and between gorillas and chimpanzees (Hoppe et al. 2015a).

Anelloviridae: Alphatorquevirus

Alphatorquevirus is a recently discovered genus in the recently established family of Anelloviridae which includes the torque teno virus (TTV) species (Kekarainen and Segalés 2012). TTV viruses have been identified in dogs, cats, nonhuman primates, and wild and domesticated swine (Ssemadaali et al. 2016). TTV is a ubiquitous virus, found in water and sewage, in the air, and on surfaces; infection occurs in all major organs, secretions, excretions, and the blood (Ssemadaali et al. 2016). TTV has a high prevalence in the human population, is typically asymptomatic, and may be a commensal (Béland et al. 2014). In one study of 205 Japanese children aged 1–12, over 98% were positive at two years of age (Ninomiya et al. 2008). However, TTV can be an opportunistic co-infection with a variety of afflictions, including viral hepatitis, asthma, autoimmune disorders, and respiratory illnesses (Ssemadaali et al. 2016). It has also been associated with post-transfusion and organ transplant infections (Béland et al. 2014). Two additional *Alphatorqueviruses* have been identified in humans: TTMV (torque teno mini virus) and TTMDV (torque teno midi virus) (Ninomiya et al. 2009). Wild and domesticated pigs are frequently infected with TTVSuV (torque teno sus virus), which has been transmitted zoonotically to humans through contact with pork products (Ssemadaali et al. 2016).

Few studies have been conducted to identify the presence of TTV-like viruses in wild primates. However, one study has found an *Alphatorquevirus* in wild chimpanzees (Calvignac-Spencer et al. 2012). Due to the ability of TTVSuV to be transmitted zoonotically from swine to humans, it is possible that the *Alphatorquevirus* in chimpanzees may represent a pathogen that could be passed to humans through bushmeat consumption or other environmental contamination. In addition, in a study of captive chimpanzees in a zoological park, both human TTV and TTMV DNA were identified, which suggests the potential for anthroponotic transfer to wild primates (Ninomiya et al. 2009). Alternatively, the viruses designated as human TTVs may not be unique to humans and may have broader diversity within wild primate populations.

Herpesviridae

Herpesviruses affect a wide range of animal species, including insects, fish, mollusks, reptiles, birds, and mammals (Wozniakowski and Samorek-Salamonowicz 2015). Most are species-specific, but a few affecting horses, swine, and nonhuman primates do have the potential to infect humans (Wozniakowski and Samorek-Salamonowicz 2015). Eight species of human herpesvirus have been identified: herpesvirus-1, herpesvirus-2, varicella-zoster virus (HHV-3), Epstein-Barr virus (HHV-4), cytomegalovirus (HHV-5), human herpes viruses 6A, 6B, and 7, and Kaposi's sarcoma-associated herpesvirus (HHV-8) (Grinde 2013; Wozniakowski and Samorek-Salamonowicz 2015).

Herpes simplex viruses include two types: HSV-1 and HSV-2. Both can cause oral and genital ulcerations characterized by an initial infection and latency with recurrent infections; however, HSV-1 is more likely to result in oral lesions and HSV-2 in genital lesions (Grinde 2013). HSV-1 is extremely common, with approximately 90% of adults developing antibodies by middle adulthood (Schiffer and Corey 2015). HSV-2 is also common globally, with an estimated 23 million new cases per year (Schiffer and Corey 2015). Neonates exposed to HSV-2 secretions can develop serious complications of visual and central nervous system infection (Schiffer and Corey 2015).

Varicella-zoster virus (human herpes virus 3), is the agent of chicken pox (varicella) and shingles (herpes zoster), with chicken pox occurring as a primary infection and shingles as a later expression of latent infection (Whitley 2015). Chicken pox typically occurs as a relatively benign childhood disease with low-grade fever, muscle ache, headache, and nausea with an accompanying itchy vesicular rash (Grinde 2013). Up through the latter part of the 20th century, varicella infection was a ubiquitous childhood infection, but a vaccine was developed in the 1970s and licensed in the U.S. in 1995 (Baxter et al. 2013). Shingles manifests as a painful unilateral vesicular eruption along a dermatome; thoracic and lumbar dermatomes are most commonly involved, but if cranial nerves are involved, it can cause a sight-threatening condition (Whitley 2015). Although shingles may develop at any age, it is more common in older adults who had primary varicella infection before the vaccine was available (Whitley 2015).

Human herpesvirus 4, or Epstein-Barr, is a *Lymphocryptovirus* and the agent of mononucleosis; it is a common virus worldwide with most individuals exposed by adulthood (Johannsen and Kaye 2015). It is transmitted through saliva and for this reason is sometimes referred to as the "kissing disease" (Grinde 2013). In children, it is often asymptomatic, but after adolescence, symptoms may include fever, sore throat, fatigue, and lymphadenopathy (Grinde 2013). Epstein-Barr has also been associated with malignant disease, including Burkitt's lymphoma and Hodgkin's lymphoma (Johannsen and Kaye 2015).

Human herpesvirus 5 is a *Cytomegalovirus* that is widespread and usually asymptomatic, but it can cause severe congenital abnormalities in infants infected *in utero* and may also cause severe disease in immunocompromised patients (Crumpacker 2015). *Cytomegalovirus* is also associated with a number of lymphomas (Grinde 2013). As with the other herpesviruses, after the initial infection, it can persist as a latent virus (Crumpacker 2015). Herpesviruses 6–8 are relatively rare. Types 6–7 are referred to as roseola viruses and can cause skin lesions and fever in infants less than two years of age (Grinde 2013). Human herpesvirus type-8 is associated with Kaposi's sarcoma in immunocompromised individuals with HIV-AIDS (Grinde 2013). However, classic Kaposi's sarcoma is not associated with immune dysfunction has been documented for over a century in people of Mediterranean, Eastern European, and Middle Eastern heritage, particularly in men (Iscovich et al. 2000).

Among humans and wild primates, the herpesviruses tend to be species specific, but some cases have been identified in humans acquiring simian herpesviruses and wild primates acquiring human herpesviruses. The zoonotic form of herpes virus that is of most concern to humans is the Herpes B virus, also known as monkey B virus, *Cercopithecine herpesvirus*, or *Herpesvirus simiae*. Macaques are considered the likely natural hosts, since *Macaca mulatta* and *M. fascicularis* are commonly infected with only mild symptoms (Tischer and Osterrieder 2010). Humans are most at risk in laboratory or research settings. Although only 50 cases of Herpes B have been documented in humans, 21 of the cases were fatal (CDC 2014). If untreated, humans can develop severe encephalitis and paralysis (Wozniakowski and Samorek-Salamonowicz 2015).

Nonhuman primates have some susceptibility to human HSV-1. It has been identified in pet primates, including one gorilla and two New World marmoset species (Gilardi et al. 2014; Imura et al. 2014). In captivity, fatal cases have been documented in New World monkeys (*Aotus* sp., *Callithrix* sp., and *Pithecia* sp.) and in gibbons (Wozniakowski and Samorek-Salamonowicz 2015). Although HSV-1 has been documented in captive nonhuman primates and pets, it has not yet been documented in wild primates. HSV-3 (varicella zoster) has been identified in gorillas in captivity (Masters et al. 2010; Myers et al. 1987) and presumably acquired anthroponotically. In older literature, outbreaks of varicella-like disease have been reported in nonhuman primates in captivity (see Brack 1987). However, simian varicella virus, which infects Old World monkeys, has similar clinical symptoms to chicken pox (Gray 2003).

Lymphocryptovirus and *Cytomegalovirus* have also been documented in several primate species in the wild. *Lymphocryptovirus* has been identified in orangutans, gorillas, bonobos, and chimpanzees, while *Cytomegalovirus* has been documented in baboons, gorillas, and chimpanzees. Although HHV-4 is a *Lymphocryptovirus* species and HHV-5 is a *Cytomegalovirus* species, the virus forms found in wild primates are not likely to be anthroponotic.

Papovaviridae: SV40

Considerable controversy surrounds the potential role of the *Polyomavirus* simian virus 40 (SV40) and its potential role in causing human disease. SV40 was first identified in 1960 in the Rhesus macaque kidney cell stocks of the Sabin poliovirus vaccine; potentially 100 million people may have

Table 2.1 DNA Viruses

ADENOVIRIDAE		
Mastadenovirus A–F		
Gorilla beringei *Gorilla gorilla* *Pan troglodytes*	Africa (W)	Calvignac-Spencer et al. 2012
HAdV-A		
Gorilla beringei	DRC (W), Uganda (W)	Hoppe et al. 2015b
Gorilla gorilla	Cameroon (W), Gabon (W)	Hoppe et al. 2015b
Pan paniscus	DRC (W)	Hoppe et al. 2015b
Pan troglodytes	CAR (W), Côte d'Ivoire (W), Gabon (W), Uganda (W)	Hoppe et al. 2015b; Wevers et al. 2011
HAdV-B		
Gorilla beringei	DRC (W), Uganda (W)	Hoppe et al. 2015a, 2015b
Gorilla gorilla	Cameroon (W), DRC (W), Gabon (W), Rwanda (W), Republic of Congo (W)	Hoppe et al. 2015b; Nkogue et al. 2016; Seimon et al. 2015; Wevers et al. 2011
Pan troglodytes	Côte d'Ivoire (W), Gabon, Republic of Congo (W), Uganda (W)	Hoppe et al. 2015b; Seimon et al. 2015; Wevers et al. 2011
HAdV-C		
Gorilla beringei	Rwanda (W), Uganda (W)	Duncan et al. 2013; Hoppe et al. 2015b
Gorilla gorilla	Cameroon (W), Côte d'Ivoire (W), Gabon (W), Republic of Congo (W), Uganda (W)	Hoppe et al. 2015b; Nkogue et al. 2016; Seimon et al. 2015; Wevers et al. 2011
Pan paniscus	DRC (W)	Hoppe et al. 2015b

(*Continued*)

Table 2.1 (Continued)

ADENOVIRIDAE		
Pan troglodytes	Côte d'Ivoire (W), DRC (W), Gabon (W), Republic of Congo (W), Rwanda (W), Uganda (W)	Hoppe et al. 2015b; Seimon et al. 2015; Wevers et al. 2011
HAdV-D		
Pan troglodytes	Uganda (W)	Wevers et al. 2011
HAdV-E		
Gorilla gorilla	Gabon (W), Republic of Congo (W)	Hoppe et al. 2015b; Nkogue et al. 2016; Seimon et al. 2015
Pan paniscus	DRC (W)	Hoppe et al. 2015b; Wevers et al. 2011
Pan troglodytes	CAR (W), Côte d'Ivoire (W), Gabon (W), Republic of Congo (W), Tanzania (W), Uganda (W)	Hoppe et al. 2015b; Seimon et al. 2015; Wevers et al. 2011
HAdV-F		
Gorilla gorilla	Cameroon (W), Gabon (W)	Hoppe et al. 2015b; Wevers et al. 2011
Pan troglodytes	Gambia (W), Uganda (W)	Hoppe et al. 2015b; Wevers et al. 2011
	Uganda (W)	
ANELLOVIRIDAE		
Alphatorquevirus		
Pan troglodytes	Africa (W)	Calvignac-Spencer et al. 2012
HERPESVIRIDAE		
***Herpes simplex* (HSV-1)**		
Callithrix jacchus *Callithrix pygmaea*	Japan (P)	Imura et al. 2014
Gorilla beringei	DRC (P)	Gilardi et al. 2014
***Lymphocryptovirus* (HHV-4 related)**		
Pongo pygmaeus	Borneo (W/SC)	Kilbourn et al. 2003
Gorilla gorilla	Africa (W)	Calvignac-Spencer et al. 2012
Pan paniscus	DRC (W)	Yoshida et al. 2016
Pan troglodytes	Africa (W)	Calvignac-Spencer et al. 2012; Levy et al. 1971
***Cytomegalovirus* (HHV-5 related)**		
Papio ursinus	South Africa (W)	Drewe and O'Riain 2012
Gorilla gorilla *Pan troglodytes*	Africa (W)	Calvignac-Spencer et al. 2012

been exposed to the parasite between 1955 and 1963 (Garcea and Imperiale 2003). The virus is typically asymptomatic in wild macaques, but experimental inoculation of high levels of the virus into rodents has led to tumor development (Garcea and Imperiale 2003). Some researchers have found SV40 in association with human brain tumors, osteosarcomas, mesotheliomas, and non-Hodgkin lymphoma, but others have argued that there is no clear association (see Shah 2007 for review). In 2002, the U.S. Immunization Safety Review Committee reported that there was inadequate evidence to conclude whether receipt of the contaminated polio vaccine later caused cancer.

RNA Viruses

Bunyaviridae: Bunyamwera, Oropouche

Bunyaviridae is a large family of viruses occurring worldwide that can infect plants, invertebrates, and vertebrates (Bente 2015). Four genera are capable of causing zoonotic infection in humans: *Hantavirus*, *Nairovirus*, *Orthobunyavirus*, and *Phlebovirus*, but only *Orthobunyaviruses* are a concern among wild primates. With the exception of *Hantavirus*, which can be acquired through contact with rodent secretions, the Bunyaviridae viruses are vector-borne (Bente 2015). *Nairovirus* and *Phlebovirus* are both zoonotic, but they have not yet been found in nonhuman primates. The most serious *Nairovirus* is Crimean-Congo hemorrhagic fever virus. Antibodies to the virus have not yet been documented in wild primates that have been surveyed, although antibodies have been found in other wild animals including hares, buffalo, rhinoceros, and bats (Spengler et al. 2016). Wild primates may not be susceptible, for laboratory attempts to infect several Old World monkeys species with the virus have not been successful (Bente et al. 2013). The most serious *Phlebovirus* is Rift Valley Fever virus, which occurs in domesticated animals in Africa, but it has been difficult to induce experimentally in nonhuman primates, suggesting they may not be readily susceptible (Smith et al. 2012).

Orthobunyaviridae includes Bwamba, Bunyamwera, California encephalitis, and Oropouche viruses, of which, Bunyamwera and Oropouche have been detected in wild primates in the Old World and New World respectively. Bunyamwera virus is found in East Africa with symptoms including fever, headache, arthralgia, rash, and sometimes central nervous system involvement (Odhiambo et al. 2014). *Anopheles gambiae* appears to be the most efficient vector, but it may also be transmitted by *Aedes aegypti* and possibly other vectors. One of the most serious concerns regarding Bunyamwera and other members of *Orthobunyaviridae* is potential reassortment into more virulent viruses. Ngari virus is a reassortment of

Bunyamwera virus and another Bunyavirus, which has been responsible for large outbreaks of acute hemorrhagic fever in Kenya and Somalia (Gerrard et al. 2004). Antibodies to Bunyamwera have been found in several species of Old World monkeys in Uganda, suggesting that they may be a potential reservoir.

Oropouche virus infection is typically a self-limiting disease with symptoms of fever, headache, myalgia, nausea, arthralgia, and less commonly, meningitis (Bente 2015). It is characterized by both an urban and a sylvatic cycle. The sylvatic cycle involves *Aedes* and *Culex* mosquitoes, where it infects sloths, marsupials, primates, and birds (Mourão et al. 2009). The human-adapted urban cycle involves transmission through midges (*Culicoides paraensis*) (Mourão et al. 2009). Epidemic outbreaks can infect thousands (Bente 2015), but the number may be underestimated due to the similarity in symptoms to dengue, chikungunya, Mayaro, and Zika viruses (Navarro et al. 2016). Oropouche virus has been isolated in wild howlers (*Alouatta guariba*), capuchins (*Cebus olivaceus*), and marmosets (*Callithrix jacchus*), and antibodies to Oropouche have been detected in wild howlers and capuchins (references in table). In addition, antibodies to the Oropouche virus have also been found in captive howlers (*Alouatta caraya*) and capuchins (*Cebus libidinosus*) housed in Brazil (Gibrail et al. 2016; Laroque et al. 2014).

Filoviridae: Ebola, Marburg

Three genera of filoviruses have been identified: *Ebolavirus*, *Marburgvirus*, and *Cuevavirus*. *Cuevavirus* infects bats in Spain and is not known to infect humans (Rougeron et al. 2015). Ebola and Marburg virus produce severe and often fatal hemorrhagic fever transmissible through blood and body fluids with headache, malaise, vomiting, diarrhea, coagulation disorders, and multi-organ failure (Geisbert 2015).

Five species of The genus *Ebolavirus* have been identified: *Zaire ebolavirus* (EBOV), *Taï Forest ebolavirus* (TAFV), *Sudan ebolavirus* (SUDV), *Bundibugyo ebolavirus* (BDBV), and *Reston ebolavirus* (RESTV) (Rougeron et al. 2015). The reservoir host for Ebola viruses are believed to be fruit bats (Leendertz et al. 2016; Leroy et al. 2005).

Zaire ebolavirus is the most virulent and has been responsible for outbreaks in central and western Africa, documented since 1976 with mortality rates ranging from 36% to 90% (Tseng and Chan 2015). The 1976 outbreak was worsened by the inadvertent spread of the disease through the reuse of unsterilized needles and syringes, as well as causes of nosocomial transmission through the health care system (Geisbert 2015). The most recent epidemic occurred between 2014 and 2016 with 28,000 cases and 11,000 deaths, primarily in Guinea, Liberia, and Sierra Leone (Shagari et al. 2016). In addition, the disease was exported by travelers to the U.S., U.K., Spain, and Sardinia. The virus is extremely contagious and if strict body fluid precautions are not taken, it can spread to health care workers and other patients and as a community infection (Geisbert 2015).

Epidemics of *Sudan ebolavirus* have also been documented since 1976, with mortality rates ranging from 36% to 53% (Tseng and Chan 2015). An outbreak of *Bundibugyo ebolavirus* occurred in 2007 in Uganda with a 25% mortality rate (Tseng and Chan 2015). The reservoir is currently unknown but is suspected to also be linked to bats (Cárdenas and Basler 2013). Only one case of *Taï Forest ebolavirus* has been documented in humans, which occurred in a researcher performing a necropsy on a chimpanzee; she survived (Rougeron et al. 2015).

Reston ebolavirus causes severe hemorrhagic fever in long-tailed macaques (*Macaca fascicularis*) but is nonpathogenic in humans (Rougeron et al. 2015). In 1989–1990, the virus was identified after an outbreak among macaques in a laboratory in Reston, Virginia, that had originated in the Philippines (Cárdenas and Basler 2013). Two subsequent outbreaks in macaques occurred in 1992 and 1994 that were linked to the same exporter in the Philippines (Cárdenas and Basler 2013).

Zaire and Taï Forest ebolaviruses have been isolated in wild chimpanzees and gorillas and result in significant mortality. In a 2002–2003 Zaire Ebola outbreak in the Lossi sanctuary in the DRC, 56% of the gorilla population and 89% of the chimpanzee population died (Leroy et al. 2004a). An outbreak of Ebola in the Taï National Park resulted in a loss of 25% of the chimpanzee population (Formenty et al. 1999). Although chimpanzees and gorillas are not the reservoir host, they have been implicated in the spread of Ebola due to the consumption of bushmeat. In Liberia, one of the countries hardest hit by the 2014–2016 epidemic, it is estimated that three-fourths of the country's meat use derives from bushmeat (Alexander et al. 2015). Leroy et al. (2005) has noted that mortality in great apes increases in the dry season, when fruit is scarcest, leading to closer contact among animals competing for food. If bats are indeed verified as the reservoir, great apes would be more likely to come into contact with bat droppings or with fruit contaminated with bat saliva during times of increased food competition.

Other primate species are apparently susceptible to *Ebolavirus* in captivity. A survey of 783 primates belonging to 20 species in Gabon and the Republic of Congo found not only gorillas and chimpanzees to be serologically positive, but also five species of Old World monkeys: *Cercopithecus neglectus*, *Mandrillus leucophaeus*, *M. sphinx*, and *Papio anubis* (LeRoy et al. 2004b). The monkeys with evidence of exposure to *Ebolavirus* were not ill at the time of the study, and it is not known how they were exposed or if they manifest clinical disease. One additional note is that Nidom et al. (2012) reported in *PLOS One* that they had identified serological evidence of exposure to *Ebolavirus* in orangutans in Indonesia. However, the editors of *PLOS One* have flagged the article with a cautionary note of concern due to questions that have been raised about the sources of the samples that the authors have not satisfactorily explained.

As described above, *Marburgvirus* is a hemorrhagic fever with symptoms similar to that of *Ebolavirus*. Two significant outbreaks have been recorded. One occurred from 1998 to 2000 in the DRC with 154 cases and an 83% case fatality rate; the second occurred between 2004 and 2005 in Angola with 252 cases and a 90% case fatality rate (Geisbert 2015). The Egyptian fruit bat, *Rousettus aegyptiacus*, has been identified as a reservoir (Pigott et al. 2015).

In the laboratory setting, humans have been infected with Marburg virus through exposure to grivet monkeys (*Chlorocebus aethiops*). In 1967, and outbreak occurred in laboratory workers who had contact with grivets imported from Uganda (Martini 1973). Thirty-one people were infected, primarily through caring for infected monkeys, but secondary infections also occurred. One was through medical staff caring for a sick patient (human), another through an accidental needle stick, and another through sexual contact with a laboratory worker. No case has been identified of transmission of Marburg from wild primates to humans outside of the laboratory setting (Pigott et al. 2015).

Flaviviridae: dengue, Japanese encephalitis group, Kyasanur Forest disease, yellow fever, Zika

Dengue

Dengue is a vector-borne disease occurring throughout the tropics. Infections range from asymptomatic, to mild fever, to potentially fatal dengue hemorrhagic shock syndrome (Bhatt et al. 2013). In 2010, approximately 96 million symptomatic infections were documented with 70% occurring in Asia, 16% in Africa, 14% in the Americas, and 0.2% in Oceania (Bhatt et al. 2013). Four serotypes of dengue have long been recognized (I, II, III, and IV), but a new serotype, dengue V, has recently been identified in Asia. (Guebler 2014). Dengue is transmitted by several species of *Aedes* mosquitoes, with *Aedes aegypti* being the principal vector in humans (Thomas et al. 2015).

The ecology of dengue differs according to region. It is believed to have originated in Asia, based on both ecological and phylogenetic evidence

(Guebler 2014). In Asia, all four types of dengue occur in a sylvatic cycle involving nonhuman primates and a human urban cycle (Guebler 2014). In Asia, the virus has been detected in several species of wild macaques and in orangutans. Dengue I, II, III, and less commonly IV occur in Africa (Messina et al. 2014). However, a sylvatic-urban cycle only occurs with dengue II (Guebler 2014). Dengue II has been identified in several species of Old World monkeys apparently as a spillback from human urban dengue. An urban cycle of all four types of dengue occur in the tropical Americas (Messina et al. 2014), but currently, there is no evidence that it has spilled back and is being maintained in New World monkeys in a sylvatic cycle (Guebler 2014).

Japanese encephalitis group

Japanese encephalitis is a vector-borne infection endemic to Asia. In the 1960s, an effective vaccine was developed, but there are still an estimated 35,000–50,000 cases and 10,000–15,000 deaths per year in Southeast Asia, India, Nepal, and northern Australia (Thomas et al. 2015). Most of those who are infected are asymptomatic or have mild influenza-type symptoms; however, in approximately 1 in 250 people, the disease progresses to encephalitis and is fatal in about 1/3 of those patients (Sachan 2015). The ecology of Japanese encephalitis involves pigs and migratory birds with *Culex* mosquito vectors and humans as accidental hosts (Sachan 2015; Thomas et al. 2015). Only a few studies have shown wild primates to be seropositive for Japanese encephalitis. In Borneo, both free-ranging and wild orangutans have demonstrated exposure to the disease, and in Thailand, macaques in an open-air enclosure were seropositive. In addition, captive macaques (*Macaca fascicularis* and *M. fuscata*) have tested seropositive (Inoue et al. 2003; Shimoda et al. 2014). According to Shimoda et al. (2014) the viral load in humans is not sufficient to infect mosquitoes. Wild primates may also be dead-end hosts.

St. Louis encephalitis virus is a vector-borne disease occurring primarily in North America, but with cases also in Central and South America. The first documented outbreak occurred in St. Louis, with more than 1,000 cases (Diaz et al. 2013). The infection now occurs throughout North America with more recent cases documented in the Caribbean, Central America, and South America (Thomas et al. 2015). The ecology of transmission is between *Culex* species mosquitoes and a variety of birds with humans as accidental hosts (Thomas et al. 2015). Only about 1 in 300 people exposed to the virus exhibit symptoms, which can range from mild influenza-like symptoms to neuroinvasive disease with meningitis and encephalitis; the mortality rate if encephalitis develops is between 4% and 27% (Oyer et al.

2014). Several species of wild howler monkeys and spider monkeys have tested seropositive for St. Louis encephalitis.

West Nile virus is a vector-borne infection that occurs in Africa, the Middle East, Europe, North America, and Central America. The virus was first isolated in Uganda in 1937, but spread to the Middle East in the 1950s, to Europe in the 1960s, and to the Americas in the late 1990s (Thomas et al. 2015). West Nile virus is transmitted primarily between mosquito vectors and numerous species of bird, but other vertebrate species may be infected with the virus (Suthar et al. 2013). Humans are typically infected through the bite of *Culex* spp. mosquitoes, but the virus can also be transmitted through blood products, through organ transplantation, transplacentally, and possibly through breast milk (Thomas et al. 2015). Most infections are asymptomatic with only 20% developing clinical symptoms, which typically manifest in a self-limiting febrile illness; however, approximately 1% of those infected develop neurological illness including meningitis, encephalitis, and a poliomyelitis-like syndrome (Sejvar 2014). Before the 1990s, only sporadic outbreaks of the infection were documented, but it has become a significant emerging global disease, increasing in frequency and severity (Petersen et al. 2013). It is now the leading cause of mosquito-borne encephalitis in the United States (Suthar et al. 2013). Among wild primates, West Nile virus has been detected in several species of African monkeys and in gorillas. In South America, it has been documented in horses (Thomas et al. 2015), but not yet in either human or wild primate populations. Humans are dead-end hosts for West Nile virus, but some mammalian and reptile species carry sufficient viral loads to infect mosquitoes. It is not yet known if wild primate species are dead-end hosts or are capable of transmitting the virus (Suthar et al. 2013).

Kyasanur Forest disease virus

Kyasanur Forest disease virus is a vector-borne infection occurring in southwest India (Hensgens and Kuijper 2013). It is spread through the bite of *Haemaphysalis* species of ticks (Mourya et al. 2014). Symptoms include high fever, severe myalgia, and bleeding from the nasal cavity, throat, and gingivae, and hemorrhagic pulmonary edema in 40% of the cases (Thomas et al. 2015). The case fatality rate is 2–10% (Thomas et al. 2015). Although a vaccine is available, approximately 100–500 people are infected each year (Hensgens and Kuijper 2013). Rodents or related species are believed to be the natural hosts, since neutralizing antibodies have been found in a number of species of rodents, as well as squirrels and bats (Pattnaik 2006). Epizootic outbreaks have been documented in macaques (*Macaca radiata*) and langurs (*Semnopithecus entellus*), which also experience severe febrile illness (Hensgens and Kuijper 2013). The primary means through which humans become infected is likely through contact with infected monkeys. The first documented outbreak of the disease occurred in 1956, when there was a simultaneous outbreak in forest monkeys and local villagers (Work and Trapido 1957). The most recent human outbreak in 2013 occurred in workers in the Bandipur National Reserve in India who were caring for sick langurs (Hensgens and Kuijper 2013).

Yellow fever virus

Yellow fever is a vector-borne pathogen that is endemic in the Afrotropics and the Neotropics. There is evidence that suggests that both the yellow fever virus and the *Aedes aegypti* mosquito vector were introduced from Africa into the Americas during the slave trade (Dobyns 1993; Kiple and Higgins 1992; Wirsing 1985). New World monkeys presumably acquired the disease from humans. Additional evidence that yellow fever was a virgin soil epidemic is that African human populations and Old World primate populations have some immunological resistance to yellow fever that is lacking among Native Americans and New World monkeys (Kiple and Higgins 1992). Although a vaccine is available, approximately 84,000–170,000 cases of yellow fever occur each year with up to 60,000 deaths, primarily in Africa (WHO 2017a). Symptoms can range from a mild febrile illness to acute liver infection and hemorrhagic disease, with a 50% mortality rate among those with acute illness (WHO 2017a).

Yellow fever is maintained in both Africa and Latin America in a sylvatic cycle involving wild primates and forest-dwelling mosquitoes, primarily *Aedes* sp. (Gubler 2004). In South and Central America, yellow fever causes clinical disease similar to that found in humans among several species of howlers in the wild (Brack 1987). Other wild Neotropical monkeys that have tested seropositive include owl monkeys (*Aotus* sp.), spider monkeys (*Ateles* sp.), sakis (*Pithecia* sp.), tamarins (*Saguinus* sp.), and marmosets (*Callithrix* sp.). In the past, epidemic urban cycles of the disease occurred in South and Central America involving primarily *Aedes aegypti*, but the last urban outbreak was in 1999 in Bolivia (Gubler 2004). In Africa, by the 1970s, vaccination programs led to urban yellow fever being largely under control, but it has resurged in a number of epidemic outbreaks over the last decades (Gubler 2004). A number of African monkey species demonstrate serological evidence of exposure to yellow fever, but in laboratory experimental infections, they demonstrate only mild and transient symptoms (Brack 1987).

Zika virus

Zika virus is a vector-borne pathogen that has recently become a global health concern due to its rapid spread and association with neurological disorders. The Zika virus was first isolated in 1947 in a captive Rhesus monkey (*Macaca mulatta*) in the Zika forest of Uganda (Dick et al. 1952). The monkey (of Asian origin) was being used as a sentinel to detect yellow fever in the area and was housed in an outdoor cage. After the monkey became febrile, the Zika virus was identified and also detected in local *Ae. africanus* mosquitoes. Subsequently, in the 1950s and early 1960s, the virus was detected sporadically in human cases from in Africa (Uganda, the former Tanganyika, Egypt, and Nigeria), Southeast Asia (Philippines, Thailand, Vietnam, and Malaysia), and India (Petersen et al. 2016). From the 1950s until 2007, only 13 human cases were reported, all presenting with a relatively mild, febrile illness (Petersen et al. 2016).

Two lineages of the Zika virus have been identified, an African strain and an Asian strain (Haddow et al. 2012). The Asian strain is responsible for infections in Southeast Asia, the Pacific Islands, and the Americas (Ogden et al. 2016). It has spread aggressively and is associated with neurological disorders. The first detection of Asian strain Zika occurred in 2007 with an outbreak on Yap Island, Federated States of Micronesia, with approximately 900 cases identified (Duffy et al. 2009). The researchers estimated that three-quarters of the island's residents had been infected, approximately 5,000 individuals. Another major outbreak occurred in French Polynesia in 2013 with an initial estimate of 19,000 cases (Cao-Lormeau et al. 2014). In early 2015, the first cases of Zika virus infection were reported in northeastern Brazil, and it has now spread more widely in Central and South America (Campos et al. 2015; Zanluca et al. 2015). As of April 2016, over 1.5 million people have been affected by Zika in Brazil alone (Carod-Artal 2016).

Zika is primarily spread through the bite of *Aedes* species mosquitoes (Thomas et al. 2015). It can also be sexually transmitted (vaginal, oral, and anal sex) and through blood transfusions (Ramos da Silva and Gao 2016). Approximately 80% of the infections with Zika are asymptomatic, and most of those infected have a mild, self-limiting febrile illness that may be accompanied by fever, rash, headache, arthralgia, and conjunctivitis (Thomas et al. 2015). However, some cases are associated with neurological symptoms, particularly with the Asian strain that spread to South America. A rise in the incidence of the neurological disorder Guillain-Barré syndrome was reported in association with the 2013 Zika outbreak in French Polynesia; in the Americas, an association has also been reported in Brazil, Colombia, El Salvador, Martinique, Panama, Puerto Rico, Suriname, and Venezuela (Broutet et al. 2016).

In South and Central America, fetal and neonatal microcephaly is associated with mothers infected by the Zika virus. By the end of 2015, Brazil reported approximately 4,000 cases of microcephaly, which was a 20-fold increase in the rate reported between 2010 and 2014, before the Zika epidemic (Fauci and Morens 2016). Zika was declared a public health emergency by the CDC in 2016, primarily due to its association with neonatal microcephaly (Ramos da Silva and Gao 2016).

The natural reservoir for the Zika virus is currently unknown. Several primates are susceptible to the virus. In Uganda, where the virus was first isolated, it has been found in three species of primates in the wild: the grey-cheeked mangabey (*Lophocebus albigena*), the red-tailed guenon (*Cercopithecus ascanius*), and the guereza (*Colobus guereza*). In Asia, the virus has been isolated in both wild and semi-captive Bornean orangutans (*Pongo pygmaeus*).

In the Neotropics, the virus has been detected in two species: the common marmoset (*Callithrix jacchus*) and the bearded capuchin (*Sapajus libidinosus*) (Favoretto et al. 2016). All of the New World monkey Zika infections involved monkeys living in close association with humans and also in an area with high incidence of microcephaly, suggesting that the Zika virus was anthroponotically acquired by the monkeys. Three capuchins tested positive – two were pets and one was being held in a wildlife screening facility. Four marmosets that were free ranging but co-habitating with humans tested positive. When monkeys are habituated to humans but also spend time in the forest, it sets up the potential for the initiation of a sylvatic cycle among nonhuman primates.

Paramyxoviridae: Rubeola, Respirovirus (HPIV-1, -3) *and* Rubulavirus (HPIV-2, -4, *and* Mumps*)*

Measles or Rubeola is a *Morbillivirus* and a highly contagious disease that is spread by respiratory aerosols (Gershon 2015). Measles typically occurs in children as a self-limiting illness with symptoms of cough, fever, congestion, conjunctivitis, and a distinctive maculopapular rash (Gershon 2015). However, measles infection also causes immunosuppression with secondary bacterial respiratory, gastrointestinal, or central nervous system infection (Coughlin et al. 2017). Deaths in infants are most likely to be due to pneumonia and in older children, encephalitis (Gershon 2015). Measles remains a significant problem in the developing world despite the availability of a vaccine. In 2000, there were an estimated 750,000 deaths due to measles globally; however, over the last 15 years, vaccination programs have reduced the rate by 60%, particularly in Africa (Gershon 2015). There were still 9.7 million cases of measles reported in 2015 (Coughlin et al. 2017).

Many nonhuman primate species are susceptible to measles. Prior to the 1970s and the availability of the measles vaccine, numerous outbreaks of measles were documented in nonhuman primates in laboratory and research environments (Brack 1987). Species affected include New World monkeys (*Aotus trivirgatus, Callithrix jacchus, Saguinus fuscicollis, S. oedipus, and Saimiri sciureus*), Asian monkeys (*Macaca fascicularis, M. mulatta, M. radiata, Trachypithecus cristatus*), African monkeys (*Colobus guereza*), and chimpanzees (*Pan troglodytes*). In the wild, an apparent outbreak of measles occurred among gorillas in Rwanda, with 6 deaths and 27 others becoming ill (Ferber 2000). Although the gorillas were free ranging, they were on a reserve that sponsored ecotourism, which facilitated the anthroponotic infections.

Human parainfluenza viruses belong to two genera. HPIV-1 and -3 are members of the genus *Respirovirus*, and HPIV-2 and -4 belong to the genus *Rubulavirus*, which also includes the mumps virus. Both *Respirovirus* and *Rubulavirus* are transmitted through direct contact, respiratory droplets, or fomites (Ison 2015; Litman and Baum 2015). The parainfluenza viruses occur worldwide and are responsible for upper and lower respiratory tract infections, particularly in children (Ison 2015). Most infections are mild and self-limiting, but HPIV-3 can be more severe and is the most likely of the four types to be associated with bronchiolitis and pneumonia (Ison 2015). Mumps infection also occurs worldwide and typically occurs in children and adolescents but is less common since the development of a vaccine in the late 1960s (Litman and Baum 2015). Mumps is typically mild and self-limiting with characteristic swelling of the parotid or salivary glands; rarely it progresses to meningitis, encephalitis, epididymo-orchitis, and oophoritis (Litman and Baum 2015). A few cases of HPIV and mumps have been documented in wild primates, with HPIV-2 and HPIV-3 in Kenyan baboons and HPIV-3 and mumps in Bornean orangutans.

Picorniviridae: Enteroviruses *(coxsackie, poliovirus)*

Picorniviridae includes a wide range of viruses including the rhinoviruses, responsible for the common cold. Two genera that have relevance to nonhuman primates will be considered here: *Enterovirus* and *Hepatovirus*. The human enteroviruses include over 100 different serotypes, most of which are transmitted through the alimentary, fecal-oral, or respiratory routes (Pons-Salort et al. 2015). Most enteroviruses present with subclinical infections, but some may cause severe neurological and cardiac symptoms. One of the most severe is the poliovirus, which can cause poliomyelitis that affects the central nervous system causing paralysis (Romero and Modlin 2015). Although a vaccine is available, it remains endemic in Afghanistan, Nigeria, and Pakistan and has been recently reintroduced into several sub-Saharan African and Eastern Mediterranean countries (Romero and Modlin 2015). In the wild, outbreaks of polio have been documented in chimpanzees in Tanzania and Zaire (Wallis and Lee 1999). In both of these cases, the diagnosis was inferential, based on clinical symptoms and the presence of polio in humans in neighboring areas. In the laboratory, both macaques and great apes are susceptible to experimental infection, and one outbreak was documented in colobus monkeys in captivity in Kenya (Brack 1987).

Of the non-polio enteroviruses, coxsackie and enteric cytopathic human orphan virus (ECHO) have been identified in wild primates. Coxsackie virus is one of enteroviruses responsible for hand-foot-and-mouth disease. Hand-foot-and-mouth disease is typically a mild and self-limiting illness occurring commonly in children under the age of five with symptoms of fever, rash, and blisters on the hands, feet, and buttocks and in the mouth (Pons-Salort et al. 2015). Coxsackie virus has been identified in wild baboons in Kenya and in orangutans in Borneo. More severe forms of hand-foot-and-mouth disease that may cause cardiopulmonary and neurological symptoms are primarily associated with *Enterovirus* A71 virus (rather than coxsackie), which has not yet been identified in wild primates. In addition, a variety of ECHO viruses have been documented in wild primates, primarily in Asian monkeys. Although ECHO viruses typically only cause mild respiratory tract infection, diarrhea, or rash, some have been associated with hand-food-and-mouth disease, as well as more severe neurological symptoms (Lum et al. 2002).

As a brief note, one study identified Hepatitis A in wild South African baboons. Hepatitis A is primarily transmitted through the fecal-oral route and typically manifests as a self-limiting illness with fever, jaundice, diarrhea, nausea, and fatigue, although fulminant hepatitis may develop in a small number of cases (Dienstag and Delmos 2015).

***Pneumoviridae:* Human metapneumovirus *and* Human Respiratory Synctial Virus**

Human metapneumovirus (HMPV) and human respiratory syncytial virus (HRSV) are extremely common respiratory infections in humans with worldwide distribution. Both are transmitted through contact with respiratory secretions (Falsey 2015; Walsh and Hall 2015). Globally, most children have been infected with HMPV by the age of five and infections can be recurrent (Falsey 2015). Most children have been infected with HRSV by the age of two, and it may also be a recurrent infection (Walsh and Hall 2015). HMPV causes upper respiratory infections which may resemble the common cold, but more severe cases may involve bronchiolitis and pneumonia (Falsey 2015). HRSV typically begins as an upper respiratory infection with cough, congestion, and fever and can progress to a more severe lower respiratory tract infection with bronchiolitis and/or pneumonia (Walsh and Hall 2015). HRSV is of particular concern in young children.

HMPV and HRSV have both been identified in the great apes. HRSV was first identified in chimpanzees that were experiencing cold symptoms with nasal inflammation and was originally termed Chimpanzee Coryza Agent (CCA) before it was recognized in humans (Walsh and Hall 2015). Chimpanzees and humans are the only known natural hosts for HRSV (Walsh and Hall 2015). HRSV has since been identified not only in chimpanzees in the wild, but also in wild and semi-captive orangutans. HMPV has also been identified in chimpanzees and gorillas in the wild.

Reoviridae

Viruses in the family Reoviridae commonly infect human beings, as well as plants and animals, but most are not considered significant causes of human disease (DeBiasi and Tyler 2015). One important exception is the genus *Rotavirus*. Three groups of *Rotavirus* are capable of infecting humans (A, B, and C), with group A capable of causing severe disease. *Rotaviruses* is transmitted through the fecal-oral route with symptoms of fever and gastroenteritis with nausea, vomiting, diarrhea, and subsequent dehydration, particularly in infants and children (Dormitzer 2015). Although most children worldwide are exposed to *Rotavirus* within the first few years of life, most of the deaths occur in the developing world (Dormitzer 2015).

Rotavirus has been identified in New World and Old World primates in the wild and more specifically, *Rotavirus A* in macaques and orangutans. The zoonotic potential for rotaviruses is unclear. Although the various serotypes/genotypes are generally considered species specific, animal strains have been found in humans and animals are capable of being infected experimentally with human strains (Cook et al. 2004). In Cook et al.'s (2004) review, they describe both animal strains (including those that infect wild primates) and properties of animal strains in humans, the latter of which may be genetic reasssortants.

Other genera of Reoviridae capable of causing symptomatic infection in humans are *Orthoreovirus*, *Orbivirus*, *Coltivirus*, and *Seadornavirus* (DeBiasi and Tyler 2015). Of these, *Orthoreovirus* and *Orbivirus* species have been found in wild primates. *Orthoreovirus* includes *Reovirus* types 1, 2, and 3. Infection with *Reovirus* is common in humans but is typically either asymptomatic or presents as a mild respiratory tract infection or gastrointestinal illness; rarely, it is the causative agent for meningitis, encephalitis, pneumonia, or myocarditis (DeBiasi and Tyler 2015). Few surveys of

Reovirus in wild primates have been conducted, but it has been identified in Asian macaques and langurs as well as African baboons. *Orbiviruses* capable of causing disease in humans include the Kemerovo complex viruses, Lebombo virus, and Changuinola virus (DeBiasi and Tyler 2015). Of these, only the *Orungo* virus has been found in wild primates. The *Orungo* virus is a vector-borne parasite that is transmitted by *Anopheles*, *Aedes*, and *Culex* species of mosquitoes (Attoui and Mohd 2015). It is widely distributed in tropical Africa where it has been isolated in monkeys, cattle, camel, sheep, goats as well as humans (Attoui and Mohd 2015). *Orungo* virus infection is often asymptomatic, but when symptoms occur they include fever, headache, and myalgia with one documented case of it progressing to encephalitis in a child (DeBiasi and Tyler 2015). In humans, seroprevalence rates in some areas of sub-Saharan Africa are between 24% and 35% (DeBiasi and Tyler 2015). A similar rate of 24% has been found in grivets and Mona monkeys in Nigeria (Tomori and Fabiyi 1976), and as such, they should be considered a potential reservoir.

Retroviridae:* Deltaretrovirus *(HTLV/STLV)*, Lentivirus *(HIV/SIV), Spumavirus (Simian foamy virus)

Deltaretrovirus*: HTLV/STLV*

Deltaretrovirus includes the Primate T-lymphotropic virus (PTLV), which consists of four human types, HTLV (I–IV) and four corresponding wild primate counterparts STLV (I–IV) (Ahuka-Mundeke et al. 2011; Richard et al. 2015). HTLV-I was first isolated in 1979 from a patient with T-cell lymphoma, and the case represented the first identification of a retrovirus in humans (Poiesz et al. 1980). In 1982, HTLV-II was described in a patient with hairy cell leukemia (Kalyanaraman et al. 1982). HTLV-I has a number of subtypes: A has spread worldwide, B is found in central Africa, C in Melanesia/Australia, and D also in central Africa (Ayouba and Peeters 2015; Vandamme et al. 1998). It is estimated that 10–20 million people have been infected (Johnson et al. 2001). The prevalence of HTLV-II is not well known, but has been identified in several Amerindian populations and in drug abusers in the U.S., Europe, and Asia (Rosadas et al. 2014). Only a few cases of HTLV-III have been identified in African individuals living in the vicinity of infected primates, and only one case of HTLV-IV has been identified to date in a hunter from Cameroon (Richard et al. 2015).

HTLV-I is asymptomatic in the majority of cases, but in 2–5% of the cases, it may progress to lymphoma, leukemia, inflammatory diseases, neurological disorders, and predisposition to opportunistic infections (Vandamme et al. 1998; Verdonck et al. 2007). The presence of disease in

HTLV-II infection is rare, but has been associated with myelopathy (Rosadas et al. 2014) and hairy cell leukemia (Kalyanaraman et al. 1982). No clear information is yet available on any symptomology that may be associated with HTLV-III or HTLV-IV. HTLV-I can be transmitted through blood or blood products, sexual contact, and breastfeeding (Verdonck et al. 2007).

Molecular phylogenetic evidence suggests that the origin of PTLV-I is in wild African primates (STLV-I) and that the HTLV-I subtypes arose from separate transmissions from wild primates into humans (Vandamme et al. 1998; Van Dooren et al. 2001; Verdonck et al. 2007). The relationships among the various subtypes of STLV-I and HTLV-I are not completely understood. While human and wild primate viruses are interspersed for some subtypes, subtypes A and C do not have a close simian analogue (Ayouba and Peeters 2015). STLV-II has only been found in the wild among bonobos (*Pan paniscus*) (Ahuka-Mundeke et al. 2011). One molecular study suggested that the ancestor of HTLV-II is humans (Vandamme et al. 1998), which may be one reason that HTLV-II is less pathogenic than HTLV-I is. It also raises the possibility that STLV-II was anthroponotically acquired by bonobos from humans. Interestingly, Chen et al. (1994) described STLV-II in five of nine spider monkeys (*Ateles fusciceps*) housed in U.S. zoos and in a single owl monkey (*Aotus trivirgatus*). It has not been found in any free-ranging New World monkeys. Its existence in zoos suggests that it may have been acquired by the New World monkeys from other Old World primates housed at the zoo, or possibly by anthroponotic transfer from humans. STLV-III has been found in a number of central African monkeys and the common chimpanzee. STLV-IV has only been found in gorillas; some were wild-born, but appear to have been in captivity (LeBreton et al. 2014; Richard et al. 2015). Indirect evidence of the presence of STLV-IV derives from a hunter who was infected with STLV-IV after reporting a severe gorilla bite when hunting (Richard et al. 2015). Hunting of bushmeat is likely the key source of transmission of STLV from wild primates to humans, given that several studies have demonstrated significant seroprevalence in bushmeat: 7.9% in the DRC (Ahuka-Mundeke et al. 2012) and 8–11% in Cameroon (Liégois et al. 2008; Sintasath et al. 2009).

Lentivirus: *HIV and SIV*

The primate lentiviruses include HIV 1 and 2 (human immunodeficiency virus) and SIV (simian immunodeficiency virus). HIV was first isolated in 1983 from a 33-year-old male and determined to be the cause of AIDS (acquired immunodeficiency syndrome) (Barré-Sinoussi et al. 2004). HIV affects the CD_4 lymphocytes, resulting in immunosuppression and vulnerability to opportunistic infections (Reitz and Gallo 2015). HIV is transmitted through body fluids including blood, semen, rectal fluids, vaginal fluids, and breast milk and vertically from mother to fetus (CDC 2017). At the end of 2015, 36.7 million people were living with HIV in the world, with approximately 70% of the cases occurring in sub-Saharan Africa (UNAIDS 2016). Although the rates of HIV infection have been declining in recent years, there were still 2.1 million newly infected people in 2015 (UNAIDS 2016). HIV-1 is more widely distributed and pathogenic than HIV-2 is (Reitz and Gallo 2015).

SIV in nonhuman primates was first isolated in 1984 when Rhesus macaques (*Macaca mulatta*) in the New England Primate Research center developed AIDS-like symptoms (Ayouba and Peeters 2015). Ultimately, it was determined that the captive macaques had contracted SIV from contact with captive sooty mangabeys (*Cercocebus atys*, SIVsmm) that are naturally infected and asymptomatic. The AIDS-like symptoms in the Rhesus macaques suggested that HIV could be of nonhuman primate origin. Simian immunodeficiency viruses are widespread in wild primate populations. Of the 73 African species of wild primates, 45 (approximately 60%) demonstrate serological evidence of SIV infection (Locatelli and Peeters 2012). Among wild primates, evidence suggests that cross-species transmission has occurred, including recombination of SIV viruses (Locatelli and Peeters 2012). In humans, the evidence suggests that the origin of HIV-1 is in chimpanzees and gorillas and the origin of HIV-2 is in sooty mangabeys, with multiple instances of lateral transmission.

HIV-1 is believed to have crossed from chimpanzees and gorillas at least four times, represented by the subgroups of M, N, O, and P. The west central African chimpanzee subspecies *Pan troglodytes troglodytes* is the reservoir for SIVcpz*Ptt* that crossed into humans' HIV-1 group M, responsible for the human pandemic, and HIV-1 group N which affected only a few individuals in Cameroon (Van Heuverswyn et al. 2007). Both HIV-1 groups O and P have been linked to SIVgor in western lowland gorillas (*Gorilla gorilla gorilla*). HIV-1 group O–like viruses have been found in a gorilla subspecies (*Gorilla gorilla gorilla*) (Van Heuverswyn et al. 2007) and Group P (from a Cameroon woman in France) is closely related to SIVgor (Neel et al. 2010; Plantier et al. 2009). However, it cannot yet be said with certainty whether western lowland gorillas are the reservoir for O and P, since both fall within the SIVcpz radiation (Neel et al. 2010). However, Neel et al. (2010) were unable to identify SIVcpz*Ptt* strains that were closely enough related to SIVgor to constitute their source. They suggest several possibilities: that the ancestral SIVcpz that gave rise to SIVgor is extinct or that O and P actually originated in chimpanzees.

SIVsmm is endemic and nonpathogenic in the sooty mangabey (*Cercocebus atys*) and is recognized as the progenitor of HIV-2 (Chen et al. 1996;

Gao et al. 1992). In the Côte d'Ivoire, 59% of wild sooty mangabeys were found to harbor the virus (Santiago et al. 2005). SIVsmm has crossed into human populations on at least eight different occasions. Groups A and B have infected substantial numbers in West Africa, but each of groups C to H has only been identified in single individuals (de Silva et al. 2008; Santiago et al. 2005)

Much remains unclear about how and why wild primate SIVs cross into human beings. While the proximate cause is most likely in blood-to-blood contact with wild primates through bushmeat hunting, what is not well understood is why only a few of the SIVs have crossed into humans. For example, the important SIVcpz has two lineages: SIVcpz*Ptt* in *Pan troglodytes troglodytes* and SIVcpz*Pts* in *Pan troglodytes schweinfurthii*; the former is responsible for the human pandemic, but the latter is not known to infect humans (Keele et al. 2006). Although SIV has crossed into human populations on multiple occasions, only a few strains have had significant human-to-human transmission (HIV-1 group M and HIV-2 groups A and B). Given that SIV exists naturally in multiple primate species and given the multiple times of crossover, the emergence of a new human HIV pandemic remains a distinct possibility.

Spumavirus: *Simian foamy virus*

Simian foamy viruses are often described as "ubiquitous" in nonhuman primates, with many different strains in prosimians, New World monkeys, and Old World primates documented both in the wild and in captivity (e.g., Locatelli and Peeters 2012; Muniz et al. 2013). The virus can be spread to humans from exposure to saliva or blood in occupational settings or hunting contexts but is apparently nonpathogenic to either humans or wild primates (Murray and Linial 2006).

A study of zoo and research institute workers in contact with primates found 3.35% (n = 418) to be seropositive (Switzer et al. 2004). All were healthy and spouses were not infected. A similar study found 3% (n = 322) of zoo workers to be seropositive (Sandstrom et al. 2000).

Several studies have documented low levels of seropositivity among bushmeat hunters (Switzer et al. 2012; Wolfe et al. 2014), but one study reported a 18.6% rate among individuals who had been bitten or scratched by a wild primate while hunting (Betsem et al. 2011).

The evidence suggests that SFV is not pathogenic in humans. Although humans can be infected with the virus, they are a dead-end host, and it is not spread from human to human. Nonetheless, SFV is important to the extent that it demonstrates the transfer of retroviruses from wild primates to humans, particularly in the context of the hunting and butchering of animals, which may have implications for other infectious agents that can be transferred through blood and body fluids.

Togaviridae: chikungunya, Eastern equine encephalitis, Mayaro, O'nyong-nyong virus, Semliki Forest virus, Sindbis virus

Togaviridae consists of two genera: *Alphavirus* and *Rubivirus*. The latter is the agent of Rubella and appears to be specific to human hosts. There are over 30 species of *Alphavirus*, which are typically mosquito-borne, and infect mammals, fish, birds, and invertebrates (Markoff 2015). Many of the alphaviruses are of concern as emerging and re-emerging infections, and a number of alphaviruses that infect humans also infect wild primates.

A number of the alphaviruses that cause infection in humans belong to the Semliki Forest virus complex, including chikungunya, Mayaro, O'nyong-nyong, Ross River virus, and the Semliki Forest virus. All have similar symptoms of fever, arthralgia, and rash (Markoff 2015). While the genetic relatedness of the viruses is clear, the evolutionary history of their geographic distribution is not (Powers et al. 2001). Most viruses of the Semliki Forest complex occur in Africa, but Mayaro virus occurs in South America and Ross River virus occurs in Australia and the South Pacific (Markoff 2015).

Chikungunya (CHIKV) is of particular concern as a re-emerging infection due to large-scale outbreaks affecting millions since 2004. CHIKV is transmitted primarily through the bite of *Aedes* species mosquitoes (and to a lesser extent, *Culex*), but can also be transmitted vertically from mother to fetus (Bandeira et al. 2016). Symptoms of infection are rapid onset of fever with arthralgia, myalgia, headache, and rash (Weaver and Lecuit 2015). The arthralgia can be debilitating and may persist for several years after the initial infection (Mavalankar et al. 2007). Four lineages of CHIKV have been identified: (1) West African, (2) East/Central/South African (ESCA), (3) Asian, and (4) Indian Ocean (IOL) (Weaver 2014). Phylogenetic evidence suggests the recent IOL CHIKV derived from ESCA CHIKV and is monophyletic in that taxon (Volk et al. 2010). The IOL strain of CHIKV has been associated with cases of encephalitis in neonates and adults (Gérardin et al. 2016).

Chikungunya was first identified in Tanzania during an outbreak in Tanzania in 1953 (Markoff 2015); soon after, chikungunya outbreaks occurred in the 1950s and 1960s (Weaver and Lecuit 2015). However, it has been hypothesized that chikungunya may have also been spread from Africa to Asia and the Americas as early as the 18th century by *Aedes* mosquitoes inhabiting water storage containers on sailing ships, much as yellow fever was spread outside of Africa (Carey 1971). Nonetheless, chikungunya appeared to be largely contained to East Africa up until the beginning of the 21st century. In 2004, an outbreak occurred in Kenya affecting 500,000 people (Markoff 2015). From there it spread to the Indian Ocean island of La Réunion and into India, affecting over 1.5 million people, and by 2014, over a million cases were suspected in the Americas (Inglis et al. 2016). A few cases have also occurred in Florida (Weaver and Lecuit 2015).

Chikungunya has been identified in both African and Asian monkeys. The ancestral cycle is believed to have originated among forest-dwelling African wild primates and *Aedes* sp. mosquitoes, with regular spillovers into human urban populations (Kumar and Gopal 2010; Weaver 2014). Geographically, CHIKV seropositive wild monkeys are widely distributed in Africa occurring in eastern, western, and southern Africa. Off the coast of Africa, prosimians in Mayotte and Mauritius have also been detected as seropositive. In captivity, gorillas and chimpanzees have also tested seropositive (Harrison et al. 1967). In Asia, there is evidence of some spillback into wild primates, but no clear indication that a sylvatic cycle has become established. A few cases of seropositive macaques have been identified in the Philippines, Mauritius, and La Réunion. In South and Central America, despite the large numbers of cases identified in humans, no spillback into wild primates has yet been documented. But it should remain a concern that it may follow the yellow fever pattern since it is transmitted by *Aedes* vectors.

O'nyong-nyong (ONNV) virus is also mosquito-borne, but is primarily spread by *Anopheles* species mosquitoes (Rios-González 2017). ONNV was first isolated in 1959 in Uganda during an epidemic outbreak that spread to the west as far as Senegal and south as far Mozambique, affecting over two million people; a second smaller outbreak occurred in Uganda in 1996 (Tappe, Kapaun et al. 2014). Although it has not been detected outside of Africa except in travelers, concern exists that it could spread in a pattern similar to chikungunya (Rios-González 2017). ONNV and CHIKV both had mid-century outbreaks in Africa with a subsequent long hiatus before another outbreak was documented. Although ONNV appears currently confined to Africa, it could potentially be spread by *Anopheles* vectors in other parts of the world. Thus far, seropositivity to O'nyong-nyong has only been detected in one wild monkey, *Mandrillus sphinx*.

Semliki Forest virus was first isolated in Uganda in the early 1940s (Smithburn and Haddow 1944). In surveys in sub-Saharan Africa from the 1950s to the 1980s, up to half of those tested had antibodies to the virus; it has also been detected in Russia and Vietnam (Pfeffer 2001). Semliki Forest virus appears to be spread primarily through *Aedes* species of mosquitoes (Markoff 2015). Although Semliki Forest virus may be asymptomatic, some may experience symptoms similar to other viruses within the complex of fever, arthralgia, myalgia, and headache; one case of fatal encephalitis has

Table 2.2 RNA Viruses

BUNYAVIRADAE		
Bunyamwera virus		
Cercopithecus ascanius	Uganda (W)	McCrae and Kirya 1982
Colobus guereza[1]		
Lophocebus albigena[2]		
Oropouche virus		
Alouatta sp.	Trinidad (W)	Roberts et al. 1977
Alouatta caraya	Brazil (W)	Gibrail et al. 2016
Alouatta guariba	Brazil (W)	Rocha et al. 2015
Cebus sp.	Trinidad (W)	Roberts et al. 1977
Cebus libidinosus	Brazil (W)	Gibrail et al. 2016
Cebus olivaceus	Venezuela (W)	Navarro et al. 2016
FILOVIRIDAE		
Ebolavirus		
Gorilla gorilla	Gabon/RC (W)	Leroy et al. 2004a; Wittmann et al. 2007
Pan troglodytes	RC (W)	Leroy et al. 2004a
	Gabon/RC (W)	Wittmann et al. 2007
***Ebola virus* – Taï Forest**		
Pan troglodytes	Côte d'Ivoire (W)	Formenty et al. 1999; Le Guenno et al. 1995; Wyers et al. 1999
FLAVIVIRIDAE		
***Dengue* (not specified)**		
Macaca fascicularis	Philippines (W/SC)	Inoue et al. 2003
Macaca nemestrina	Thailand (SC)[3]	Nakgoi et al. 2014
Macaca sinica	Sri Lanka (W)	De Silva et al. 1999
Dengue 1		
Cercopithicini spp.[4]	Nigeria (W)	Monath et al. 1974
Dengue 2		
Cercopithicini spp.[4]	Nigeria (W)	Monath et al. 1974
Chlorocebus sabaeus	Senegal (W)	Sylla et al. 2014
Erythocebus patas	Senegal (W)	Sylla et al. 2014
Mandrillus sphinx	Gabon (W)	Kading et al. 2013
Macaca sinica	Sri Lanka (W)	Peiris et al. 1993
Pongo pygmaeus (Bornean)	Borneo (W/SC)	Kilbourn et al. 2003; Wolfe et al. 2001

(*Continued*)

Table 2.2 (Continued)

Japanese encephalitis		
Macaca nemestrina	Thailand (C[3])	Nakgoi et al. 2014
Pongo pygmaeus (Bornean)	Borneo (W/SC)	Kilbourn et al. 2003; Wolfe et al. 2001
Kyasanur Forest disease virus		
Macaca radiata	India (W)	Work and Trapido 1957
Semnopithecus entellus	India (W)	Hensgens and Kuijper 2013; Work and Trapido 1957
St. Louis encephalitis		
Ateles chamek	Bolivia (W)	Karesh et al. 1998
Alouatta guariba	Brazil (W)	Rocha et al. 2015
Alouatta villosa	Panama (W)	Seymour et al. 1983
Ateles geoffroyi[5]	Panama (W)	Galindo and Srihongse 1967
West Nile virus		
Cercopithicini spp.[4]	Nigeria (W)	Monath et al. 1974
Cercopithecus ascanius	Uganda (W)	Kirya and Okia 1972; McCrae and Kirya 1982
Cercopithecus mona	Uganda (W)	McCrae and Kirya 1982
Chlorocebus pygerythrus[9]	South Africa (W)	Kaschula et al. 1978
Colobus guereza[1]	Uganda (W)	McCrae and Kirya 1982
Gorilla beringei	Gabon (W)	Kading et al. 2013
Yellow Fever		
Alouatta belzebul	Brazil (W)	Hoch et al. 1981
Alouatta caraya	Brazil (W)	Almeida et al. 2012
	Argentina (W)	Holzmann et al. 2010
Alouatta guariba	Argentina (W)	Holzmann et al. 2010
Alouatta guariba[7]	Brazil (W)	Almeida et al. 2012; Sallis et al. 2003
Alouatta pigra[8]	Panama (W)	Seymour et al. 1983
Alouatta seniculus	French Guiana (W)	de Thoisy et al. 2004, 2001
Aotus trivirgatus	Panama (W)	Seymour et al. 1983
Ateles chamek	Bolivia (W)	Karesh et al. 1998
Callithrix (Mico)argentata	Brazil (W)	Hoch et al. 1981
Callithrix pencillata	Brazil (W)	Laemmert and Ferreira 1945
Pithecia pithecia	French Guiana (W)	de Thoisy et al. 2004, 2001
Saguinus geoffroyi	Panama (W)	Seymour et al. 1983

Saguinus midas	French Guiana (W)	de Thoisy et al. 2004, 2001
Cercopithicini spp.[4]	Nigeria (W)	Monath et al. 1974
Cercopithecus ascanius	Uganda (W)	Kirya and Okia 1972; Simpson et al. 1965
Chlorocebus aethiops[8]	Uganda (W)	Kirya and Okia 1972; McCrae and Kirya 1982
Chlorocebus sabaeus	Gambia (W)	Monath et al. 1980
Procolobus badius	Gambia (W)	Monath et al. 1980
Erythrocebus patas	Senegal (W)	Sylla et al. 2014
Lophocebus albigena[2]	Uganda (W)	McCrae and Kirya 1982
Mandrillus sphinx	Gabon (W)	Kading et al. 2013
Papio sp.	Kenya (W)	Kalter et al. 1966
Zika virus		
Callithrix jacchus	Brazil (P/W)	Favoretto et al. 2016
Sapajus libidnosus[2]	Brazil (P)	Favoretto et al. 2016
Cercopithicini spp.[4]	Nigeria (W)	Monath et al. 1974
Lophocebus albigena[2]	Uganda (W)	McCrae and Kirya 1982
Cercopithecus ascanius	Uganda (W)	Kirya and Okia 1972; McCrae and Kirya 1982
Chlorocebus aethiops[8]	Uganda (W)	Kirya and Okia 1972
Colobus guereza[1]	Uganda (W)	McCrae and Kirya 1982
Pongo pygmaeus (Bornean)	Borneo (W/SC)	Kilbourn et al. 2003; Wolfe et al. 2001
ORTHOMYXOVIRUS		
***Influenza* A2**		
Macaca mulatta	India (W)	Bhatt et al. 1966
Macaca radiata		
Semnopithecus entellus		
African monkeys		
Papio sp.	Kenya (W)	Kalter et al. 1966
PARAMYXOVIRIDAE		
Morbillivirus: Rubeola/measles		
Gorilla beringei[10]	Rwanda (W)	Ferber 2000
Respirovirus: HPIV-3		
Papio sp.	Kenya (W)	Kalter et al. 1966
Pongo pygmaeus (Bornean)	Borneo (SC)	Kilbourn et al. 2003

(*Continued*)

Table 2.2 (Continued)

Rubulavirus: Mumps virus		
Pongo pygmaeus (Bornean)	Borneo (W/SC)	Kilbourn et al. 2003
Rubulavirus: HPIV-2		
Papio sp.	Kenya (W)	Kalter et al. 1966
PICORNIVIRIDAE		
Coxsackie B2		
Papio sp.	Kenya (W)	Kalter et al. 1966
Coxsackie B4		
Pongo pygmaeus (Borneo)	SC/FR	Kilbourn et al. 2003
Enteric Cytopathic Human Orphan (ECHO)		
***Echovirus* 3, 11, 12, 19**		
Macaca mulatta	India (W)	Bhatt et al. 1966
Macaca radiata		
Semnopithecus entellus[11]		
***Echovirus* 7**		
Macaca mulatta	India (W)	Bhatt et al. 1966
Macaca radiata		
Semnopithecus entellus[11]		
Papio sp.	Kenya (W)	Kalter et al. 1966
Hepatitis A		
Papio ursinus	South Africa (W)	Drewe and O'Riain 2012
PNEUMOVIRIDAE		
Metapneumovirus: HMPV		
Pan troglodytes	Africa (W)	Calvignac-Spencer et al. 2012
	Côte d'Ivoire (W)	Köndgen et al. 2008
Gorilla beringei	Africa (W)	Calvignac-Spencer et al. 2012
	Rwanda (W)	Palacios et al. 2011
Orthopneumovirus: HRSV		
Pan troglodytes	Côte d'Ivoire (W)	Köndgen et al. 2008
Pongo pygmaeus (Bornean)	Borneo (W/SC)	Kilbourn et al. 2003
REOVIRIDAE		
Orungo virus		
Chlorocebus aethiops[9]	Nigeria (W)	Tomori and Fabiyi 1976
Cercopithecus mona		

***Reovirus* 1**		
Macaca mulatta	India (W)	Bhatt et al. 1966
Macaca radiata		
Papio sp.	Kenya (W)	Kalter et al. 1966
***Reovirus* 2, 3**		
Macaca mulatta	India (W)	Bhatt et al. 1966
Macaca radiata		
Semnopithecus entellus		
Rotavirus		
Alouatta seniculus	Venezuela (W)	Zavala et al. 2006
Semnopithecus entellus	India (W)	Hrdy 1981
Pan troglodytes	Tanzania (W)	Kaur et al. 2008
Pongo pygmaeus (Bornean)	FR/SC	Kilbourn et al. 2003
Rotavirus Group A		
Macaca fascicularis	Malaysia (W)	Awang and Yap 1990
Pongo pygmaeus (Bornean) (SA11)	FR/SC	Kilbourn et al. 2003
RETROVIRIDAE		
Deltaretrovirus STLV-I		
Macaca fascicularis	Cambodia (W)	Ayouba et al. 2013
Hylobates pileatus		
Presbytis cristata		
Cercocebus atys	Sierra Leone (B)	Traina-Dorge et al. 2005
Cercocebus agilis	Cameroon (B)	Courgnaud et al. 2004; Liégeois et al. 2008; Sintasath et al. 2009
Cercocebus torquatus	Gabon (B)	Liégeois et al. 2012
Cercopithecus ascanius	DRC (B)	Ahuka-Mundeke et al. 2012
Cercopithecus cephus	Cameroon, Gabon (B)	Courgnaud et al. 2004; Liégeois et al. 2012; Liégeois et al. 2008
Cercopithecus neglectus	DRC (B)	Ahuka-Mundeke et al. 2012
Cercopithecus nictitans	Cameroon, Gabon (B)	Courgnaud et al. 2004; Liégeois et al. 2012; Liégeois et al. 2008; Sintasath et al. 2009

(*Continued*)

Table 2.2 (Continued)

Cercopithecus pogonias	Cameroon (B)	Courgnaud et al. 2004; Liégeois et al. 2008
	CAR (W)	Saksena et al. 1994
	Gabon (B)	Liégeois et al. 2012
Cercopithecus wolfi	DRC (B)	Ahuka-Mundeke et al. 2012
Chlorocebus aethiops[9]	Ethiopia, CAR, Senegal (W)	Saksena et al. 1994; Takemura et al. 2002
Chlorocebus tantalus	Cameroon (B)	Courgnaud et al. 2004
Colobus guereza	Cameroon (B)	Liégeois et al. 2008
Erythrocebus patas	Central African Republic; Senegal (W)	Saksena et al. 1994
Lophocebus albigina	Cameroon (B)	Liégeois et al. 2008
Mandrillus sphinx	Cameroon (B)	Courgnaud et al. 2004
Mandrillus sphinx	Gabon (B)	Liégeois et al. 2012
Miopithecus ogouensis	Cameroon (B)	Courgnaud et al. 2004
Papio anubis	South Africa, Ethiopia (W)	Mahieux et al. 1998; Takemura et al. 2002
Papio cynocephalus	Tanzania (W)	Voevodin et al. 1997
Papio doguera	CAR (W)	Saksena et al. 1994
Papio ursinus	South Africa (W)	Mahieux et al. 1998
Piliocolobus badius	Côte d'Ivoire (W)	Leendertz et al. 2010
Piliocolobus tephrosceles	Uganda (W)	Goldberg et al. 2009
Piliocolobus tholloni	DRC (B)	Ahuka-Mundeke et al. 2012
Gorilla gorilla	Cameroon (B)	Courgnaud et al. 2004: Nerrienet et al. 2004
Deltaretrovirus: STLV-II		
Pan paniscus	DRC (B)	Ahuka-Mundeke et al. 2011
Deltaretrovirus: STLV-III		
Cercocebus torquatus	Gabon (B)	Liégeois et al. 2012
Cercocebus agilis	Cameroon (B)	Courgnaud et al. 2004; Liégeois et al. 2008; Sintasath et al. 2009
Cercopithecus cephus	Cameroon (B)	Liégeois et al. 2008
Cercopithecus mona	Cameroon (B)	Sintasath et al. 2009
Cercopithecus nictitans	Cameroon (B)	Courgnaud et al. 2004; Sintasath et al. 2009

Cercopithecus torquatus	Cameroon (B)	Liégeois et al. 2008
Colobus angolensis	DRC (B)	Ahuka-Mundeke et al. 2012
Colobus guereza	Cameroon (B)	Liégeois et al. 2008
Lophocebus albigena	Cameroon (B)	Liégeois et al. 2008; Sintasath et al. 2009
Lophocebus aterrimus	DRC (B)	Ahuka-Mundeke et al. 2012
Piliopithecus tholloni		
Pan paniscus	DRC (B)	Ahuka-Mundeke et al. 2011
***Lentivirus:* HIV-1 related**		
SIVcpz		
Pan troglodytes troglodytes	Tanzania (W)	Santiago et al. 2002
	DRC (W)	Worobey et al. 2004
	Cameroon (W)	Keele et al. 2006; Neel et al. 2010; Van Heuverswyn et al. 2006; Van Heuverswyn et al. 2007
SIVgor		
Gorilla gorilla	Cameroon (W)	Neel et al. 2010; Takehisa et al. 2009; Van Heuverswyn et al. 2006
***Lentivirus:* HIV-2 related**		
SIVsmm		
Cercocebus atys	Côte d'Ivoire (W)	Santiago et al. 2005
	Sierra Leone (W)	Apetrei et al. 2005; Chen et al. 1996
	Liberia and Sierra Leone (P)	Chen et al. 1996; Marx et al. 1991
TOGAVIRIDAE		
Chikungunya virus		
Eulemur fulvus	Mayotte (W)	Vourc'h et al. 2014
Galago senegalensis	Senegal (W)	Diallo et al. 1999
Macaca fascicularis	Reunion, Mauritius (W)	Vourc'h et al. 2014
	Philippines (W)	Inoue et al. 2003
Macaca nemestrina	Thailand (SC)	Nakgoi et al. 2014
Cercopithicini spp.[4]	Nigeria (W)	Monath et al. 1974

(*Continued*)

Table 2.2 (Continued)

Cercopithecus ascanius	Uganda (W)	Kirya and Okia 1972; McCrae and Kirya 1982
Chlorocebus aethiops[8]	Senegal (W)	Diallo et al. 1999
	Uganda (W)	Kirya and Okia 1972
	Zimbabwe (W)	McIntosh et al. 1963
	South Africa (W)	Kaschula et al. 1978
Colobus guereza[1]	Uganda (W)	McCrae and Kirya 1982
Lophocebus albigena[2]		
Mandrillus sphinx	Gabon (W)	Kading et al. 2013
Papio ursinus	Zimbabwe (W)	McIntosh et al. 1963
Eastern equine encephalitis virus		
Ateles chamek	Bolivia (W)	Karesh et al. 1998
Mayaro virus		
Alouatta belzebul	Brazil (W)	Hoch et al. 1981
Alouatta caraya	Argentina and Paraguay (W)	Díaz et al. 2007
Alouatta seniculus	French Guiana (W)	de Thoisy et al. 2003; Talarmin et al. 1998
Alouatta villosa	Panama (W)	Seymour et al. 1983
Callithrix (Mico)argentata	Brazil (W)	Hoch et al. 1981
Pithecia pithecia	French Guiana (W)	de Thoisy et al. 2003
Saguinus midas	French Guiana (W)	de Thoisy et al. 2003; Talarmin et al. 1998
Saimiri sciureus	French Guiana (W)	de Thoisy et al. 2003
Mayaro subtype UNA		
Alouatta caraya	Argentina and Paraguay (W)	Díaz et al. 2007
O'nyong-nyong Virus		
Mandrillus sphinx	Gabon (W)	Kading et al. 2013
Semliki Forest virus		
Cercopithecus ascanius	Uganda, Kenya (W)	Haddow 1952
Cercopithecus mitis	Uganda (W)	Haddow 1952
Cercopithecus mona		
Cercopithecus nictitans	Uganda (W)	Smithburn et al. 1944
Colobus guereza[8]	Uganda (W)	Haddow 1952

Lophocebus albigena[12]		
Papio anubis[13]		
Sindbis		
Pongo pygmaeus	Borneo (W)	Kilbourn et al. 2003; Wolfe et al. 2001

1. formerly *Colobus abyssinicus*
2. formerly *Cercocebus albigena*
3. Captive, but held in an open-air environment in their indigenous region in Thailand
4. Aggregated for *Cercopithecus mona*, *C. nictitans martini*, and *Chlorocebus aethiops tantalus* (= *Cercopithecus aethiops tantalus*)
5. = *Ateles grisescens*
6. formerly *Cercopithecus aethiops pygerythrus*
7. *Alouatta fusca* = *Alouatta guariba*
8. *Alouatta villosa* = *Alouatta pigra*
9. formerly *Cercopithecus aethiops*
10. Diagnosis by clinical symptoms
11. *Semnopithecus entellus* = former *Presbytis entellus*
12. *Lophocebus albigena* = former *Cercocebus albigena*
13. *Papio anubis* = former *Papio doguera*

been documented in a German researcher who was exposed to the virus in a laboratory setting (Pfeffer 2001). Shortly after the virus was first isolated, several species of African monkeys were found to be seropositive in the same region including *Cercopithecus*, *Colobus*, *Lophocebus*, and *Papio* species (Haddow 1952), suggesting that wild monkeys may be a possible reservoir.

Mayaro virus was first isolated in Trinidad in the 1950s with sporadic outbreaks since then in Brazil, Bolivia, and Venezuela (Auguste et al. 2010). The symptoms are similar to those of other Semliki Forest virus complex members with fever, arthralgia, and rash (Markoff 2015). The virus is believed to be maintained among wild monkeys and *Haemagogus* species of mosquitoes with urban spillover into human populations and *Aedes* species mosquitoes (Auguste et al. 2010). A number of New World monkey species have been found seropositive, including those of the genera *Alouatta*, *Callithrix*, *Pithecia*, *Saguinus*, and *Saimiri*. UNA virus, a subtype of Mayaro virus, has been found in *Alouatta* species in Argentina and Paraguay (Díaz et al. 2007).

Alphaviruses outside of the Semliki Forest complex that have been detected in both humans and wild primates are eastern equine encephalitis virus (EEEV) and Sindbis virus. EEEV is maintained in an avian/mosquito transmission cycle in North America, South America, and the Caribbean (Markoff 2015). *Culiseta* species mosquitoes are most important in avian transmission, with *Coquillettidia* and *Aedes* species mosquitoes being important bridge vectors to humans, horses, and other mammals (Go et al. 2014). In Bolivia, seropositivity has been identified in *Ateles* species monkeys in the wild. Wild monkey, like humans and other mammals, appear to be incidentally infected. Sindbis virus belongs to the western equine encephalitis complex and, like EEEV, is maintained in an avian/mosquito transmission cycle (Markoff 2015). *Culex*, *Culiseta*, and *Aedes* mosquito species have been identified as important vectors (Adouchief et al. 2016). Sindbis virus occurs in Eurasia, Oceania, and South Africa (Adouchief et al. 2016). Symptoms are similar to those of the Semliki Forest complex with fever, arthralgia, and rash (Markoff 2015). Among wild primates, seropositivity has been identified in orangutans in Borneo.

3 Protozoa

Enteric protozoa

Balantidium coli

Balantidium coli is a food- and water-borne infection with pigs being the primary reservoir (Suh et al. 2015). It is often asymptomatic but may lead to chronic diarrhea, if it invades the large intestine, or present as a fulminating infection, particularly in immunocompromised individuals, with bloody, mucoid explosive diarrhea, and in severe cases, perforation of the colon (Schuster and Ramirez-Avila 2008). It has a widespread distribution worldwide, essentially in any location where pigs are raised (Schuster and Ramrez-Avila 2008). It also has a wide host range; one study identified *B. coli* in 59 mammalian species just in Japan (Nakauchi 1999). It is considered a neglected disease that has not been extensively studied (Schuster and Ramirez-Avila 2008).

Although studies identifying *Balantidium coli* are limited, the parasite appears to have a wide host range in wild primates. It has been found in a prosimian (*Eulemur*), one New World monkey species (*Ateles paniscus*), two Asian primate species (*Macaca seniculus*, *Pongo pygmaeus*), several African monkey species (*Cercopithecus* spp., *Chlorocebus aethiops*, *Mandrillus sphinx*, *Papio* spp.), and gorillas (*Gorilla* spp.) and the chimpanzee (*Pan troglodytes*). In captivity, it has been found in many New World primates (*Alouatta*, *Ateles*, *Brachyteles*, *Cacajao*, *Callibella*, *Callicebus*, *Callimico*, *Callithrix*, *Cebus*, *Cebuella*, *Chiropotes*, *Leontopithecus*, *Mico*, *Pithecia*, *Saguinus*, and *Saimiri* spp.) (da Silva Barbosa et al. 2015). Given that pigs are the host reservoir, wild primate infections are likely due to water contamination from runoff water from pig farming. Thus, *B. coli* is likely an anthroponosis in wild primates.

Blastocystis

Blastocystis occurs worldwide in humans and infects a wide range of animals, including mammals, amphibians, birds, and reptiles (Vassalos et al. 2008). Some debate exists as to whether it is pathogenic in humans, but symptoms of diarrhea and abdominal pain have been reported in some patients (Dagci et al. 2014), and some evidence suggests it may be linked to irritable bowel syndrome (Poirier et al. 2012). The prevalence is highest in developing countries, at between 30% and 50% (Vassalos et al. 2008), but prevalence is also high in some areas of developed countries, including the U.S. at 22.5% (Yoshikawa 2012). The mode of transmission has not yet been conclusively determined between human-human, human-animal, and animal-animal, but it is likely the fecal-oral route through contaminated food and water (Yoshikawa 2012). *Blastocystis* was at one time considered a yeast infection and although now known to be a protozoa, the taxonomy of its species has not yet been resolved (Basak et al. 2014). *Blastocystis hominis* is the designation when it occurs in humans.

Blastocystis spp. have been identified in a number of species of wild New World monkeys (*Alouatta*, *Aotus*, *Ateles*, *Saimiri*, *Sapajus* spp.), Asian monkeys (*Macaca* spp.), African monkeys (*Cercopithecus*, *Colobus*, *Lophocebus*, *Papio*, *Presbytis* spp.) and in the chimpanzee (*Pan troglodytes*). Two studies have identified *Blastocystis hominis* in pet monkeys. In Ethiopia, pet monkeys (*Chlorocebus*, *Papio*) had a prevalence rate of 16% (Legesse and Erko 2004). In Indonesia, *B. hominis* was found in nine species of macaques (*Macaca*) with a prevalence rate of 42.5% (Jones-Engel et al. 2004). The pet studies suggest the possibility that *Blastocystis* may be anthroponotically acquired by wild primates. In addition, *Blastocystis* sp. has been identified in captive prosimians (*Lemur*, *Varecia* spp.), New World monkeys (*Alouatta*, *Ateles*, *Pithecia*), Asian monkeys (*Macaca* sp.), African monkeys (*Cercocebus*, *Cercopithecus*, *Erythrocebus* spp.), Asian apes (*Hylobates*, *Pongo* spp.), and African apes (*Gorilla* and *Pan* spp.) (Gómez et al. 1996; Maesano et al. 2014; Montoya et al. 2013).

Cryptosporidium

Cryptosporidiosis is primarily a waterborne infection with a worldwide distribution that is particularly prevalent in developing countries but has been associated with waterborne epidemics in the developed world (White 2015). It is estimated that 5–10% of people in developing countries are hosts to *Cryptosporidium* and that it is the cause of 15–25% of cases of diarrhea in children (Checkley et al. 2015). Oocysts are able to survive outside the body for several months, particularly in cooler climates (Fayer 2004). In the

1980s, large numbers of cases began to be identified in immunocompromised AIDS patients, and in 1993, it was associated with a large outbreak in Milwaukee, Wisconsin, that affected over 400,000 people (White 2015). In children, it is associated with malnutrition and impaired growth, which is believed to be due to inflammatory changes in the small intestine (Checkley et al. 2015).

Cryptosporidium has a broad host range, infecting domesticated and wild mammals as well as insects, fish, amphibians, reptiles, and birds (Fayer 2004; Xiao and Feng 2008). At one time, it was thought to be a single species, but it has now been differentiated into approximately 15 species (Fayer 2004). *C. hominis* is the primary cause of infection in humans, followed by *C. parvum* (White 2015). However, AIDS patients have been diagnosed with *C. canis* (dogs), *C. felis* (cats), and *C. melagridis* (turkeys) (Xiao and Feng 2008). Host specificity is variable with some species appearing to be host-specific and others, such as *C. parvum*, being more cosmopolitan (Fayer 2004). *Cryptosporidium* spp. have been identified in prosimians, New World monkeys, Asian monkeys, and African monkeys and apes in the wild. Only two specific species have been identified in wild primates, with *C. bovis* infecting gorillas and *C. parvum* infecting spider monkeys (*Ateles*), howler monkeys (*Alouatta*), and gorillas (*Gorilla*). *Cryptosporidium* spp., including *C. hominis*, *C. andersoni*, and *C. parvum*, have also been commonly found in nonhuman primates in captivity, and undifferentiated *Cryptosporidium* spp. have been found in New World monkeys (*Alouatta*, *Saimiri*, *Callithrix*) and Asian monkeys (*Macaca*) (da Silva et al. 2009; Hahn et al. 2010; Montoya et al. 2013).

Cyclospora

Cyclospora cayetanensis is an intestinal parasite that is spread by ingesting food or water that has been contaminated with feces (CDC 2013). It has a worldwide distribution but is most common in developing areas (Suh et al. 2015). *C. cayetanensis* is a common cause of traveler's diarrhea, but it has become a concern as an emerging disease due to several large-scale food-borne outbreaks in the late 1990s in the United States and Canada (Shields and Olson 2003). *C. cayetanensis* infection is sometimes asymptomatic, but common symptoms are watery diarrhea, vomiting, headache, fever, and other flu-like-symptoms (CDC 2013). It is also of concern because it has been associated with more serious sequelae including Guillain-Barré syndrome, reactive arthritis syndrome, and cholecystitis (Shields and Olson 2003).

Cyclospora cayetanensis has been detected in a few species of wild primates: spider monkeys (*Ateles*) and howler monkeys (*Alouatta*) in the

New World and macaques (*Macaca*) from Nepal. A *Cyclospora* sp. that may be *C. cayetanensis* has been detected in baboons (*Papio anubis*) and vervets (*Chlorocebus aethiops*) that were living in the premises of a hotel in Ethiopia (Legesse and Erko 2004). Due to their human habitation and adaptation to an urban setting, the monkeys are best considered as pets. However, they may represent simian-adapted *Cyclospora* species. Recently, several *Cyclospora* species have been identified in wild primates in Kenya and Ethiopia that appear to have some degree of host specificity at the level of the tribe and perhaps the genus (Eberhard et al. 1999, 2001). Two species of colobus monkeys (*Colobus angolensis* and *C. guereza*, subfamily Colobines) harbor *Cyclospora colobi*. In the Cercopithicinae subfamily, differences occur at the level of the tribe. The cercopithecine *Chlorocebus aethiops* harbors *Cyclospora cercopitheci* and two Papionines (baboons, *Papio anubis* and *P. cynocephalus*) harbor *Cyclospora papionis*. Although it is not known whether these simian *Cyclospora* species are capable of infecting humans, given their host specificity, it is likely a low risk. *Cyclospora* species have also been identified in captive chimpanzees and macaques in a research center in Italy (Marangi et al. 2015).

Entamoeba histolytica

Entamoeba histolytica is a gastrointestinal parasite spread through the fecal-oral route through ingestion of contaminated food or water (Petri and Rashidul 2015). Approximately 80% of the cases are asymptomatic, and when symptoms appear, they are often mild with diarrhea (CDC 2015a). However, in some cases, amebic dysentery may develop with more severe symptoms of bloody diarrhea, amebic colitis, and liver abscess (Petri and Rashidul 2015). Approximately 34–50 million symptomatic cases occur worldwide each year with approximately 100,000 deaths (Petri and Rashidul 2015). It is most common in tropical areas of the developing world and associated with poverty and poor sanitation (CDC 2015a). Young children and immunocompromised individuals are most at risk (Petri and Rashidul 2015).

A significant problem in determining the extent of *E. histolytica* in wild primates is that it is morphologically indistinguishable from the nonpathogenic *E. dispar*; the two can only be distinguished through PCR and ELISA (Gonin and Trudel 2003). In the wild primate literature, it is often described as the *E. histolytica/dispar* complex. When studies have described broadly an *Entamoeba* sp., it could also refer to the common nonpathogenic commensal parasite *Entamoeba coli* or the nonpathogenic *E. hartmanni.* One additional species, *E. moshkoviskii*, may also infect humans and cause amebic dysentery (Petri and Rashidul 2015), but this species was not found in wild primates in the review of the literature. Fifteen studies in the literature review specifically identified *E. histolytica* in wild primates. However, the methodologies appeared to identify the species by morphology, and none provided specific information as to how *E. histolytica* and *E. dispar* were differentiated. Although it seems likely that *E. histolytica* could parasitize wild primates, the studies currently available do not provide sufficient evidence of occurrence of the infection in primates in the wild.

Giardia lamblia

Giardia lamblia (also known as *G. intestinalis* or *G. duodenalis*) has been described as the most common waterborne human parasite worldwide (Halliez and Buret 2013). It is most common in developing regions where nearly all children have been infected by the age of ten (Hill and Nash 2015). It is most often spread through drinking contaminated water, but can also be spread through contact with food, soil, or other objects contaminated with feces (CDC 2015b). *Giardia lamblia* is capable of surviving outside the body for weeks or months (CDC 2015b). Symptoms vary considerably. Individuals may be asymptomatic, experience a self-limiting diarrheal disease, or develop a chronic infection (Hill and Nash 2015). Chronic infection is of concern, for it may lead to chronic diarrheal disease manifesting in growth and cognitive deficiencies in children or irritable bowel syndrome in adults (Halliez and Buret 2013).

A number of *Giardia lamblia* genotypes (assemblages) infect a broad range of animal species. Assemblages A and B are found in humans, wild primates, and other wild and domesticated animals; assemblages G–H are not known to usually infect humans or wild primates (Hill and Nash 2015). *Giardia lamblia* has been identified in a number of wild primate species in the Old World and the New World. Studies that have only been able to determine to the level of genus, *Giardia* sp., are likely *Giardia lamblia* since this is the only species yet known to infect wild primates. It should be noted that the literature review did not locate studies identifying *Giardia* in either prosimians or Asian primates in their natural habitats. *Giardia* is widespread in Asia (e.g., Yong et al. 2000), so it may be that sufficient research has not yet been conducted to identify these parasites in Asian monkeys. Studies from zoos have identified *Giardia* in Asian primates, including langurs (*Semnopithecus*), lutungs (*Trachypithecus*), macaques (*Macaca*), gibbons (*Hylobates*, *Nomascus*), and orangutans, as well as prosimians (*Lemur*, *Nycticebus*), suggesting that they are at least susceptible to the infection (Beck et al. 2011; Karim et al. 2015).

Sarcocystis

The genus *Sarcocystis* is a ubiquitous parasite with almost 190 identified species in multiple species of animals (Poulsen and Stensvold 2014). Self-limiting gastrointestinal symptoms in humans have been primarily due to *S. hominis* (from infected beef) and *S. suihominis* (from infected pork) (Suh et al. 2015); however, the infection is typically asymptomatic (Poulsen and Stensvold 2014). Between 2012 and 2014, three outbreaks of invasive muscular sarcocystitis in Malaysia have made *Sarcocystis* a concern as an emerging infection. Two outbreaks occurred on Tioman Island (Esposito et al. 2012; Tappe et al. 2014) and one on Pangkor Island (Abubakar et al. 2012). DNA analysis revealed the Pangkor Island outbreak to be due to *S. nesbitti* (Abubakar et al. 2012). Previously (as of 2004), only about 100 cases of human invasive sarcocystitis had been reported, with most discovered accidentally (Esposito et al. 2012).

Apart from the identification of a *Sarcocystis* sp. in wild baboons (*Papio ursinus*), the literature is scarce for this parasite in nonhuman primates in the wild. In captive studies, *Sarcocystis kortei* has been documented in African primates (*Macaca*, *Erythrocebus*, *Cercopithecus*) and *S. nesbitti* in New World (*Saimiri*, *Saguinus*), and Asian (*Macaca*) and African primates (*Papio*) (Dubey et al. 2015; Karr and Wong 1975; Yang et al. 2005). Invasive muscular *Sarcocystis* has been identified in captive baboons (*Papio*), macaques (*Macaca*), and tamarins (*Saguinus*) (Kan et al. 1979; Kuncl and Richter 1988; Mehlhorn et al. 1977; Prathap 1973). In captivity, it appears to be particularly common in the lion-tailed macaque (*Macaca fascicularis*). Although captive studies must be viewed with extreme caution in interpreting the existence of a parasite in the wild, it is noteworthy that the lion-tailed macaque inhabits both Pangkor and Tioman Islands (the sites of recent outbreaks), which have resort hotels. A Google image search of these two islands showed these monkeys in hotel areas, eating from garbage bins and interacting with humans. In one image, a juvenile monkey is sitting on a woman's lap. Given the level of human habituation of these monkeys, the presence of *S. nesbitti* in captive primate lab studies, and the recent human outbreaks of invasive muscular sarcocystosis (at least one of which was *S. nesbitti*), it seems likely these monkeys do play a role in human infection.

Toxoplasma gondii

Toxoplasma gondii is a parasite found worldwide. In the United States, it is estimated that approximately 22.5% of the population over age 12 have been infected, with rates up to 95% in hot, humid climates in other parts of the world (CDC 2015c). *T. gondii* is spread through ingestion of

Table 3.1 Enteric Protozoa

***Balantidium* sp.**		
Alouatta palliata	Ecuador (W)	Helenbrook et al. 2015
Papio ursinus	South Africa (W)	McConnell et al. 1974
Balantidium coli		
Eulemur fulvus	Madagascar (W)	Clough 2010
Ateles paniscus	Bolivia (W)	Karesh et al. 1998
Macaca seniculus	Sri Lanka (W)	Ekanayake et al. 2006
Pongo pygmaeus	Borneo (SC/W)	Kilbourn et al. 2003
Cercocebus agilis	CAR (W)	Lilly et al. 2002
Cercopithecus neglectus	Kenya (W)	Muriuki et al. 1998
Cercopithecus mitis		Munune et al. 1998; Muriuki et al. 1998
Chlorocebus aethiops[1]		Muriuki et al. 1998
Mandrillus sphinx	Gabon (W)	Poirotte et al. 2016
	Gabon (SC)	Setchell et al. 2007
Papio anubis[2]	Kenya (W)	Munune et al. 1998; Muriuki et al. 1998; Myers and Kuntz 1968
	Ghana (W)	Ryan et al. 2012
	Tanzania (W)	McGrew et al. 1989
	Nigeria (W)	Weyher et al. 2006
Papio cynocephalus	Tanzania (W)	Kooriyama et al. 2012
Papio hamadryas	Saudi Arabia (W)	Ghandour et al. 1995
Papio papio[3]	Senegal (W)	Howells et al. 2011; McGrew et al. 1989
Papio ursinus[4]	Namibia (W)	Appleton and Brain 1995; Benavides et al. 2012
Gorilla beringei	Rwanda (W)	Hassell et al. 2013
Gorilla gorilla	CAR (W)	Lilly et al. 2002
Pan troglodytes	CAR (W)	Lilly et al. 2002
	Tanzania (W)	Gillespie et al. 2010
	Senegal (W)	Howells et al. 2011
***Blastocystis* sp.**		
New World Monkeys		
Alouatta palliata	Ecuador (W)	Helenbrook et al. 2015
Alouatta seniculus	Peru (W)	Phillips et al. 2004
Aotus azarae	Argentina (W)	Perea-Rodriguez et al. 2010

(*Continued*)

Table 3.1 (Continued)

Ateles belzebuth	Peru (W)	Phillips et al. 2004
Saimiri sciureus		
Sapajus apella[5]		
Cercopithecus ascanius	Uganda (W)	Chapman et al. 2012
Cercopithecus mitis		
Colobus guereza		
Colobus vellerosus	Ghana (W)	Teichroeb et al. 2009
Lophocebus albigena	Uganda (W)	Chapman et al. 2012
Presbytis femoralis	Singapore (W)	Srivathsan et al. 2016
Pan troglodytes	Uganda (W)	Ashford 2000; Muehlenbein 2005
Blastocystis hominis		
Alouatta seniculus	Peru (W)	Phillips et al. 2004
Saimiri sciureus		
Sapajus apella[5]		
Macaca fascicularis	Indonesia (P)	Jones-Engel et al. 2004
Macaca hecki		
Macaca maura		
Macaca nemestrina		
Macaca nigra		
Macaca nigrescens		
Macaca ochreata		
Macaca tokeana		
Macaca hybrid		
Chlorocebus aethiops[1]	Ethiopia (P)	Legesse and Erko 2004
Papio anubis		
Pan troglodytes	Guinea-Bissau (W)	Sá et al. 2013
***Cryptosporidium* sp.**		
Microcebus rufus	Madagascar (W)	Rasambainarivo et al. 2013
Prolemur simus		
Saguinus mystax	Peru (W)	West et al. 2013
Macaca seniculus	Sri Lanka (W)	Ekanayake et al. 2006
Semnopithecus priam		
Trachypithecus vetulus		
Chlorocebus aethiops[1]	Ethiopia (P)	Legesse and Erko 2004
Papio anubis[2]	Ethiopia (P), Uganda (W)	Legesse and Erko 2004; Hope et al. 2004

Piliocolobus tephrosceles	Uganda (W)	Salzer et al. 2007
Gorilla beringei	Uganda (W)	Nizeyi et al. 1999
Cryptosporidium bovis		
Gorilla gorilla	CAR (W)	Sak et al. 2013
Cryptosporidium parvum		
Alouatta seniculus	Ecuador (W)	Roncancio-Duque and Montaño 2013
Ateles hybridus		
Gorilla beringei	Uganda (W)	Graczyk et al. 2001; Kalema-Zikusoka et al. 2005
***Cyclospora* sp.**		
Alouatta palliata	Ecuador (W)	Helenbrook et al. 2015
Chlorocebus aethiops[1]	Ethiopia (P)	Legesse and Erko 2004
Mandrillus leucophaeus	Equat. Guinea (W)	Eberhard et al. 2014
Papio sp.	Tanzania (W)	Smith et al. 1996
Papio anubis[2]	Ethiopia (P)	Legesse and Erko 2004
Pan troglodytes	Tanzania (W)	Smith et al. 1996
Cyclospora cayetanensis		
Alouatta seniculus	Ecuador (W)	Roncancio-Duque and Montaño 2013
Ateles hybridus		
Macaca mulatta	Nepal (W)	Chu et al. 2004
***Giardia* sp.**		
Alouatta caraya	Argentina (W)	Kowalewski et al. 2011
Alouatta palliata	Costa Rica (W)	Carmona et al. 2005
Alouatta pigra	Belize, Mexico (W)	Vitazkova and Wade 2006
Aotus azarae	Argentina (W)	Perea-Rodriguez et al. 2010
Papio anubis[2]	Uganda (W)	Hope et al. 2004
Gorilla beringei	Rwanda (W), Uganda (W)	Hogan et al. 2014; Nizeyi et al. 1999; Sleeman et al. 2000
Pan troglodytes	Uganda (W)	Ashford et al. 2000
Giardia lamblia		
Alouatta caraya		Stuart et al. 1998
Alouatta pigra	Belize, Mexico (W)	Vitazkova and Wade 2006
Cebus capucinus	Costa Rica (W)	Parr et al. 2013
Saimiri oerstedi		Appleton and Boinski 1991
Cercopithecus ascanius	Uganda (W)	Gillespie et al. 2005; Johnston et al. 2010; Salzer et al. 2007

(*Continued*)

Table 3.1 (Continued)

Cercopithecus ascanius		Chapman et al. 2012
Chlorocebus pygerythrus[6]		Petrášová et al. 2010
Colobus guereza		Johnston et al. 2010
Colobus vellerosus	Ghana (W)	Teichroeb et al. 2009
Papio hamadryas	Saudi Arabia (W)	Ghandour et al.1995; Nasher 1988
Papio ursinus[4]	Namibia	Appleton and Brain 1995
Piliocolobus tephrosceles[7]	Uganda (W)	Johnston et al. 2010; Salzer et al. 2007
Gorilla beringei	Rwanda (W)	Graczyk et al. 2002; Sleeman et al. 2000
	DRC (W)	Kalema-Zikusoka et al. 2005
	Uganda (W)	
Pan troglodytes	Tanzania (W)	Huffman et al. 1997
	Guinea-Bissau (W)	Sá et al. 2013
***Sarcocystis* sp.**		
Papio ursinus	South Africa (W)	McConnell et al. 1973
Toxoplasma gondii		
Eulemur macaco	Madagascar (W)	Junge and Louis 2007
Propithecus diadema		Irwin et al. 2010
Alouatta caraya	Brazil (W)	Garcia et al. 2005; Molina et al. 2014
Alouatta seniculus	French Guiana (W)	Carme et al. 2002; de Thoisy et al. 2003
Callithrix pencillata	Brazil (W)	Molina et al. 2014
Cebus sp.		Garcia et al. 2005
Saguinus midas	French Guiana (W)	de Thoisy et al. 2003
Saimiri sciureus	Mexico (P)	Cedillo-Peláez et al. 2011
Sapajus apella[4]	Brazil (W)	Silva et al. 2013
Chlorocebus aethiops[1]	South Africa (W)	Kaschula et al. 1978
Chlorocebus sabaeus[8]	Caribbean (W)	Hamilton et al. 2014
Macaca sinica	Sri Lanka (W)	Ekanayake et al. 2004
Papio ursinus	South Africa (W)	McConnell et al. 1973

SC = Semi-Captive; P = Pet; W = Wild (free-ranging)

Note: See end of Table 3.2 (Vector-Borne Protozoa) for notes to all Protozoa.

contaminated food or water, accidental ingestion of fecal material, or vertical transmission from mother to child *in utero* (Montoya et al. 2015). The only known definitive hosts are felids, including both domesticated cats and wild felids, such as lions, tigers, jaguars, and bobcats (Fayer et al. 2004). A wide range of mammals and birds are susceptible to infection in the wild due to its presence in the environment in soil and water (Montoya et al. 2015). Infection in humans is typically asymptomatic, but congenital infection may cause severe symptoms in infants including neurological disease, ocular disease leading to blindness, and cardiac and cerebral abnormities (Paquet et al. 2013). Congenital transmission often occurs when pregnant women are infected when cleaning the litter boxes of pet cats (CDC 2015c). In immunocompromised individuals (such as those with HIV/AIDS), symptoms present typically as a reactivation of a latent infection, rather than one that has been newly acquired (Montoya et al. 2015).

Several studies have found wild primates to be seropositive for *Toxoplasma gondii* including prosimians, New World monkeys, and African monkeys. Among green monkeys (*Chlorocebus sabeus*) in St. Kitts, 48.1% were found to be seropositive (Hamilton et al. 2014).

Likely many more species are susceptible in the wild. Studies from zoo animals have found seropositive prosimians (*Lemur* sp.), New World monkeys (*Ateles*, *Cebus*), Asian monkeys (*Macaca*), African monkeys (*Erythrocebus*) and apes (*Gorilla*, *Hylobates*, *Pan*, *Pongo*). Another study of note identified *T. gondii* infection as the cause of death for two pet squirrel monkeys brought to a veterinary clinic in Mexico City (Cedillo-Peláez et al. 2011). Although *T. gondii* infection is typically asymptomatic in humans, this study raises the possibility that it may cause more serious disease in wild primates.

Vector-borne protozoa

Plasmodium

Plasmodium species are widespread and responsible for malaria infections in humans and other animals. In humans, *Plasmodium* parasites are spread by several *Anopheline* species of mosquito vectors (Fairhurst and Wellems 2015). Sinden and Gilles (2002) estimated that *Plasmodium* infects approximately 120 species of mammals, reptiles, and birds. That figure is likely an underestimate, for it is known to occur in at least 65 species of wild primates (Cormier 2011). Four *Plasmodium* species are classified as human parasites: *P. falciparum*, *P. vivax*, *P. malariae*, and *P. ovale* (Fairhurst and Wellems 2015). In addition, the simian parasite *P. knowlesi* has recently been called the "fifth human malaria," due to recent human outbreaks in Southeast Asia

(McCutchen 2008; White 2008). Public health interventions have led to a significant decline in malaria cases over the last 15 years; however, in 2015, approximately 214 million cases and 438,000 deaths occurred worldwide (WHO 2015a). Malaria primarily occurs in the tropical regions of sub-Saharan Africa, Asia, Oceania, and Latin America (Fairhurst and Wellems 2015), but mostly (88%) in Africa (WHO 2015a).

All forms of malaria are characterized by cyclical fevers with the length of periodicity depending on the plasmodial species (Fairhurst and Wellems 2015). Falciparum malaria and vivax malaria constitute the greatest health concerns, with *P. falciparum* being the most prevalent form in Africa and *P. vivax* having a wider geographic distribution (WHO 2015a). *P. vivax* is rare in sub-Saharan Africa due to RBC Duffy negativity, which is a homozygous state of red blood cell antigens that confer complete resistance to *P. vivax* (Marsh 2002). Over 97% of the indigenous peoples in sub-Saharan Africa exhibit RBC Duffy negativity (Carter and Mendis 2002). The sickle cell trait and other RBC polymorphisms provide some resistance to *P. falciparum*, but do not confer immunity in the way that RBC Duffy negativity does for *P. vivax* (see Cormier 2011 for a review). *P. falciparum* is a malignant form of malaria, which in addition to the characteristic fever can cause severe anemia, respiratory distress, renal failure, cerebral malaria, severe malaria of pregnancy, shock, multi-system organ failure, and death (Fairhurst and Wellems 2015). The other forms of malaria are considered more benign. *P. malariae* is often asymptomatic with low levels of parasitemia; however, *P. vivax* and *P. ovale* do sometimes cause serious and fatal illness (Fairhurst and Wellems 2015).

The relationships among the plasmodia that cause human and wild primate malaria are complicated and characterized by a long evolutionary history of host switching (Cormier 2011). Cormier (2011) suggested that the distinction between human versus nonhuman plasmodia is misleading, and instead proposed classifying by the four broad types of malaria, each of which have species that affect both human and nonhuman primates. Falciparum-type malaria includes African ape *P. reichenowi*, human *P. falciparum*, and a number of newly identified species affecting chimpanzees and gorillas. Recent molecular studies have placed the origin of human *P. falciparum* in gorillas; ironically, its evolution is linked to a human enzyme mutation involving sialic acids that conferred immunity to *P. reichenowi* (Chou et al. 1998; Irie et al. 1998; Muchmore et al. 1998). Thus, *P. falciparum* arose in humans by taking advantage of an enzyme mutation that protected them from *P. reichenowi*. Interestingly, New World monkeys have a similar enzyme mutation that appears to have arisen independently that also makes them susceptible to *P. falciparum* (Martin et al. 2006). Beginning in 2001, a number of New World monkey species including *Alouatta*, *Callicebus*, *Lagothrix*, *Pithecia*, and *Saimiri* species began to be documented with *P. falciparum* infections in the wild in Brazil, French Guiana, and Peru. Monkey infections are most certainly anthroponotic, given the evidence that *P. falciparum* was introduced into the Americas from Africa during colonization (see Cormier 2011 for review). The evidence of *P. falciparum* in South American monkeys is disturbing, for it presents the possibility that they could become a new reservoir and potentially increase the prevalence of *P. falciparum* in the Neotropics.

Vivax-type malaria is particularly prominent in Neotropical monkeys and Asian monkeys but also affects Asian apes, and to a lesser extent, African apes and monkeys.

In the New World, the relationships between *P. simium* and *P. vivax*, as well as *P. brasilianum* and *P. malariae*, are so close that many malaria researchers have argued that they should be considered indistinguishable conspecifics (e.g., Ewald 1983; Escalante et al. 1995; Fandeur et al. 2000; Lal et al. 1988; LeClerc et al. 2004; Rich and Ayala 2000). *P. simium/vivax* has a limited host range in New World monkeys, occurring only in *Alouatta*, *Brachyteles*, and *Saguinus* species, with most of the cases occurring in the Atlantic forest of Brazil. Like *P. falciparum* in the New World, both *P. simium/vivax* and *P. brasilianum/malariae* are likely anthroponotic infections in monkeys introduced during colonization. Eight simian vivax-type species affect Asian primates and one is specific to African monkeys; *P. vivax* itself can infect gorillas and chimpanzees and *P. vivax/P. simium* is found in New World monkeys (Cormier 2011). The vivax-type species in Asian monkeys are variable as to host specificity with some plasmodia species infecting multiple species of monkeys, some monkeys being infected with multiple species of plasmodia, and others being more host-specific. Given the broad host range of some of the vivax-type malarias, they are of concern as potential zoonoses. In 2004, simian *P. knowlesi* (vivax type) was identified as the parasite responsible for a large-scale outbreak of severe malaria in Borneo (Cox-Singh et al. 2008; Singh et al. 2004). Since then, cases have been identified in Thailand (Jongwutiwes et al. 2004; Putaporntip et al. 2009), the Philippines (Luchavez et al. 2008), and Singapore (Ng et al. 2008). *P. cynomolgi* (vivax type) is also of concern, since it is also capable of infecting humans. The first cases were identified in the 1960s among primate researchers who were accidentally infected with *P. cynomolgi* (Eyles et al. 1960), and a recent case occurred in Malaysia (Ta et al. 2014).

P. brasilianum/malariae is extremely widespread in New World monkeys, documented in all families, nearly all genera, and multiple species. Cases of *P. malariae* may be underestimated in the Neotropics, particularly among indigenous peoples. WHO (2015a) statistics indicate that *P. malariae* is not detected at a statistically appreciable level in Amazonian South America. However, high rates have been reported in indigenous tribes. Seropositive rates of 38.8–45.4% have been found in adults among the Wayana, Emerillon, and Wayampi, 90% of Asurini, and 100% of the Metuktire (Volney et al. 2002; de Arruda et al. 1989). In Africa, a few cases of *P. malariae* have been identified in chimpanzees (*Pan troglodytes*) and bonobos (*Pan paniscus*). The bonobo case was in a sanctuary primate, so it may be a case of anthroponotic infection. *P. ovale* at one time was considered to be exclusive to human beings, but recently, cases have been identified in chimpanzees and gorillas. Overall, the *Plasmodia* of most concern for potential host switching between human and wild human primates are the vivax-type occurring in Asian monkeys, since *P. knowlesi* has had a recent host switch into humans and *P. cynomolgi* has been documented to infect at least one human.

African trypanosoma

Human African trypanosomiasis (HAT) is commonly known as African sleeping sickness. It is a vector-borne disease transmitted by the tsetse fly (*Glossina* spp.) and, rarely, through vertical transmission or blood transfusion (Kirchhoff 2015). It is caused by two related protozoal subspecies in the *Trypanosoma brucei* complex: *T. brucei gambiense* and *T. brucei rhodesiense*. A third type, *T. brucei brucei*, is an animal parasite that is non-pathogenic in humans (Bengis et al. 2002). The Gambian form accounts for 98% of the cases, 95% of which occur in the Democratic Republic of Congo (Franco et al. 2015). The Rhodesian form occurs in East Africa and is a zoonotic disease of a variety of domesticated and wild animals that occasionally infects humans (Franco et al. 2015). HAT manifests in a hemolymphatic stage and a central nervous system stage (Kirchhoff 2015). The hemolymphatic stage involves fever, headache, anemia, and lymphadenopathy. In the second stage, the central nervous system is invaded with neuropsychiatric signs and symptoms. The Rhodesian form tends to follow a more rapid course and can lead to death if untreated, whereas the Gambian form typically develops into chronic disease if untreated. Over the last 15 years, control efforts have significantly decreased the number of new cases, with less than 10,000 new cases in 2009 (the lowest in 50 years) and less than 4,000 new cases in 2014 (WHO 2016c).

The three members of the *Trypanosoma brucei* complex have been characterized as anthroponotic (*T. b. gambiense*), zoonotic with humans as accidental host (*T. b. rhodesiense*), and strictly zoonotic (*T. b. brucei*). *T. gambiense* has only been identified in a few species of western and central

African monkeys (*Cercocebus torquatus*, *Cercopithecus ascanius*, *C. nictitans*, and *Lophocebus albigena*). Given the limited number of cases identified, they likely represent spillover infections into wild primates from humans, but it cannot yet be ruled out that they may serve as reservoirs. The Rhodesian type infects a wide number of domesticated and wild animals, including bovids (e.g., cattle, impala), suids (wild and domesticated pigs), giraffes, zebras, lions, and hyenas (Franco et al. 2015). Nagana is the common name for *T. b. brucei* infection, which also infects wild and domesticated animals including bovids and suids, as well as horses, dogs, and elephants (Bengis et al. 2002).

Humans and some nonhuman primate species possess what is termed the trypanocidal (or trypanolytic) factor (TC) due to the APOL1 gene, which makes them resistant to nagana (*T. b. brucei*) (Thomson et al. 2014). TC is present in humans and in a few primate species, including Western lowland gorillas (*Gorilla gorilla*), mandrills (*Mandrillus sphinx*), the sooty mangabey (*Cercocebus atys*) and two species of baboon (*Papio cynocephalus* and *P. hamadryas*) (Lugli et al. 2004; Seed et al. 1990; Seed et al. 1993). However, TC was absent in a number of other species tested, including other apes (chimpanzees, bonobos, orangutans, and gibbons), African cercopithecines and colobines, and Asian macaques, suggesting they may be potentially susceptible to nagana (Seed et al. 1990).

Infection with undifferentiated *T. brucei* s.l. has been identified in a several species of free-ranging African prosimians, monkeys, and chimpanzees. Based on geographic location, they may possibly represent both *T. b. gambiense* and *T. b. rhodesiense* infections. However, *T. b. rhodesiense* is not known to infect wild primates despite its ability to infect humans and cause HAT. In western and central Africa, two species of prosimians, ten species of monkeys, and the Western chimpanzee were positive for *T. brucei* s.l. Of note is that the sooty mangabey is infected. Given that this species is immune to *T. brucei brucei* at the West African location, it suggests the possibility of Gambian trypanosoma infection. In East Africa, the eastern chimpanzee, the olive baboon (*Papio cynocephalus*), and the vervet monkey (*Chlorocebus aethiops*) have been found positive for *T. brucei* s.l. These may represent infections with Rhodesian trypanosoma, although it has not yet been documented in primates. Nagana is also a possibility, as is the possibility that the trypanosoma responsible is another *T. brucei* complex member not yet identified. In summary, it can be established that *T. b. gambiense* is capable of infecting some western and central African primates, but it is unclear if they are accidental hosts or potentially reservoirs. *T. b. rhodesiense* is suspect in East African nonhuman primate infections; *T. b. brucei* cannot be ruled out in primates that lack the TC factor.

In addition, a number of wild primates in Africa and Asia are infected with a variety of other trypanosomes. These include:

- African prosimians: *T. congolese*, *T. irrangiense*, *T. peridictici*, and *T. vivax* (Berghe et al. 1963; Herder et al. 2002; Keymer 1971; Njiokou et al. 2004)
- Asian monkeys: *T. conorrhini* in *Macaca* spp. (Cross et al. 1983; Weinman 1972)
- African monkeys: *T. congolese* in *Cercopithecus*, *Colobus* spp., *T. simiae* in *Cercocebus* and *Cercopithecus* spp., and *T. vivax* in *Cercocebus*, *Cercopithecus*, *Miopithecus* sp. (Herder et al. 2002; Njiokou et al. 2004)

American trypanosoma

American trypanosomiasis, commonly known as Chagas disease, is a vector-borne disease caused by the protozoan parasite *Trypanosoma cruzi*. The vectors are triatomine insects that infect when their feces come into contact with tissues, such as the conjunctivae, mucosal surfaces, or skin abrasions (Bennett et al. 2014). Although there are over 100 different species of triatomine insects capable of transmitting the parasites, the most important species are *Rhodnium prolixus* and *Triatoma infestans*, which infest houses (Kollien and Schaub 2000). The parasites can also be transmitted vertically, through blood transfusion, or through consuming infected food and water (WHO 2012).

Today, approximately 6–7 million people are infected in 21 Latin American countries where the disease is endemic (WHO 2017b). Due to insect control measures, the rates have decreased significantly from the 1980s, when an estimated 24 million people were infected (WHO 2012). Cases of *T. cruzi* infection have also been found in several southern U.S. states, including Alabama, Arizona, California, Florida, Georgia, Louisiana, New Mexico, Tennessee, Texas, and Utah (Zeledon et al. 2012). The acute phase of infection is often asymptomatic, but may involve fever, headache, enlarged lymph glands and/or muscle, and abdominal or chest pain (WHO 2016c). In less than 50% of the cases, an inflammatory lesion called a chagoma may develop at the site of entry of the infection (Bennet et al. 2014; WHO 2017b). Chagas may develop into a chronic, long-term infection, with 20–30% of those with chronic infection developing irreversible cardiovascular, gastrointestinal, and/or neurological disorders (WHO 2012).

Trypanosoma cruzi has been documented in all families and multiple species New World primates. When zoos and research centers in Brazil are included, *T. cruzi* has been documented in almost every genus of

New World primate, including *Aotus nigriceps*, *Brachyteles arachnoides*, *Cacajao calvus*, *Callicebus personatus*, *Callimico goeldi*, *Callithrix* spp., *Chiropotes satanas*, *Leontopithecus* spp., *Mico* spp., *Pithecia irrorata*, *Saguinus* spp., and *Saimiri boliviensis* (Eberhard and D'Alessandro 1982; Lisboa, Mangia, Rubião et al. 2004; Minuzzi-Souza et al. 2016; Ziccardi et al. 2000). Although these are not natural infections, strictly speaking, the captive primates are in geographic areas where the triatomine bug is endemic. In addition, a number of *T. cruzi* infections have also been identified in captive Old World primates in zoos, research centers, and colonies in southern U.S. states (Louisiana, Texas, and Georgia). They include the prosimians (*Lemur catta*), Old World monkeys (*Macaca and Papio* spp.), and a chimpanzee (*Pan troglodytes*) (Bommineni et al. 2009; Hall et al. 2007; Kasa et al. 1977; Olson et al. 1986; Pung et al. 1998; Schielke et al. 2002; Williams et al. 2009). Since *T. cruzi* does not naturally exist in the Old World, they may represent novel cross-infections from being housed with New World primates at the facilities. Alternatively, these primates may represent sentinels for the presence of *T. cruzi* in the human population in the U.S. South. In addition, it should be noted that New World primates harbor several nonpathogenic species of trypanosomes with *T. devei*, *T. minasense*, *T. rangeli*, and *T. saimiri* being most often reported (Da Silva et al. 2004; Dunn et al. 1963; Ziccardi et al. 1998)

Leishmania

Leishmaniasis is a vector-borne disease with approximately one million cases and 20,000–30,000 deaths per year (WHO 2016d). Approximately 30 species have been identified, with about 15–20 capable of infecting humans, most of which are zoonotic (Ashford 2000; Gramiccia and Gradoni 2005). A variety of suspected reservoir hosts have been identified, which vary by geographic location and include dogs, horses, rodents, rock hyraxes, opossum, squirrels, anteaters, kinkajou, porcupines, sloths, and nonhuman primates (Ashford 2000). The vectors are phlebotomine sandflies with almost 100 species proven or suspected vectors, including *Phlebotomus* spp. in the Old World and *Lutzomyia* spp. in the New World (Maroli et al. 2013). *Leishmania* can also be transmitted by blood transfusions, needle sharing among drug users, vertical transmission, and in rare cases, sexual transmission (Magill 2015).

Three main forms of leishmaniasis exist: visceral (VL), cutaneous (CL), and muco-cutaneous (MCL). VL (or kala azar) is the most serious form with symptoms of fever, weight loss, anemia, and enlargement of the spleen and liver; if untreated, it is fatal in 95% of the cases (WHO 2016d). VL primarily affects infants and immunosuppressed individuals and is due specifically to *L. infantum* infection (Ashford 2000). VL is endemic in East Africa and the Indian subcontinent and is also common in Bangladesh, Brazil, Ethiopia, India, South Sudan, and Sudan (WHO 2016d). CL, the most common form of leishmaniasis, results in ulcerative skin lesions, with 95% of the cases occurring in the Americas, the Mediterranean Basin, and Central Asia (WHO 2016d). MCL leads to partial or total destruction of mucus membranes of the nose, mouth, and throat, with almost 90% of the cases occurring in Bolivia, Brazil, and Peru (Magill 2015; WHO 2016d).

Leishmania spp. have been identified in both New World and Old World primates. In South America, *L. brasiliensis* has been found in owl monkeys (*Aotus* spp.) and squirrel monkeys (*Saguinus geoffroyi*); *L. mexicana* has been found in howlers (*Alouatta* spp.); and *L. shawi* in capuchins (*Sapajus apella*) and bearded sakis (*Chiropotes satanas*). Rovirosa-Hernández et al. (2013) found a prevalence rate of 30% (n = 55) among howlers sampled, suggesting the possibility that they are a reservoir. In addition, *L. amazonensis* and *L. chagasi/infantum* has been found in a variety of captive monkey genera housed in zoos in Brazil (*Ateles*, *Alouatta*, *Aotus*, *Callicebus*, *Leontopithecus*, *Pithecia*, *Saguinus*, and *Sapajus*) (De Lima et al. 2012; Malta et al. 2010). Similar to American trypanosoma, while the monkeys are not in their natural habitat, they are in a geographic region where *Leishmania* spp. occurs in the human population. Among Old World species, the presence of *L. major* has been identified in three wild monkey species and a gorilla. Gicheru et al. (2009) found prevalence rates of anti-*L. major* antibodies in 48.5% of baboons (n = 101, *Papio anubis*), 48% of vervets (n = 213, *Chlorocebus aethiops*), and 37.5% of Sykes monkeys (n = 64, *Cercopithecus mitis*). In addition, *L. major* was identified in 13% (12/91) of gorillas (*Gorilla gorilla*) in Cameroon (Hamad et al. 2015).

Babesia

Babesiosis is a vector-borne disease spread by ticks with malaria-like symptoms that can lead to hemolytic anemia and death (Gray et al. 2010). The genus *Babesia* is geographically widespread and diverse with more than 100 known species (Homer et al. 2000). The two of most concern to humans are *B. microti*, which occurs primarily in the U.S., and *B. divergens*, which occurs primarily in Europe; less commonly, it has been found Asia and Africa (Homer et al. 2000). A few recent studies have documented *B. microti*-like parasites in wild primates in Africa (*Chlorocebus aethiops*, *Papio anubis and P. cynocephalus*). This raises the possibility of zoonotic transmission to humans. However, given that babesiosis has only rarely been documented in humans in Africa (Homer et al. 2000), it does not seem to be a significant threat at this time.

Table 3.2 Vector-Borne Protozoa

PLASMODIA		
Plasmodia **– Falciparum Type**		
P. falciparum cluster/P. falciparum-like		
Gorilla gorilla	Cameroon (NI)	Duval et al. 2010
	Rep. of Congo (W)	Liu et al. 2010
Pan paniscus	DRC (S)	Krief et al. 2010
P. falciparum		
Alouatta, Ateles, Cebus, Chiropotes, Saimiri spp.[9]	Brazil (P)	De Arruda et al. 1989
Alouatta, Saimiri spp.[9]	Brazil (W)	De Arruda et al. 1989
Alouatta caraya	Brazil (W)	de Castro Duarte et al. 2008
Alouatta guariba		
Alouatta seniculus	French Guiana (W)	Volney et al. 2002
Callicebus brunneus	Brazil (W)	Araújo et al. 2013
Lagothrix cana		
Pithecia pithecia	French Guiana (W)	Volney et al. 2002
Saimiri sciureus	Peru (W)	Gonzalo and Tantaleán 1996
Gorilla gorilla	Cameroon (W)	Prugnolle et al. 2010
Pan troglodytes	Cameroon (NI)	Duval et al. 2010
Plasmodium **– Vivax Type**		
P. knowlesi		
Macaca cyclopis	Asia (NI)	Warren and Wharton 1963
Macaca fascicularis[10]	Asia (NI)	Coatney 1971; Coatney et al. 1971; Eyles 1963; Garnham 1963; Warren and Wharton 1963
	Malaysia (W)	Vythilingam et al. 2008; Warren et al. 1970
Macaca nemestrina	Asia (NI)	Coatney et al. 1971; Eyles 1963; Garnham 1963; Warren and Wharton 1963
Presbytis melalophos	Asia (NI)	Coatney et al. 1971; Eyles 1963; Warren and Wharton 1963

(*Continued*)

Table 3.2 (Continued)

P. simium/vivax		
Alouatta caraya	Brazil (W)	de Castro Duarte et al. 2008
Alouatta guariba[11]	Neotropics (NI)	Coatney 1971; Coatney et al. 1971; Eyles 1963; Garnham 1963; Warren and Wharton 1963
	Brazil (W)	da Fonseca 1951; Deane 1992, 1972, 1964; de Castro Duarte et al. 2008; Lourenço-de Oliveria and Deane 1995
Alouatta seniculus	French Guiana (W)	Volney et al. 2002
Brachytelesarachnoides	Neotropics (NI)	Coatney 1971; Coatney et al. 1971
	Brazil (W)	Lourenço-de Oliveria and Deane 1995
	Brazil (NI)	Deane 1992
Saguinus midas	French Guiana (W)	Volney et al. 2002
P. vivax		
Gorilla gorilla	CAR (W)	Mapua et al. 2015
Pan troglodytes	Côte d'Ivoire (W)	Kaiser et al. 2010
***P. vivax*-like**		
Pan troglodytes	DRC (S)	Krief et al. 2010
	Uganda (W)	
***Plasmodium* – Malariae Type**		
P. brasilianum/malariae		
Alouatta sp.	Neotropics (NI)	Warren and Wharton 1963
	Brazil (W)	De Arruda et al. 1989
	Brazil (P)	
Alouatta belzebul	Neotropics (NI)	Davies et al. 1991
	Brazil (W)	Deane 1992; Deane 1972; Lourenco-de Oliveria and Deane 1995
Alouatta caraya	Brazil (W)	Deane 1992; Deane 1972; de Castro Duarte et al. 2008; Lourenço-de Oliveria and Deane 1995
Alouatta clamitans	Brazil (W)	Costa et al. 2014
Alouatta guariba[11]	Brazil (NI)	Coatney et al. 1971
	Brazil (W)	Deane 1992, 1972; de Castro Duarte et al. 2008; Lourenço-de Oliveria and Deane 1995

Alouatta palliata	Neotropics (NI)	Coatney et al. 1971; Eyles 1963
	Brazil (W)	Deane 1992; Lourenço-de Oliveria and Deane 1995;
Alouatta seniculus	Neotropics (NI)	Coatney et al. 1971; Davies et al. 1991
	Brazil (W)	Deane 1972; Lourenço-de Oliveria and Deane 1995
	French Guiana (W)	de Thoisy et al. 2001; Fandeur et al. 2000; Volney et al. 2002
Alouatta pigra[12]	Neotropics (NI)	Coatney et al. 1971; Eyles 1963
	Brazil (W)	Lourenço-de Oliveria and Deane 1995
Aotus nigriceps	Brazil (W)	Araújo et al. 2013
Aotus vociferans	Brazil (W)	Lourenço-de Oliveria and Deane 1995
	Peru (W)	Collins et al. 1985
Ateles sp.	Neotropics (NI)	Warren and Wharton 1963
	Brazil (P)	De Arruda et al. 1989
Ateles belzebuth	Brazil (W)	Lourenço-de Oliveria and Deane 1995
Ateles chamek[13]	Neotropics (NI)	Coatney et al. 1971
	Brazil (W)	Araújo et al. 2013; Deane 1992, 1972
Ateles fusciceps	Neotropics (NI)	Coatney et al. 1971; Eyles 1963
Ateles geoffroyi[14]	Neotropics (NI)	Coatney et al. 1971; Eyles 1963
	Brazil (W)	Lourenço-de Oliveria and Deane 1995;
Ateles paniscus	Neotropics (NI)	Coatney et al. 1971; Davies et al. 1991; Eyles 1963
	Brazil (W)	Deane 1992, 1972; Deane et al. 1989; Lourenço-de Oliveria and Deane 1995
Brachyteles arachnoides	Neotropics (NI)	Coatney et al. 1971
	Brazil (W)	Deane 1992, 1972; Lourenço-de Oliveria and Deane 1995
Cacajao calvus	Neotropics (NI)	Coatney 1971; Davies et al. 1991; Eyles 1963; Warren and Wharton 1963
	Brazil (W)	Deane 1992, 1972, 1964

(*Continued*)

Table 3.2 (Continued)

Callicebus brunneus	Neotropics (NI)	Davies et al. 1991
	Brazil (W)	Deane 1992; Deane et al. 1989; Lourenço-de Oliveria and Deane 1995
Callicebus caligatus	Brazil (W)	Bueno et al. 2013
Callicebus dubius	Brazil (W)	Araújo et al. 2013; Bueno et al. 2013
Callicebus moloch	Neotropics (NI)	Coatney et al. 1971; Davies et al. 1991
	Brazil (W)	Deane 1992, 1972; Lourenço-de Oliveria and Deane 1995
Callicebus moloch Complex	Neotropics (NI)	Davies et al. 1991
Callicebus ornatus	Neotropics (NI)	Coatney et al. 1971
	Brazil (W)	Lourenço-de Oliveria and Deane 1995
Callicebus torquatus	Neotropics (NI)	Coatney et al. 1971; Davies et al. 1991
	Brazil (W)	Deane 1992, 1972; Dean et al. 1969; Lourenço-de Oliveria and Deane 1995
Cebus s.l. sp.	Neotropics (NI)	Warren and Wharton 1963
	Brazil (P)	De Arruda et al. 1989
Cebus albifrons	Neotropics (NI)	Coatney et al. 1971; Davies et al. 1991; Eyles 1963
Cebus capucinus	Neotropics (NI)	Coatney et al. 1971; Eyles 1963
	Brazil (W)	Lourenço-de Oliveria and Deane 1995;
Chiropotes sp.	Brazil (P)	De Arruda et al. 1989
Chiropotes albinasus	Neotropics (NI)	Davies et al. 1991
	Brazil (W)	Araújo et al. 2013; Deane 1992; Lourenço-de Oliveria and Deane 1995
Chiropotes chiropotes	Neotropics (NI)	Coatney et al. 1971
	Brazil (W)	Deane 1992
Chiropotes satanas	Neotropics (NI)	Davies et al. 1991
	Brazil (W)	Deane 1992; Deane 1972; Lourenço-de Oliveria and Deane 1995

Lagothrix sp.	Neotropics (NI)	Warren and Wharton 1963
Lagothrix cana[15]	Neotropics (NI)	Coatney et al. 1971
	Brazil (W)	Araújo et al. 2013; Deane 1992, 1972
Lagothrix poeppigii[16]	Neotropics (NI)	Coatney et al. 1971; Eyles 1963
	Brazil (W)	Deane 1992
Lagothrix lagotricha	Neotropics (NI)	Coatney et al. 1971; Davies et al. 1991; Eyles 1963
	Brazil (W)	Deane 1992, 1972; Lourenço-de Oliveria and Deane 1995
Pithecia sp.	Brazil (W)	Bueno et al. 2013
Pithecia irrorata	Neotropics (NI)	Davies et al. 1991
	Brazil (W)	Araújo et al. 2013; Lourenço-de Oliveria and Deane 1995
Pithecia monachus	Brazil (W)	Deane 1992; Lourenço-de Oliveria and Deane 1995
Pithecia pithecia	Neotropics (NI)	Davies et al. 1991
	Brazil (W)	Deane 1992; Lourenço-de Oliveria and Deane 1995
	French Guiana (W)	de Thoisy et al. 2001; Fandeur et al. 2000; Volney et al. 2002
Saguinus geoffroyi	Brazil (W)	Lourenço-de Oliveria and Deane 1995
Saguinus midas	Neotropics (NI)	Davies et al. 1991
	Brazil (W)	Deane 1992; Lourenço-de Oliveria and Deane 1995
	French Guiana (W)	de Thoisy et al. 2001; Fandeur et al. 2000; Volney et al. 2002
Saimiri sp.	Neotropics (NI)	Warren and Wharton 1963
	Brazil (P)	De Arruda et al. 1989
	Brazil (W)	De Arruda et al. 1989
Saimiri boliviensis	Neotropics (NI)	Coatney et al. 1971; Davies et al. 1991; Eyles 1963
	Brazil (W)	Deane 1992, 1972; Lourenço-de Oliveria and Deane 1995

(*Continued*)

Table 3.2 (Continued)

Saimiri sciureus	Neotropics (NI)	Coatney et al. 1971; Davies et al. 1991; Eyles 1963; Garnham 1963
	Brazil (W)	Deane 1992, 1972; Lourenço-de Oliveria and Deane 1995
Saimiri ustus	Neotropics (NI)	Davies et al. 1991
	Brazil (W)	Araújo et al. 2013; Deane 1992; Deane et al. 1989; Lourenço-de Oliveria and Deane 1995
Sapajus apella[5]	Neotropics (NI)	Coatney et al. 1971; Davies et al. 1991; Eyles 1963
	Brazil (W)	Araújo et al. 2013; Deane 1992, 1972; Deane et al. 1989; Lourenço-de Oliveria and Deane 1995
P. malariae		
Pan troglodytes	Cameroon (NI)	Duval et al. 2010
	Côte d'Ivoire (W)	Kaiser et al. 2010
P. malariae-like		
Pan paniscus	DRC (SC)	Krief et al. 2010
***Plasmodium* – Ovale Type**		
P. ovale		
Gorilla gorilla	CAR (W)	Mapua et al. 2015
Pan troglodytes	Cameroon (NI)	Duval et al. 2010
	Côte d'Ivoire (W)	Kaiser et al. 2010
TRYPANOSOMA		
Trypanosoma brucei s.l.		
Arctocebus calabarensis	Cameroon (B)	Njiokou et al. 2004
Perodicticus potto	Cameroon (B)	Njiokou et al. 2004
Cercocebus atys	Côte d'Ivoire (W)	Jirků et al. 2015
Cercocebus torquatus	Cameroon (B)	Njiokou et al. 2004
Cercopithecus nictitans	Equatorial Guinea (B)	Cordon-Obras et al. 2015
Cercopithecus nictitans	Cameroon (B)	Njiokou et al. 2004
Cercopithecus mona		
Cercopithecus cephus		

Chlorocebus aethiops[1]	Kenya (W)	Jeneby et al. 2002; Jeneby 2011
Colobus guereza		
Lophocebus albigena[17]		
Miopithecus talapoin		
Cercopithecus mitis		
Papio anubis[2]		
Piliocolubus sp.	DRC (W)	Jirků et al. 2015
Piliocolobus badius	Côte d'Ivoire (W)	Jirků et al. 2015
Pan troglodytes	Côte d'Ivoire (W)	Jirků et al. 2015
	Uganda (W)	Jirků et al. 2015
T. brucei, non-gambiense		
Arctocebus calabarensis	Cameroon (B)	Herder et al. 2002
Perodicticus potto	Cameroon (B)	Herder et al. 2002; Njiokou et al. 2006
Cercocebus albigena	Cameroon (B)	Njiokou et al. 2006
Cercocebus torquatus		
Cercopithecus cephus		
Cercopithecus mona		
Cercopithecus neglectus		
Cercopithecus nictitans		
Colobus guereza		
Miopithecus talapoin		
Cercopithecus cephus	Cameroon (B)	Herder et al. 2002
Cercopithecus nictitans		
Miopithecus talapoin		
T. brucei gambiense		
Cercocebus torquatus	Cameroon (W)	Funk et al. 2013
	Cameroon (B)	Herder et al. 2002; Njiokou et al. 2006
Cercopithecus ascanius	Equat. Guinea (B)	Cordon-Obras et al. 2015
Lophocebus albigena	Equat. Guinea (B)	Cordon-Obras et al. 2015
Trypanosoma cruzi		
Alouatta sp.	Brazil (W)	Lisboa et al. 2006
Alouatta caraya		Stuart et al. 1998
Alouatta palliata	Mexico (W)	Rovirosa-Hernández 2013
Alouatta pigra		
Alouatta seniculus		Stuart et al. 1998

(*Continued*)

Table 3.2 (Continued)

Aotus sp.	Brazil (W)	Marcili, Lima et al. 2009; Marcili, Valente 2009; Lisboa et al. 2006
Aotus azarae	Brazil (W)	Deane et al. 1989
Ateles sp.	Brazil (W)	Lisboa et al. 2006
Ateles fusciceps	Panama (W)	Sousa et al. 1974
Callicebus brunneus	Brazil (W)	Deane et al. 1989
Callithrix emiliae	Brazil (W)	Deane et al. 1989
Cebuella pygmaea	Brazil (W)	Marcili, Lima et al. 2009
Cebus albifrons	Brazil (W)	Marcili, Lima et al. 2009; Marcili, Valente 2009
Cebus capucinus	Panama (W)	Sousa et al. 1974
Lagothrix sp.	Brazil (W)	Lisboa et al. 2006
Leontopithecus sp.		
Leontopithecus rosalia	Brazil (W)	Lisboa et al. 2000, Lisboa, Mangia, De Lima et al. 2004; Monteiro et al. 2006, 2007
Pithecia irrorata	Brazil (W)	Deane et al. 1989
Saguinus sp.	Brazil (W)	Lisboa et al. 2006
Saguinus fuscicollis	Brazil (W)	Deane et al. 1989; Marcili, Lima et al. 2009; Marcili, Valente 2009
Saguinus geoffroyi	Panama (W)	Sousa et al. 1974
Saguinus labiatus	Brazil (W)	Marcili, Lima et al. 2009; Marcili, Valente 2009
Saguinus midas	Brazil (W)	Marcili, Lima et al. 2009; Marcili, Valente 2009
Saguinus nigricollis[18,19]	Peru (W)	Dunn et al. 1963
Saimiri boliviensis[19]	Peru (W)	Dunn et al. 1963
Saimiri sciureus[19]	Brazil (W)	Marcili, Lima et al. 2009; Ziccardi and Lourenço-de-Oliveira 1997
	Colombia (W)	Dunn et al. 1963
	Peru (W)	Dunn et al. 1963
Saimiri ustus[20]	Brazil (W)	Deane et al. 1989; Marcili, Lima et al. 2009; Ziccardi and Lourenço-de-Oliveira 1997
Sapajus apella[5]	Brazil (W)	Deane et al. 1989; Marcili, Lima et al. 2009; Marcili, Valente 2009

Leishmania brasiliensis		
Aotus azarae	Argentina (W)	Acardi et al. 2013
Aotus trivirgatus	Panama (W)	Herrer and Christensen 1976; Herrer et al. 1973
Saguinus geoffroyi	Panama (W)	Herrer et al. 1973
Leishmania chagasi/ infantum[21]		
Alouatta guariba	Brazil (C/W)22	Lombardi et al. 2014
Leishmania mexicana		
Alouatta palliata	Mexico (W)	Rovirosa-Hernández et al. 2013
Alouatta pigra		
Leishmania shawi		
Chiropotes satanas	Brazil (W)	Lainson et al. 1988
Sapajus apella[5]		
Leishmania major		
Cercopithecus mitis	Kenya (W)	Gicheru et al. 2009
Chlorocebus aethiops	Kenya (W)	Gicheru et al. 2009; Jeneby 2011
Papio anubis[2]	Kenya (W)	Gicheru et al. 2009
Gorilla gorilla	Cameroon (W)	Hamad et al. 2015
***Babesia* sp.**		
Prosimians		
Indri indri	Madagascar (W)	Larsen et al. 2016
Propithecus diadema		
Propithecus verreauxi	Madagascar (W)	Springer et al. 2015
Babesia microti-like		
African Monkeys		
Chlorocebus aethiops	Kenya (W)	Maamun et al. 2011; Jeneby 2011
Papio anubis[2]		
Papio cynocephalus	Zambia (W)	Nakayima et al. (2014)

B = Bushmeat; C = Captive; NI = Not indicated; SC = Semi-Captive; P = Pet; W = Wild (free-ranging)

1. *Chlorocebus aethiops* = *Cercopithecus aethiops*
2. *Papio anubis* = *Papio cynocephalus anubis* and *Papio doguera*
3. *Papio hamadryas papio* = *Papio papio* (Guinea baboon)
4. *Papio ursinus* = *Papio cynocephalus ursinus*
5. *Sapajus apella* = *Cebus apella*
6. *Chlorocebus pygerythrus* = *Chlorocebus aethiops pygerythrus*

7. *Piliocolobus tephrosceles* = *Procolobus badius tephrosceles*
8. St. Kitts island *Chlorocebus sabaeus* are African monkeys that came to the island at some point during colonization and eventually became established
9. De Arruda et al. 1989 aggregated data for wild and pet monkey species, so unclear which species were affected.
10. *Macaca fascicularis* = *Macaca irus*
11. *Alouatta guariba* = *Alouatta fusca*
12. *Alouatta pigra* = *Alouatta villosa*
13. *Ateles chamek* = *Ateles paniscus chamek*
14. *Ateles geoffroyi* = *Ateles grisestens/grisecens*
15. *Lagothrix cana* = *Lagothrix lagotricha cana*
16. Described as *Lagothrix infumata.* In the older literature, this designation has been used to refer to both *Lagothrix lagotricha* and *Lagothrix poeppigii* (see Fooden 1963). Dunn et. al. (1963) identify the location as Loretto province in eastern Peru, so they are probably referring to *L. poeppigii.* Eyles (1963) and Cogwell's (2000) use of the term *Lagothrix lagotricha* is apparently following Dunn and Lambrecht's designation.
17. *Lophocebus albigena* = *Cercocebus albigena*
18. *Saguinus nigricollis* = former *Tamarinus nigricollis*
19. Monkeys cited by Dunn et al. (1963) were recent imports from South America to the U.S. for research
20. Marcili, Lima et al. (2009) identified as *Saguinus ustus*, but likely *Saimiri ustus*
21. *L. chagasi* is now largely considered to be genetically indistinguishable from *L. infantum* (Mauricio et al. 2000).
22. Lombardi et al. (2014) state that *Alouatta guariba* sampled were free-ranging and some were captive, but unclear which carried parasite

4 Bacteria

Bacillaceae: *Bacillus*

Two closely related species of bacillus have been found in both humans and wild animals: *Bacillus anthracis* and *Bacillus cereus*. Anthrax is primarily a disease of domesticated herbivores, with humans becoming exposed through skin-to-skin contact, ingestion of contaminated meat, or exposure to spores in the soil (PAHO 2003). Infected animal hosts shed the bacilli into the soil where they can persist for decades; flies may also play a role in transmission (WHO 2008). Over 95% of the cases in humans are cutaneous, with the development of skin lesions (WHO 2008). Anthrax can also be transmitted through inhalation of spores in dust, which is a concern for the potential of anthrax to be used as a biological weapon (PAHO 2003). For all forms of exposure, the bacteria itself can be treated with antibiotics, but severe reactions can occur due to the production of bacterial toxins that can lead to sepsis, toxemia, and death (WHO 2008). *B. anthracis* has only been documented in three wild primate species: baboons (*Papio ursinus*), chimpanzees (*Pan troglodytes*) and gorillas (*Gorilla gorilla*). Given that cutaneous exposure is most common in humans, bushmeat hunting poses the risk of skin-to-skin contact, and to a lesser extent, the possibility of contraction through eating contaminated bushmeat.

Bacillus cereus is closely related to *Bacillus anthrax*, but poses less of a threat. Similar to *B. anthracis*, *B. cereus* is a spore-forming soil bacterium, but it is quite ubiquitous in the environment and can also occur in water (DelVecchio et al. 2006; Rosenbaum et al. 2013). It is an opportunistic infection most commonly associated with food poisoning, sometimes referred to as "fried rice syndrome" with typical symptoms being diarrhea from bacterial toxins (Rosenbaum et al. 2013). To date, *B. cereus* has only been documented in two prosimian species (*Eulemur macaco* and *Propithecus verreauxi*), but given its characterization as being ubiquitous and opportunistic, it is likely that other wild primate species have encountered this bacteria. However, it is unlikely that it is transmitted laterally in either direction between humans and wild primates.

Bartonellaceae: Bartonella

The genus *Bartonella* currently has 30 identified species that affect a diverse range of animals, including cats, dogs, sheep, cattle, rodents, squirrels, flying squirrels, ground hogs, kangaroos, and bats (Breitschwerdt 2014). *Bartonella* species are vector-borne with three species commonly infecting humans: *B. bacilliformis*, *B. quintana*, and *B. henselae.* However, as vector-borne pathogens, other *Bartonella* species are of concern as potential human pathogens (Gandhi et al. 2015).

B. bacilliformis (Oroya fever) has a limited distribution in the Peruvian Andes and is transmitted by the *Lutzomyia* species of sandflies (Breitschwerdt 2014). Although asymptomatic in approximately 15% of the cases, *B. bacilliformis* can cause life-threatening infections, with symptoms including hemolytic anemia, high fever, myalgia, abdominal pain, jaundice, lymphadenopathy, thrombocytopenia, seizures, delirium, and hepatic and gastrointestinal dysfunction (Gandhi et al. 2015). Humans are the only known reservoir (Breitschwerdt 2014).

B. quintana (trench fever) is found globally and is transmitted through the human body louse (Gandhi et al. 2015). Historically, it was responsible for causing illness in over one million soldiers in Europe during WWI (Breitschwerdt 2014). Although often a self-limiting febrile illness, it can result in chronic bloodstream infection (Gandhi et al. 2015).

B. henselae (cat scratch fever) is a flea-borne pathogen of cats that can be zoonotically acquired by humans through a bite or scratch of a cat (Gandhi et al. 2015). *B. henselae* typically manifests as a cutaneous papule or pustule with regional lymphadenopathy, low-grade fever, fatigue, headache, sore throat, muscle pain, and sometimes an associated rash (Gandhi et al. 2015). More serious symptoms may manifest, particularly in immunocompromised individuals including encephalitis, cerebral vasculitis, pneumonia, hepatitis, transverse myelitis, and thrombocytopenic purpura (Breitschwerdt 2014).

Among wild primates, an unidentified species of the *Bartonella* genus has been identified in wild gorillas (Bittar et al. 2014). Given that the only known reservoir of *B. bacilliformis* are humans – *B. quintana* is transmitted by human body lice, and *B. henselae* is transmitted to humans via cats or their fleas – *Bartonella* species seem to be relatively low risk as a zoonotic infection from primates. However, as a vector-borne pathogen, the potential does exist.

Brucellaceae: *Brucella*

Brucella species have been identified in cattle, pigs, goats, dogs, and marine mammals (Hadush and Pal 2013). The most significant species for humans are those that parasitize domesticated animals: *B. melitensis*, *B. suis*, *B. abortis, and B. canis*, which cause disease when humans are exposed to infected animals, their tissues, or unpasteurized milk products (Gul and Erdem 2015). Brucellosis can affect any organ of the body and may present as an acute febrile illness or a chronic infection characterized by relapses; hepatomegaly occurs in one-third to one-half of those infected, but it may also cause neurological, genitourinary, cardiovascular, respiratory, and hematological symptoms, as well as cutaneous and ocular lesions (Gul and Erdem 2015).

Brucellosis is considered a re-emerging infection of global significance with approximately 500,000 new cases reported each year (Hadush and Pal 2013). It has been described as the most frequently occurring zoonotic infection worldwide (Gul and Erdem 2015). The CDC has classified *Brucella* as a category B biological weapon (second highest priority) due to its ease of dissemination (Noah et al. 2002). Among wild primates, it has only been documented in Kenyan baboons (*Papio* sp.). Baboons are notorious for raiding human garbage sites and it is likely they are infected through eating contaminated meat. The baboons then pose a potential risk to humans when consumed as bushmeat.

Campylobacteriaceae: *Campylobacter*

The genus *Campylobacter* includes approximately 25 species, many of which are pathogenic for humans and animals (Man 2011). *C. jejuni* is considered an emerging zoonotic infection and a leading cause of gastroenteritis in humans worldwide; *C. fetus* and other species are involved to a lesser extent (PAHO 2003). Humans are infected primarily through the consumption of feces-contaminated water, unpasteurized milk, or consumption of contaminated meat, particularly chicken (Kaakoush et al. 2015; PAHO 2003). Most infections are self-limiting with symptoms of diarrhea and fever, but infection may also lead to more severe conditions including autoimmune disorders (Guillain-Barré and related Miller Fisher syndrome), ulcerative colitis, inflammatory bowel syndrome, and septicemia (Kaakoush et al. 2015). The source of infection is primarily food- or water-borne with person-to-person transmission being rare (PAHO 2003).

Campylobacter jejuni has been reported in human-habituated gorillas (*Gorilla beringei*) in Rwanda, which may be anthroponotic (Whittier et al. 2010). However, the study also found a *Campylobacter* species that differed from previously published sequences and may be host-specific for *G. beringei* or other related species. Two additional studies identified *Campylobacter* species in *G. beringei* in Uganda, both of which were also in human-habituated groups. If a pathogenic species of *Campylobacter* becomes established in a wild primate population, the potential exists for human transmission through consumption of bushmeat.

Coxiellaceae: *Coxiella burnetii*

Coxiella burnetii is the only identified species of the *Coxiella* genus but is found in a wide range of animals, including arthropods, fish, birds, rodents, marsupials, livestock, dogs, camels, water buffalo, cats, and rabbits; it is maintained in arthropods (Marrie and Didier 2015).

Commonly termed “Q fever,” *Coxiella burnetii* has a nearly worldwide distribution (Arricau-Bouvery and Rodolakis 2005). Humans are typically infected through inhalation of contaminated aerosols from animal feces, urine, and birth products with windborne pathogens capable of travelling distances of at least 10 km (Marrie and Didier 2015). Clinical manifestation is highly variable, with an estimated 60% of cases being asymptomatic and most other cases presenting as a mild flu-like illness, but some infected persons may develop pneumonia, hepatitis, endocarditis, chronic fatigue syndrome, and in women, repeated abortions (Arricau-Bouvery and Rodolakis 2005).

Although only a few studies have identified *Coxiella* in wild primates, the studies are significant for the high rates of antibodies. Kalter et al. (1966) found 90% ($n = 41$) of Kenyan baboons (*Papio* sp.) to have antibodies against *Coxiella*. A recent study of Cameroon gorillas found 23.8% ($n = 21$) to have antibodies against *Coxiella* (Bittar et al. 2014). Given its capacity to travel long distances as a wind-borne aerosol and the high rates of exposure in baboons and gorillas, it may well be more common in wild primates than the current research suggests.

Enterobacteriaceae: *Klebsiella*, *Proteus*, *Salmonella*, *Shigella*, *Yersinia*, *Escherichia*

Klebsiella

Klebsiella pneumonia is considered an emerging zoonotic infection that can be transmitted through food, water, or soil contaminated with wild or domesticated animal feces. Most commonly, *K. pneumonia* occurs as an opportunistic infection that affects immunocompromised hosts. *Klebsiella* spp. are widely distributed in the environment and found in water, sewage, and soil and can also contaminate inanimate objects (Podschun and Ullman 1998). *Klebsiella* spp. can be found in the nasopharynx and intestinal tracts of humans, many nonhuman primates, and other wild and domesticated animals, where it is usually asymptomatic (Singh and Sharma 1999). As an emerging infection, it is of most concern due to the role of *K. pneumonia* (and to a lesser extent, *K. oxytoca*) as an antibiotic resistant nosocomial infection in hospital patients, causing both pneumonia and abscesses (Podschun and Ullman 1998; Singh and Sharma 1999). In patients who undergo antibiotic treatment, *K. pneumonia* can be an opportunistic colonizer; among those with the infection, antibiotic resistant strains can be difficult to treat. It is also a problem in neonatal units with the immunologically immature.

Klebsiella infections have been documented in a number of wild primate species. Unidentified species of *Klebsiella* have been documented in baboons and orangutans. *Klebsiella oxytoca* has been identified in the grivet monkey. *Klebsiella pneumoniae* has been documented in a wider range of wild primates including lemurs, New World monkeys, chimpanzees, and gorillas. Among captive primates, *Klebsiella pneumonia* is frequently responsible for fatal pneumonia and septicemia in both Old World and New World monkeys in research facilities (Pinkerton 1972; Pisharath et al. 2005). It has also been found in ill pet monkeys referred for treatment (*Lagothrix* in Peru and *Saimiri* in Grenada) (Chikweto et al. 2013; Quevedo and Lescano 2014).

Of much greater concern is the emergence of a hypervirulent variety, HMV (hypermucovisious) *K. pneumoniae* (or hvKP [hypervirulent]). Over the last several decades, HMV-*K. pneumoniae* has emerged in Asia and the West as a community-acquired illness that can cause life-threatening infection in younger and otherwise healthy hosts (Shon et al. 2013). Mortality rates have ranged from 3% to 55% due to liver abscesses, pneumonia, meningitis, bacteremia, and necrotizing fasciitis; survivors from critical infection may experience loss of vision, loss of limb, or neurological sequelae (Shon et al. 2013).

Two cases of HMV-*K. pneumoniae* have thus far have been reported in wild monkeys: a green monkey (*Chlorocebus sabaeus*) in St. Kitts and a lion tamarin (*Leontopithecus chrysomelas*) in Brazil. It has also been documented in captive primates. In 2005–2006, an outbreak of HMV-*K. pneumonia* was responsible for the deaths of six monkeys (*Chlorocebus aethiops*) at a U.S. research facility, which suffered from fatal multisystem abscesses (Twenhafel et al. 2008). Interestingly, another survey of captive African monkeys (*Chlorocebus aethiops, M. fasicularis, M. mulatta*) found that although 26% were positive for HMV-*K. pneumonia*; all were asymptomatic (Burke et al. 2009).

Proteus

Members of the genus *Proteus* have been identified in a wide range of animals, including wild and domesticated mammals and birds, insects, marine life, helminths, and plants, and are also found in soil and water (Drzewiecka 2016). *P. mirabilis*, *P. penneri*, *P. stuartii*, and *P. penneri* are pathogenic to humans, with *P. mirabilis* being responsible for approximately 90% of infections in humans (Donnenberg 2015; Morozova et al. 2016). It has been postulated that in a small percentage of the population, *Proteus* is an intestinal commensal but can cause opportunistic infection (Drzewiecka 2016). *Proteus* is a common cause of urinary tract infections, particularly in hospital environments, and can progress to chronic renal inflammation; it may also infect surgical wounds (Donnenberg 2015; Morozova et al. 2016). Multi-drug resistant strains of *P. mirabilis* have been identified in poultry and cattle, implicating the pathogen as a potential zoonosis (Nahar et al. 2014). Limited information is available on *Proteus* in wild primates. A *Proteus* sp. has been identified in baboons and *Proteus mirabilis* has been identified in gorillas. *Proteus* sp. has also been identified in macaques (*Macaca mulatta*) (Yu et al. 2013).

Salmonella

The genus *Salmonella* is complex with over 2,500 serotypes, but has been divided into two species, *S. enterica* and *S. bongori*, with six subspecies of *S. enterica*; of those, only *S. enterica* subsp. *enterica* infect humans and warm-blooded animals (Pegues 2015). The *S. enterica* serovars are divided into the non-typhoidal (NTS) and typhoidal species. The two serotypes responsible for typhoid fever, *typhi* and *paratyphi*, appear to be human-specific, while the NTS types are zoonotic and cause salmonellosis (PAHO 2003; Pegues 2015). Salmonellosis is a food- and water-borne disease that typically causes self-limiting gastroenteritis with symptoms of fever, abdominal pain, nausea, vomiting, and diarrhea (PAHO 2003). The serovars *Enteritidis* and *Typhimurium* occur most commonly in humans and occur worldwide (PAHO 2003). Approximately 94 million cases occur globally each year, with approximately 150,000 deaths (Majowicz et al. 2010). Of particular concern is the emergence of invasive non-typhoidal salmonella disease in Africa (iNTS) among immunocompromised individuals. Symptoms are fever, hepatomegaly, and respiratory symptoms, which have a case fatality rate of 20–25% (Feasey et al. 2012; MacLennan and Levine 2013). Those most at risk are HIV-infected adults and children with malnutrition, malaria, or HIV infection (Feasey et al. 2012; MacLennan and Levine 2013).

Salmonella has been documented in relatively few primate species. The serovar *Typhimurium* has been identified in lemurs and in two cases with baboons (*Papio ursinus*). The lemur infections may be due to their living in human-habituated areas and the baboon cases may be due to garbage raiding. Otherwise, the occurrence of *Salmonella* in wild primates has been either with serovars uncommon in humans or in cases where the serovars were not identified. These cases include prosimian (*Lemur* spp.), New World monkeys (*Alouatta*, *Aotus*, *Saguinus* spp.), and gorillas (*Gorilla gorilla*). The data available suggest that in most cases, wild primates are infected with nonhuman serovars. However, given that wild primates living in human-habituated areas can be infected with the *Typhimurium* serovar, consumption of primate bushmeat poses a potential risk for *Salmonella* infection.

Shigella

Four species of *Shigella* are recognized, all of which are capable of causing disease in humans: *S. dystenteriae*, *S. flexneri*, *S. boydii*, and *S. sonnei* (Dupont 2015). *Shigella* species have a worldwide distribution, but *S. flexneri* is most common in the developing regions and *S. sonnei* is most common in the developed regions (WHO 2005). Of most concern is the serovar *S. dysenteriae* serotype 1, which is the most virulent and has been responsible for causing multiple outbreaks of epidemic disease in the developing world (PAHO 2003). Annually, approximately 165 million cases occur worldwide, 100 million of which occur in the developing world, with more than one million deaths per year, particularly in children under the age of five (Dupont 2015). *Shigella* can be spread through feces-contaminated food or water or through contact with infected individuals; it is also suspected that flies may have a role in transmission (Dupont 2015; PAHO 2003; WHO 2005). Dupont (2015) describes *Shigella* as the *most* communicable bacterial infection. Symptoms of infection with *Shigella* range from asymptomatic to serious fatal disease (PAHO 2003). Symptoms include fever, abdominal cramping, and bloody diarrhea (WHO 2005).

All four species of *Shigella* have been reported in wild primates: *S. boydii* in gorillas, *S. dysenteriae* in prosimians, baboons, and gorillas, *S. flexneri* in baboons and gorillas, and *S. sonnei* in spider monkeys, baboons, and gorillas. Most of these cases are likely due to the nonhuman primate interactions with humans. The lemurs (several *Lemur* spp.) and the gorillas (*Gorilla beringei*) were both in human-habituated areas (Bublitz et al. 2015; Nizeyi et al. 2001). The baboons (*Papio ursinus*) may have been infected through garbage raiding or through contaminated water rather than being a natural reservoir (Brede 1972). The New World monkey identified with *Shigella* infection was a single case in a spider monkey (*Ateles fusciceps*) that had been recently captured and brought into a laboratory environment (Kourany and Porter 1969). Here, it cannot be ruled out that the infection happened at some point after capture through contact with humans. Although there is no clear evidence that wild primates serve as reservoirs for *Shigella*, evidence does exist that they can be infected anthroponotically from humans. A large epizootic outbreak occurred at the National Zoo affecting prosimians (*Lemur* sp.), New World monkeys (*Ateles* sp.), Asian primates (*Macaca, Hylobates, Pongo* spp.), and African primates (*Cercocebus, Colobus, Pan* spp.) (Banish et al. 1990, 1993). The captive primates had clinical symptoms similar to those of humans. Outbreaks of *Shigella* infection have also been reported periodically in laboratory primates (e.g., Cooper and Needham 1976; Galton et al. 1948; Kennedy et al. 1993).

Yersinia

Eighteen species of *Yersinia* are found in animals and in the environment, but only three are significant for humans: *Yersinia pestis*, *Y. enterocolitica*, and *Y. pseudotuberculosis* (Mead 2015). The most virulent form, *Yersinia pestis*, is the cause of historical pandemics of plague, transmitted by flea vectors from a variety of rodent species (Mead 2015). There is currently no evidence that wild primates are susceptible to *Y. pestis*, so it will not be treated further here. *Y. enterocolitica* and *Y. pseudotuberculosis* are transmitted from fecal-contaminated food and water and present with similar symptoms. Both are typically self-limiting illnesses that disproportionately affect young children with symptoms of diarrhea, fever, and abdominal pain, due to inflammation of the lymph nodes of the abdominal mesentery that can resemble appendicitis (Drummond et al. 2012; Mead 2015). Although both species occur worldwide, *Y. enterocolitica* is most common in Europe, South Africa, Canada, and the U.S., whereas *Y. pseudotuberculosis* is most common in Europe, Japan, and Asiatic Russia (PAHO 2003). Pigs are the major reservoir for *Y. enterocolitica*, but it is also found in rodents, beaver, rabbits, sheep, cattle, horses, dogs, and cats (Drummond et al. 2012; Mead 2015). *Y. pseudotuberculosis* is found in rodents, rabbits, beaver, deer, farm animals, dogs, cats, and wild and domesticated birds (Drummond et al. 2012; Mead 2015).

Thus far, only one study has found *Yersinia pseudotuberculosis* in wild primates. Here, it was found in several human-habituated lemur species (Bublitz et al. 2015). Outbreaks of both *Y. pseudotuberculosis* and *Y. enterocolitica* have been reported in a wide range of captive primates in zoos and laboratory environments, often identified after fatalities occur. Examples of *Y. pseudotuberculosis* include New World monkeys (*Saguinus, Saimiri* spp.), Asian monkeys (*Macaca* spp.), and African monkeys

(*Cercocebus*, *Erythocebus*, *Papio* spp.) (Buhles et al. 1981; Bronson et al. 1972; Kageyama et al. 2002; Taffs and Dunn 1983). Examples of *Y. enterocolitica* include prosimians, New World monkeys (*Ateles*, *Callithrix*, *Lagothrix*, *Saguinus*, *Saimiri* spp.), Asian primates (*Hylobates*, *Macaca* spp.), and African monkeys (*Cercopithecus*, *Cercocebus* spp.) (Iwata et al. 2005; Poelma et al. 1977; Van Damme et al. 1978). These studies suggest that wild primates, at least, are susceptible to enteric forms of *Yersinia* parasites. In one study of *Y. pseudotuberculosis* (Kageyama et al. 2002) and one of *Y. enterocolitica* (Iwata et al. 2005) involving captive primates, the parasite was also isolated from local rodents.

Escherichia coli

Escherichia coli is a normal part of the intestinal flora of humans and other warm-blooded animals, is involved in the synthesis of vitamin K (Bentley and Meganathan 1982), and may also help prevent infection with more pathogenic bacteria by outcompeting them (Reid et al. 2001). However, some serogroups of *E. coli* can be highly pathogenic, causing severe diarrhea and other gastrointestinal dysfunction. Six pathogenic variants have been identified that may cause significant morbidity and mortality worldwide, including EPEC (enteropathogenic *E. coli*), ETEC (enterotoxogenic *E. coli*), EIEC (enteroinvasive *E. coli*), STEC or EHEC (Shiga toxin producing or enterohemorrhagic *E. coli*), and EAEC (enteroaggregative *E. coli*) (Calik et al. 2016; Croxen et al. 2013). Humans may acquire pathogenic forms such as ETEC or EPEC from livestock, such as cattle, goats, pigs, and sheep, due to fecal contamination of meat (Julian 2016). *Escherichia coli* is commonly identified as part of the normal flora of wild primates without differentiating serogroups. However, EPEC has been identified in several species of New World primates (*Alouatta*, *Aotus*, *Ateles*, *Saguinus* spp.) and in South African baboons (*Papio ursinus*).

Enterococcaceae: *Enterococcus*

The genus *Enterococcus* includes approximately 40 different species with wide-ranging hosts, including humans, mammals, birds, reptiles, insects, and plants (Lebreton et al. 2014). Among animals, *Enterococcus* is typically a normal commensal of the gastrointestinal tract (Arias and Murray 2015). However, beginning in the 1970s, some species began to emerge as multidrug resistant nosocomial infections in hospitals (Lebreton et al. 2014). Of particular concern are drug-resistant, hospital-associated *E. faecium* and *E. faecalis*, which are considered emerging infections and can result in urinary tract infection, endocarditis, meningitis, and sepsis (Arias and Murray

2015). These two species were previously classified as *Streptococcus D group* (Arias and Murray 2015). Among wild primates, *Enterococcus faecalis* has been identified in gorillas and lemurs.

Listeriaceae: *Listeria*

Approximately 14 different species of *Listeria* have been identified (den Bakker et al. 2014). Of most concern is *Listeria monocytogenes*, a pathogen of cattle, sheep, and goats that can cause food-borne illness in humans (Saha et al. 2015). For healthy individuals, listeriosis presents as a self-limiting febrile gastroenteritis, but in the young, the elderly, and immunocompromised individuals, it can cause life-threatening bacteremia and meningoencephalitis (Lorber 2015). *Listeria monocytogenes* is now considered an emerging food-borne pathogen due to outbreaks documented since the 1980s (Saha et al. 2015). Among wild primates, a *Listeria* species has been identified in baboons (*Papio* sp.) in Kenya. Given the propensity of baboons to raid refuse areas, it is possible that this was food-borne *Listeria monocytogenes*. A few instances of *L. monocytogenes* infection have been reported in captive primates, including Asian monkeys (*Macaca* sp.), African monkeys (*Cercopithecus* sp.), and the chimpanzee (*Pan troglodytes*) (Heldstab and Rüedi 1982; Lemoy et al. 2012; Vetesi et al. 1971).

Mycobacteriacae: *Mycobacterium*

The genus *Mycobacterium* contains over 100 species that can infect humans, mammals, birds, and fish (Jagielski et al. 2014). The *Mycobacterium* are divided into three broad groups: *M. leprae*, the causative agent of Hansen's disease; the *Mycobacterium tuberculosis* complex (MTBC), responsible for tuberculosis; and nontuberculous *Mycobacterium* (NTM) (Jagielski et al. 2014; Lee et al. 2000). Members of all three groups have been identified in both human and nonhuman primates.

Mycobacterium leprae

Hansen's disease, commonly known as leprosy, involves slowly replicating bacilli that may take up to 20 years for symptoms to develop (WHO 2016e). *Mycobacterium leprae* can be transmitted through respiratory droplets, nasal secretions, and skin-to-skin contact, from mother to child (through breast milk and transplacentally), and from zoonotic exposure, particularly armadillos; evidence also exists for genetic susceptibility to leprosy (Renault and Ernst 2015). Symptoms include peripheral sensory nerve damage, disfiguring skin lesions, and damage to the limbs and eyes (Renault and Ernst 2015;

WHO 2016e). Multi-drug therapy has been successful in treating leprosy, with prevalence decreasing by 99% between 1983 and 2014 and with a prevalence of 175,554 cases worldwide in 2014 (WHO 2016e).

Mycobacterium leprae has not yet been isolated in primates in the wild, but several cases have been reported periodically in captive chimpanzees (*Pan troglodytes*) (Leininger et al. 1980; Walsh et al. 1981) and sooty mangabeys (*Cercocebus atys*) (Gormus et al. 1988; Walsh et al. 1981), which exhibit symptoms similar to those of humans. One additional case was identified in a captive long-tailed macaque (*Macaca fascicularis*) (Valverde et al. 1998). In most of these cases, information was provided that symptoms were discovered soon after the primates were imported for laboratory research; this raises the possibility that it may occur in the wild, but the parasites may have been acquired anthroponotically during the capture and transport process.

Mycobacterium tuberculosis *complex*

The *Mycobacterium tuberculosis* complex (MTBC) includes *M. tuberculosis*, *M. bovis*, *M. africanum*, and *M. microti*. Humans are the only natural reservoir for *M. tuberculosis*, which affects one-third of the world's population with 9.7 million new cases and 1.4 million deaths each year (Fitzgerald et al. 2015). Transmission is primarily through inhalation of aerosol droplets (Fitzgerald et al. 2015; PAHO 2003). The most serious clinical symptom is granuloma formation in the lungs, but every organ can be infected (Fitzgerald et al. 2015). Of particular concern is the emergence of multi-drug resistant (MDR) and extremely drug resistant (XDR) forms of *M. tuberculosis* worldwide (Abubakar et al. 2013). An additional form of human tuberculosis is caused by *M. africanum*, which has similar clinical symptoms to *M. tuberculosis* but a more limited distribution, primarily in West Africa (Sharma et al. 2016). *M. bovis* is a disease of cattle, but can be zoonotically acquired by humans (and wild primates), presenting similar clinical symptoms as *M. tuberculosis* (PAHO 2003). *M. microti* is a rodent form of tuberculosis, but cases of transmission to humans have been documented (Emmanuel et al. 2007; Panteix et al. 2010).

Infections with parasites of the MTB complex have been identified in wild primates and in pet primates. Several studies have identified *M. bovis* in wild baboons. In one of the studies, the source of the infection in *Papio anubis* was identified as eating infected meat from a human refuse site (Sapolsky and Else 1986). The cases identified in *Papio ursinus* were believed to have been acquired directly or indirectly from local buffaloes (Keet et al. 2000, 1996). *Mycobacterium tuberculosis* has been identified in a New World monkey that was being kept as a pet in South Africa (Michel and Huchzermeyer 1998). MTB complex infections (undifferentiated as to species) have also been detected in a number of species of Asian primates (*Macaca*). Most were found in pet monkeys and temple monkeys, but one case was found in a wild-living primate.

MTB complex parasites have also been documented in captive primates in zoos and research centers. Undifferentiated MTB has been found in Old World monkeys (*Macaca* and *Papio* spp.) (Engel et al. 2012; Martino et al. 2007). *M. bovis* has been identified in African monkeys (*Erythocebus*, *Colobus*, *Macaca* spp.) and Asian gibbons (*Hylobates* sp.) (Stetter et al. 1995; Wilson et al. 1984) and *M. tuberculosis* in New World monkeys (*Ateles* sp.), African monkeys (*Cercocebus*), and chimpanzees (*Pan troglodytes*) (Kesdangsakonwut et al. 2015; Michel et al. 2003; Rocha et al. 2011).

Nontuberculous Mycobacterium

NTM (nontuberculous *Mycobacterium*) includes over 150 species, half of which are potentially pathogenic to humans (Brown-Elliot and Wallace 2015). NTM are ubiquitous worldwide and found in soil, water, and dust, but they are not spread directly through person-to-person or animal-to-person contact (Gordin and Horsburgh 2015). The most important of the NTM to humans belong to the *Mycobacterium avium* complex (MAC), which are pathogenic to birds and some animals, including cattle, swine, armadillos, dogs, and cats; it has become a more significant emerging pathogen among immunocompromised individuals, such as those with HIV/AIDS (Brown-Elliot and Wallace 2015; PAHO 2003). Symptoms include pulmonary disease, lymphadenitis, and disseminated disease (Gordin and Horsburgh 2015). Chronic pulmonary symptoms are more common in adults, whereas lymphadenitis is more common in children (PAHO 2003).

NTM has been identified in semi-captive orangutans (*Pongo*) and in one pet tamarin (*Saguinus*). The orangutans were infected with *M. avium* (Kilbourn et al. 2003). The pet tamarin infected with *M. asiaticum* was living in the United States (Siegal-Willott et al. 2006). In captive primates, NTM infections of the *M. avium* complex have been identified in New World monkeys (*Saguinus* and *Sapajus* spp.) and Asian monkeys (*Macaca* spp.) (Alfonso et al. 2004; Bellinger and Bullock 1988; McClure et al. 1987; Smith et al. 1973).

Pseudomonadaceae: *Pseudomonas*

Pseudomonas is a diverse genus with over 200 species that inhabit soil, water, plants, insects, and animals (D'Agata 2015; Jun et al. 2016). As a human pathogen, the opportunistic *Pseudomonas aeruginosa* is of most concern. It is one of the leading causes of ventilator-associated pneumonia, catheter-associated urinary tract infections, and surgical wound infections (Carmeli 2014; D'Agata 2015). Increasing antibiotic resistance is a concern, as is its ability to colonize diverse human environments including sinks, ice makers, swimming pools, cleaning equipment, home humidifiers, and water-damaged homes (Carmeli 2014; D'Agata 2015). In wild primates, *Pseudomonas* species have been identified in prosimians, New World monkeys, and Old World monkeys; *P. aeruginosa* has been identified in lemurs, baboons, and gorillas.

Spirochaetaceae: *Treponema*, *Borrelia*, and *Leptospira*

Treponema

Treponema pallidum consists of three subspecies that are serologically indistinguishable, but historically have been differentiated by symptoms and the geographic area in which they occur; only very recently have genetic tests become available to distinguish the three (Knauf et al. 2013). *T. p. pallidum* has a worldwide distribution and is the agent of the venereal disease syphilis. *T. p. endemicum*, also known as Bejel, is the agent of endemic syphilis and occurs in arid regions. *T. p. pertenue* is the agent of the ulcerative skin disease yaws and primarily affects children in hot and humid areas of Africa and Asia and is the form that has zoonotic potential from nonhuman primates.

The WHO (2015b) describes yaws as a neglected tropical disease that affects millions, primarily the poor and children under the age of 15. In most cases, the disease is self-limiting, but in 10% of the cases the ulcerative lesions can cause severe disfiguration (particularly the nose), difficulty in chewing and breathing, and possibly ulcerative lesions of the bones. It is readily treatable with either azithromycin or benzathine penicillin. By mid-century, the number of cases of yaws decreased by 95%, but recently it has resurged in some areas (Knauf et al. 2013).

Treponema pallidum has been identified in several species of Old World primates, including baboons (*Papio anubis*, *P. cynocephalus*, *P. papio*), patas monkeys (*Erythocebus patas*), vervets (*C. aethiops*), and gorillas (*Gorilla gorilla*). Skin-to-skin contact in bushmeat hunting is a possible means for wild primate-to-human transmission (Knauf et al. 2013). In one experimental study in Venezuela in the 1970s, human beings inoculated with *Treponema pallidium* (unspecified subspecies) from a baboon developed yaws symptoms (Smith et al. 1971). While such a study would be unethical today, it does provide evidence for the zoonotic potential of wild primate yaws; however, much remains unclear. Two recent studies have described ano-genital ulceration in wild baboons (*P. anubis*) with *T. pallidium* (Harper et al. 2012; Knauf et al. 2012). The latter study found that although the clinical symptoms were more similar to *T. p. pallidium*, the organism was more closely related to *T. p. pertenue.* At the other end of the spectrum, a study of baboons (*Papio papio*) in Senegal found that 90% were positive for *T. pallidium* antibodies, but none showed any clinical symptoms (Knauf et al. 2015). An additional Treponema (*Treponema carateum*) is the cause of pinta, but it has not yet been documented in wild primates. *Treponema* infection has also been identified in a number of captive African monkeys (*Cercopithecus*, *Colobus*, *Erythrocebus*, *Papio* spp.) and the chimpanzee (*Pan troglodytes*) (Fribourg-Blanc and Mollaret 1969).

Borrelia *and* Leptospira

Other spirochetes of concern are *Borrelia* and *Leptospira* spp. The genus *Borrelia* has numerous species that occur worldwide with the exception of Australia, New Zealand, and Oceania (PAHO 2003). Of the most concern in humans is *Borrelia burgdorferi*, which is considered an emerging infectious disease and is the cause of tick-borne Lyme disease, but it is restricted to the Northern Hemisphere, particularly the U.S., so it does not infect primates in the wild (PAHO 2003). *Borrelia* is also responsible for a variety of relapsing fevers, including *B. recurrentis*, which is considered an emerging infection and is spread primarily by head lice but also ticks. One older study suggests the possibility of anthrozoonotic transmission between monkeys and humans (Clark et al. 1931). In an older study, a tamarin that had been recently captured as a pet developed an apparent relapsing fever that was identified by morphology as *B. recurrentis* (Clark et al. 1931). Several people were exposed to the spirochete through either inoculation with the blood of the monkey or a tick that had fed on the monkey. In both cases, the humans developed relapsing fever. Brack (1987) cites several older studies that document *Borrelia* species in wild monkeys, but in reviewing these articles, they appear to be captive primates and/or experimental studies. Recently, a *Borrelia* species was identified in a wild prosimian (*Indri indri*) in Madagascar (Larsen et al. 2016) and also in wild gorillas in Cameroon (Bittar et al. 2014). Given the wide geographic range of *Borrelia* and the diversity of its species, it is quite possible that more wild primates harbor species of these bacteria transmitted by forest arthropods than the evidence currently suggests.

The spirochete genus *Leptospira* includes approximately 17 species, occurs worldwide, and affects humans, wild animals, and domesticated animals (Bharti et al. 2003). *Leptospira interrogans* is of most concern to humans and is considered an emerging zoonotic infection with human-to-human transmission being rare (PAHO 2003). Humans infected with *L. interrogans* may be asymptomatic or have mild symptoms of fever or headache, but in severe cases, it can develop into renal failure or pulmonary hemorrhage (Bharti et al. 2003). *L. interrogans* is itself diverse with over 200 serological variants (PAHO 2003). Human infection occurs through direct exposure to the urine of mammals or indirectly through contaminated soil or water (Bharti et al. 2003). *Leptospira* has only rarely been documented in wild primates, and thus far only two cases in the vervet monkey (*Chlorocebus pygerythrus*) have been described, with one being a serovar of *L. interrogans* and another undetermined *Leptospira* species. Serovars of *L. interrogans* were documented in a number of primate species in a survey of research facilities in an older study, including Old World monkeys (*Cercocebus*, *Chlorocebus*, *Erythrocebus*, *Macaca*, *Papio*), apes (*Hylobates*, *Pan*), and one New World monkey genus (*Saguinus*) (Minette 1966). Leptospiral antibodies were also found in 15% (11 of 73) of lion tamarins (*Leontopithecus* spp.) in a Brazilian zoo (Lilenbaum et al. 2005).

Staphylococcaceae: *Staphylococcus*

The genus *Staphylococcus* includes over 30 species that colonize a wide range of animals (Harris et al. 2002; Morgan 2008; Que 2015). The species *Staphylococcus aureus* is of most concern in humans. It can occur both as a commensal and as an opportunistic infection, depending on the site the parasite colonizes and the strain of the parasite. *S. aureus* asymptomatically colonizes the anterior nostrils of approximately 20–60% of the normal human population and is also a common colonizer of the skin (Kluytmans et al. 1997; Que 2015).

As an opportunistic infection, *S. aureus* can produce a wide range of symptoms including relatively benign skin infections, food-borne illness, and severe and potential fatal invasive disease including toxic shock syndrome (Kadariya et al. 2014). *S. aureus* is the primary cause of hospital-acquired bloodstream infections and invasive infections including general sepsis, deep abscesses, endocarditis, osteomyelitis, and pneumonia (Que 2015). *S. aureus* is one of the most common food-borne diseases worldwide due to contamination of food by enterotoxins (Kadariya et al. 2014). Of particular concern is the antibiotic resistant MRSA (methicillin-resistant *S. aureus*), which occurs both as a nosocomial infection and as a community infection, including food-borne MRSA in meat products (Morgan 2008; Que 2015).

Among wild primates, *S. aureus* has been identified in a number of species including lemurs, African monkeys, orangutans, gorillas, and chimpanzees that otherwise appear healthy, suggesting that the agent may occur as a natural commensal as in human populations. Unidentified *Staphylococcus* species have also been identified in lemurs, African monkeys, and orangutans. In captivity, *S. aureus* has also been identified in Asian monkeys (Van Den Berg et al. 2011). Antibiotic-resistant *S. aureus* has also been identified in captive gorilla and chimpanzee populations (Nagel et al. 2013). One captive chimpanzee colony in Texas had a MRSA prevalence of 69% (Hanley et al. 2015). In addition, human-related drug resistant *S. aureus* has been found in semi-captive sanctuary apes (Schaumburg, Mugisha et al. 2012, 2013). This form of *S. aureus* is presumably acquired anthroponotically from humans. However, given their semi-captive status, the presence of the parasite in these populations poses the risk of transfer of more virulent forms of *S. aureus* to wild primate populations.

Streptococcaceae: *Streptococcus*

The genus *Streptococcus* is composed of approximately 100 different species that are widely distributed and often exist as part of the normal flora of humans and animals, but can opportunistically cause infection (Parks et al. 2015). *Streptococcus pneumoniae* and *S. pyogenes* are two of the most important invasive pathogenic species. *S. pneumoniae* may asymptomatically colonize the pharyngeal mucosa, cause bacterial illnesses such as otitis media, sinusitis, or pneumonia, or cause invasive infections including bacteremia, meningitis, and endocarditis (Janoff and Musher 2015). It is the leading cause of bacterial meningitis worldwide in young children and older adults (Janoff and Musher 2015). *S. pyogenes* infection occurs most commonly as streptococcal pharyngitis or superficial skin infections such as impetigo and cellulitis (Bryant and Stevens 2015). It can also cause more serious and potentially life-threatening disease, including streptococcal toxic shock syndrome, rheumatic fever, and glomerulonephritis (Bryant and Stevens 2015). In addition, *Streptococcus suis*, which occurs in swine, is considered a global emerging zoonotic disease and can cause septicemia and meningitis in individuals exposed to infected pigs or contaminated pork products (Goyette-Desjardins et al. 2014).

Several studies have identified *Streptococcus* species in wild primates. Unidentified species of the genus *Streptococcus* have been found in baboons and orangutans. *S. pneumoniae* has been identified in chimpanzees and gorillas. In the Côte d'Ivoire, three outbreaks of respiratory epidemics occurred in a nature preserve with over 90% of the population affected (Köndgen et al. 2008). The nature preserve is a site of ecotourism, and it is presumed the outbreaks were anthroponotic in the chimpanzees. *Streptococcus pyogenes* has also been identified in wild chimpanzees.

Table 4.1 Bacteria

BACILLACEAE		
***Bacillus* sp.**		
Papio sp.	Kenya (W)	Kalter et al. 1966; Pinkerton 1972
Bacillus anthracis		
Papio ursinus	Namibia (W)	Magwedere et al. 2012
Gorilla sp.[1]	Cameroon (W)	Klee et al. 2006
Gorilla gorilla	Côte d'Ivoire (W)	Leendertz et al. 2006
Pan troglodytes	Côte d'Ivoire (W)	Klee et al. 2006[1]; Leendertz et al. 2004; Leendertz et al. 2006
	Cameroon (W)	Klee et al. 2006[1]; Leendertz et al. 2006
Bacillus cereus		
Eulemur macaco	Madagascar (W)	Junge and Louis 2007
Propithecus verreauxi	Madagascar (W)	Junge and Louis 2005
BARTONELLACEAE		
***Bartonella* sp.**		
Gorilla gorilla	Cameroon (W)	Bittar et al. 2014
BRUCELLACEAE		
Papio sp.	Kenya (W)	Pinkerton 1972
CAMPYLOBACTERIACEAE		
Campylobacter jejuni		
Gorilla beringei	Rwanda (W)	Whittier et al. 2010
***Campylobacter* spp.**		
Gorilla beringei	Rwanda (W)	Whittier et al. 2010
	Uganda (W)	Kalema-Zikusoka et al. 2005; Nizeyi et al. 2001
CHLAMYDIACEAE		
***Chlamydia* sp.**		
Chlorocebus pygerythrus[2]	South Africa (W)	Kaschula et al. 1978
COXIELLACEAE		
Coxiella burnetii		
Papio sp.	Kenya (W)	Kalter et al. 1966
Gorilla gorilla	Cameroon (W)	Bittar et al. 2014
ENTEROBACTERIACEAE		
Enteropathogenic E. coli		
Alouatta villosa	Panama (W)	Kourany and Porter 1969
Aotus trivirgatus		
Ateles fusciceps		
Saguinus geoffroyi		

(*Continued*)

Table 4.1 (Continued)

Papio ursinus	South Africa (W)	Brede 1972
***Klebsiella* sp.**		
Papio sp.	Kenya (W)	Kalter et al. 1966
Pongo pygmaeus	Borneo (FR/SC)	Kilbourn et al. 2003
Klebsiella oxytoca		
Chlorocebus sabaeus[3]	St. Kitts (W)	Whitehouse et al. 2010
Klebsiella pneumonia		
Eulemur fulvus[4]	Madagascar (W)	Junge and Louis 2005
Eulemur macaco[4]	Madagascar (W)	Junge and Louis 2007
Lagothrix lagothricha	Peru (P)	Quevedo and Lescano 2014
Saimiri sciureus	Grenada (P)	Chikweto et al. 2013
Gorilla beringei	Rwanda (W)	Palacios et al. 2011
Gorilla gorilla	Cameroon (W)	Bittar et al. 2014
Pan troglodytes	Uganda (SC)	Mugisha et al. 2014
HMV *Klebsiella pneumonia*		
Leontopithecus chrysomelas	Brazil (W)	Bueno et al. 2015
Chlorocebus sabaeus[3]	St. Kitts (W)	Whitehouse et al. 2010
***Proteus* sp.**		
Papio sp.	Kenya (W)	Kalter et al. 1966
Gorilla gorilla	Cameroon (W)	Bittar et al. 2014
***Salmonella* sp.**		
Papio ursinus	South Africa (W)	de Vos et al. 1973
Gorilla beringei	Uganda (W)	Kalema-Zikusoka et al. 2005; Nizeyi et al. 2001
***Salmonella enterica* – *Typhimurium* serovar**		
Lemur spp.	Madagascar (W)	Bublitz et al. 2015
Papio ursinus	South Africa (W)	Brede 1972
Salmonella enterica* – serovars other than *Enteritidis* or *Typhimurium		
Alouatta villosa	Panama (W)	Kourany and Porter 1969
Aotus trivirgatus		
Saguinus geoffroyi		
Shigella boydii		
Gorilla beringei	Uganda (W)	Nizeyi et al. 2001

Shigella dysenteriae (Schmitzi)		
Papio ursinus	South Africa (W)	Brede 1972
Shigella flexneri		
Lemur spp.	Madagascar (W)	Bublitz et al. 2015
Papio ursinus	South Africa (W)	Brede 1972
Gorilla beringei	Uganda (W)	Nizeyi et al. 2001
Shigella sonnei		
Ateles fusciceps	Panama (W)	Kourany and Porter 1969
Papio ursinus	South Africa (W)	Brede 1972
Gorilla beringei	Uganda (W)	Nizeyi et al. 2001
Yersinia pseudotuberculosis		
Lemur spp.	Madagascar (W)	Bublitz et al. 2015
ENTEROCOCCACEAE		
Group D Enterococcus[5]		
Lemur catta	Madagascar (W)	Dutton et al. 2003
Enterococcus faecalis		
Gorilla gorilla	Cameroon (W)	Bittar et al. 2014
LISTERIACEAE		
***Listeria* sp.**		
Papio sp.	Kenya (W)	Pinkerton 1972
MYCOBACTERIACEAE		
MTB		
***Mycobacterium tuberculosis complex* – undifferentiated**		
Macaca hybrid	Sulawesi (P)	Wilbur et al. 2012
Macaca maura		
Macaca nigra		
Macaca ochreata		
Macaca nigrescens		
Macaca tonkeana		
Macaca fascicularis	Bali (T)	Wilbur et al. 2012
	Java (P)	
	Singapore (W)	
	Sulawesi (P)	
Macaca mulatta	Nepal (T)	Wilbur et al. 2012

(Continued)

Table 4.1 (Continued)

Mycobacterium bovis		
Papio anubis[6]	Kenya (W)	Sapolsky and Else 1986; Tarara et al. 1985
Papio ursinus	South Africa (W)	Keet et al. 2000, 1996
Mycobacterium tuberculosis		
Callithrix jacchus	South Africa (P)	Michel and Huchzermeyer 1998
NTM		
Mycobacterium avium		
Pongo pygmaeus	Borneo (W/SC)	Kilbourn et al. 2003
Mycobacterium asiaticum		
Saguinus midas	U.S. (P)	Siegal-Willott et al. 2006
PSEUDOMONADACEAE		
***Pseudomonas* sp.**		
Lemur catta	Madagascar (W)	Dutton et al. 2003
Alouatta caraya	Brazil (W)	Menezes-Costa et al. 2013
Alouatta belzebul		
Papio sp.	Kenya (W)	Pinkerton 1972
Pseudomonas aeruginosa		
Lemur catta	Madagascar (W)	Dutton et al. 2003
Papio sp.	Kenya (W)	Kalter et al. 1966
Gorilla gorilla	Cameroon (W)	Bittar et al. 2014
SPIROCHETACEAE		
Borrelia sp.		
Indri indri	Madagascar (W)	Larsen et al. 2016
Gorilla gorilla	Cameroon (W)	Bittar et al. 2014
Borrelia recurrentis[7]		
Saguinus geoffroyi[8]	Panama (W/P)	Clark et al. 1931
***Leptospira* sp.**		
Chloroecebus pygerythrus	Botswana (W)	Jobbins and Alexander et al. 2015
Leptospira interrogans		
Pongo pygmaeus	Borneo (FR/SC)	Kilbourn et al. 2003
Leptospira pomona		
Chlorocebus pygerythrus[2]	South Africa (W)	Kaschula et al. 1978
Treponema pallidum pertenue[9,10]		
Chlorocebus pygerythrus[2]	Kenya (W)	Felsenfeld and Wolf 1971

Erythrocebus patas	West Africa (W)	Felsenfeld and Wolf 1971
Papio anubis[6]	Kenya (W)	Harper et al. 2012
	Tanzania (W)	Harper et al. 2012; Knauf et al. 2012; Wallis and Lee 1999[7]
Papio cynocephalus	Kenya (W)	Harper et al. 2012
	Tanzania (W)	Harper et al. 2012
Papio papio[11]	Guinea (W)	Fribourg-Blanc et al. 1963
Papio papio	Senegal (W)	Baylet et al. 1970; Knauf et al. 2015
Gorilla gorilla	Rep. of Congo (W)	Levréro et al. 2007
STAPHYLOCOCCACEAE		
***Staphylococcus* sp.**		
Eulemur macaco	Madagascar (W)	Junge and Louis 2007
Indri indri	Madagascar (W)	Junge and Louis 2002
Avahi sp.		
Lepilemur sp.		
Varecia sp.		
Papio sp.	Kenya (W)	Pinkerton 1972
Pongo spp.	Borneo and Sumatra (W)	Pettersson et al. 2013
S. aureus		
Eulemur rufifrons	Madagascar (W)	Schaumburg et al. 2013
Propithecus verreauxi		
Cercopithecus ascanius	Gabon (B)	Schaumburg, Alabi et al. 2012
Cercopithecus nictitans		
Lophocebus albigena		
Miopithecus ogouensis		
Colobus polykomos	Côte d'Ivoire (W)	Schaumburg, Alabi et al. 2012
Piliocolobus badius		
Gorilla gorilla	Cameroon (W)	Bittar et al. 2014
	Gabon	Schaumburg, Alabi et al. 2012
Pan troglodytes	Côte d'Ivoire (W)	Schaumburg, Alabi et al. 2012; Schaumburg et al. 2013
	Uganda (SC)	Mugisha et al. 2014

(*Continued*)

Table 4.1 (Continued)

***S. aureus* – human related**		
Pan troglodytes	Uganda (SC)	Schaumburg et al. 2013
Pan troglodytes – sanctuary (drug-resistant)	Uganda and Zambia (SC)	Schaumburg Mugisha et al. 2012
STREPTOCOCCACEAE		
***Streptococcus* sp.**		
Papio sp.	Kenya (W)	Kalter et al. 1966; Pinkerton 1972
Asian apes		
Pongo spp.	Borneo and Sumatra (W)	Pettersson et al. 2013
Streptococcus pneumoniae		
Pan troglodytes	Côte d'Ivoire	Köndgen et al. 2008
Gorilla beringei	Rwanda (W)	Palacios et al. 2011
Streptococcus pyogenes		
Pan troglodytes	Uganda (SC)	Mugisha et al. 2014

P = Pet; SC = Semi-Captive; W = Wild (i.e., free-ranging)

1. Klee et al. 2006: *Bacillus anthracis*-like
2. *Chlorocebus pygerythrus* = former *Cercopithecus aethiops pygerythrus*
3. *Chlorocebus sabeus* = former *Chlorocebus aethiops sabaeus*
4. *Klebsiella ozaenae*, subspecies *Klebsiella pneumoniae ozaenae*
5. Includes Enterococcus faecalis and E. faecium
6. Papio anubis (olive baboon) = former P. cynocephalus anubis and P. hamadryas Anubis
7. *Borrelia recurrentis* = former *Treponema recurrentis*
8. Species identified as *Leontocebus geoffroyi*, and is likely *Saguinus geoffroyi*
9. See discussion for *Treponema pallidum* subspecies differentiation
10. Diagnosis by observation of symptoms
11. Fribroug-Blanc, Neil, and Mollaret (1963) characterize as "cynocéphale de Guinée," which would make them *Papio papio* (Guinea baboon) rather than *Papio cynocephalus* (yellow baboon). Also note that these were wild monkeys that were recently imported to Paris when examined.

5 Helminths

The helminths are broadly categorized into three groups: Nematodes (roundworms), Cestodes (tapeworms), and Trematodes (flukes). In the review of the literature, many helminth species were found that are capable of being transmitted between humans and wild primates. Many, but not all, are intestinal parasites. Particularly in the developing world, chronic intestinal worm parasitism may demonstrate few clinical symptoms and rarely cause mortality (Wammes et al. 2014). According to Taylor et al. (2001), virtually all helminths are zoonotic. Many helminths among humans and wild primates have been described as "heirloom" species, sharing a long evolutionary history among anthropoid primates (Kliks 1983, 1990; Sprent 1969). Recently, attention has been given to co-evolutionary relationships between vertebrates and helminths, whereby helminths may play a beneficial role in maintaining and regulating the immune response (Allen and Maizels 2011). In this brief section on helminths, two types of vector-borne worms will be highlighted that have greater potential to cause serious disease: filariasis and schistosomiasis, both of which are considered to be neglected tropical diseases and have the potential to be transmitted from wild primates.

Onchoceridae: *Wuchereria* and *Brugia*

Lymphatic filariasis is a vector-borne nematode infection caused by filarial worms that can invade the lymphatic vessels, blood vessels, and subcutaneous tissues (da Rocha et al. 2017). The majority of cases do not manifest in overt clinical symptoms, but others may lead to short-term lymphedema or more serious chronic infection (Kazura 2015). Short-term infection includes fever with swelling of the leg, arm, or male genitalia; chronic infection can lead to the extreme swelling of elephantiasis or bacterial infections and sclerosis of the skin (Kazura 2015). Worldwide, lymphatic filariasis is endemic in 73 countries in Asia, Africa, and the Americas and is considered a neglected disease by the WHO (da Rocha et al. 2017).

Three species of parasites that may infect humans are *Wuchereria bancrofti*, *Brugia malayi*, and *Brugia timor*. *Wuchereria bancrofti* is responsible for 90% of the documented cases of lymphatic filariasis, but humans appear to be the only reservoir, which is also true for *B. timor* (Kazura 2015). Only *Brugia malayi has* been found in wild primates. *Brugia malayi* has been documented in Malaysian macaques (*Macaca fascicularis*) and colobine monkeys (*Presbytis melalophos*, *Trachypithecus cristatus*, and *T. obscurus*) (Edeson and Wilson 1964; Mak et al. 1982; Masbar et al. 1981). The colobine species are considered to be reservoir hosts for *B. malayi*, with 55% of those examined ($n = 88$) testing as seropositive (Mak et al. 1982; Wood et al. 2014).

Some studies have suggested the possibility of other filiariases that cause human disease existing in nonhuman primates, including *Loa loa* (eye worm), *Onchocerca volvulus* (river blindness), and *Mansonella streptocerca* (subcutaneous filariasis). *Loa loa* species have been identified in gorillas and monkeys (Bain et al. 1995; Kalema-Zikusoka et al. 2005). But the strains or subspecies that affect forest simians appear to have separate host-vector complexes, making human and wild primate cross-infection unlikely (Duke 1972). *Onchocerca volvulus* was reported in 1964 in a gorilla from the Congo (Van den Berghe et al. 1964). Given the age of the report and lack of other confirming studies, there is insufficient evidence to consider the parasite as infecting wild primates. Mak et al. (1982) indicate that *Onchocerca volvulus* has no nonhuman reservoir. Another older article identifies *Mansonella streptocerca* in the bonobo and chimpanzee (Peel and Chardome 1946) and other older articles suggest that it occurs in gorillas as well, but the literature review did not find other studies suggesting it occurs in nonhuman primates. Unfortunately, these older studies have been frequently cited in more recent literature, giving the impression that *Mansonella streptocerca* is commonly found in gorillas and chimpanzees.

Schistosomatidae: schistosoma

Schistosoma are trematode flatworms or flukes found worldwide. Each year approximately 237 million individuals are infected in 74 countries with 120 million exhibiting symptoms, 20 million having severe disease, and 100,000–200,000 deaths (Maguire 2015). It is endemic in Africa, Latin America, the Caribbean, Southeast Asia, Europe, the Mediterranean, and the Western Pacific (WHO 2015c). Some species of freshwater snails harbor schistosomes, and when larval schistosoma are released into the water, humans can become infected; snails in turn become infected through water contamination with human feces or urine (WHO 2015c). Infection may be asymptomatic, but the clinical presentation may manifest in a febrile illness

Table 5.1 Helminths

ONCHOCERCIDAE		
Brugia malayi		
Macaca facicularis[1]	Malaysia (W)	Edeson and Wilson 1964
Presbytis melalophos	Malaysia (W)	Edeson and Wilson 1964; Mak et al. 1982
Trachypithecus cristatus[2]	Malaysia (W)	Edeson and Wilson 1964; Mak et al. 1982
	Malaysia (W)	Masbar et al. 1981
Trachypithecus obscurus[3]	Malaysia (W)	Edeson and Wilson 1964; Laing et al. 1960; Mak et al. 1982
SCHISTOSOMATIDAE		
***Schistosoma* sp.**		
Papio sp.	Kenya (W)	Kalter et al. 1966
Schistosoma haematobium		
Cercopithecus mitis	Kenya (W)	Else et al. 1982; Nelson 1960
Chlorocebus aethiops[4]	Kenya (W)	Nelson (1960)
Papio ursinus[5]	Zimbabwe (W)	Purvis et al. 1965
Schistosoma japonicum		
Macaca fascicularis	Borneo (W)	Kuntz 1978
Schistosoma mansoni		
Aotus vociferans	Peru (W)	Phillips et al. 2004
Chlorocebus aethiops[4]	South Africa (W)	Kaschula et al. 1978
	Kenya (W)	Else et al. 1982; Muriuki et al. 1998
	Ethiopia (W)	Fuller et al. 1979
Cercopithecus mitis	Kenya (W)	Munune et al. 1998
Erythrocebus patas	Cameroon (P)	Pourrut et al. 2011
Papio anubis[6]	Ethiopia (W)	Fuller et al. 1979
	Ethiopia (P)	Legesse and Erko 2004
	Kenya (W)	Hahn et al. 2003; Miller 1960; Munune et al. 1998; Muriuki et al. 1998; Nelson 1960
	Tanzania (W)	Fenwick 1969; Müller-Graf et al. 1997; Murray et al. 2000
	Nigeria (W)	Mafuyai et al. 2013; Weyher et al. 2006
Papio hamadryas	Saudi Arabia (W)	Ghandour et al. 1995

(*Continued*)

Table 5.1 (Continued)

Papio papio[7]	Senegal (W)	McGrew et al. 1989; Howells et al. 2011
Papio ursinus	Zimbabwe (W)	Goldsmid 1974
Pan troglodytes	Uganda (SC)	Stothard et al. 2012
Schistosoma mattheei		
Chlorocebus aethiops[4]	South Africa (W)	Pitchford and Pienaar 1974
Papio ursinus	South Africa (W)	McConnell et al. 1974; Pitchford and Pienaar 1974

P = Pet; SC = Semi-Captive; W = Wild (i.e., free-ranging)

1. *Macaca fascicularis* = former *Macaca irus*
2. *Trachypithecus cristatus* = former *Presbytis cristatus/cristata*
3. *Trachypithecus obscurus* = former *Presbytis obscurus/obscura*
4. *Chlorocebus aethiops* = former *Cercopithecus aethiops*
5. *Papio ursinus* = former *Papio rhodesiae*
6. *Papio anubis* includes former *Papio cynocephalus anubis* and *Papio doguera*
7. Includes *Papio hamadryas papio*

with myalgia, diarrhea, and abdominal pain; cough with chest infiltrates; spleen, lymph node, and liver enlargement; urticaria with skin lesions; and anemia (Maguire 2015). Of the eight species of *Schistosoma* found in humans, four have also been found in wild primates: *S. mansoni*, *S. haematobium*, *S. japonicum*, and *S. mattheei*. The most significant species in humans are *S. mansoni*, *S. haematobium*, and *S. japonicum*. Schistosomes have been most frequently found in baboons (*Papio* spp.), although they have also been found in other Old World monkeys, great apes, and New World monkeys. The finding may relate to the tendency of baboon species to raid crops, which may place them in close contact with human water sources.

6 Concluding remarks

Human and wild primates have a long history of sharing many types of parasites, but recent human cultural behaviors are changing primate habitats and the ecological niches of the parasites and vectors and increasing the potential for host switching and the emergence of new diseases. Vector-borne parasites are particularly challenging, because direct contact is not needed between humans and wild primates when there is an intervening mobile vector. Old human afflictions such as yellow fever are difficult to eradicate, even if a vaccine is available, because the parasite can be maintained in forest mosquitoes and wild primate reservoirs. The newly emerging disease of *Plasmodium knowlesi* in Southeast Asia involved not only a host switch from wild primates, but also an adaptation of the mosquito vector to human-modified agricultural zones.

Water-borne parasites are also mobile when fecal matter or other infectious body fluids contaminate water sources that humans may use for drinking, bathing, or cooking. Water-borne parasites also pose a risk to wild primates, which may be exposed to novel human parasites. Domesticated animals, such as cattle and swine, may also be a source of introduction of novel parasites to wild primates through water sources, including antibiotic resistant strains of bacteria. While helminths are generally of the least concern, a number of studies were discussed that demonstrated that helminth load is often increased in nonhuman primates that live near areas of human disturbance. Heavy parasite loads have been demonstrated to impair the overall health of wild primates.

The RNA viruses tend to have broad host ranges and higher mutation rates than DNA viruses have, with potential for evolution of virulent strains in humans. Viruses such as HIV/SIV, Ebola, and Zika have caused human pandemics in the last decades. Continued deforestation eliminates buffer zones between human and wild animal habitats, creating more forest fragments, edges, and potential hot spots for parasite sharing. But equally important is the ease of travel, both locally with roads connecting rural and urban areas, and internationally with airports connecting major cities of the world. Today, local disease outbreaks have the potential to quickly become global problems. The week that this manuscript was completed (in March 2017), the first cases of Zika virus were reported in India.

The behavior, characteristics, and ecological niches of wild primates affect the transmission of parasites. Among the primates, humans are closest in evolutionary history to the African great apes (bonobos, chimpanzees, and gorillas). The baboons of Africa and the macaques of Asia are notorious crop raiders that commonly enter into human areas, posing risks for host switching of parasites. Wild primate species that prefer disturbed habitats are more likely to come into contact with humans than are those species that prefer more densely forested areas. Wild primates that are more terrestrial also have greater chance to come into contact with humans than are those that occupy the higher canopy layers of the forest. The Neotropical primates are largely arboreal, and this may contribute to why many of the emerging primates zoonoses have originated in Africa or Asia.

Hunting choices also affect which wild primates are more likely to come into contact with humans. Generally, larger primates are more likely to be hunted than very small primates are. Primates that live in large groups are easier to locate than those that are solitary or live in small groups. Primates with large group sizes are also more likely to sustain and spread parasites than are those with smaller group sizes. Bushmeat hunting poses a number of potential ways for parasites to be transferred, but blood-borne parasites are a particular problem from injury from a hunted animal or the processing or consumption of bushmeat. Primate pet keeping often occurs in the context of bushmeat hunting when orphaned juveniles or infants are taken back into human domestic settings. Pets are not only in direct contact, but may also expose their owners to parasites in urine, feces, and other body fluids. Another problem with pets is that they may move between the forest and the household, with potential to bring wild primate parasites to humans and human parasites to wild primates.

The concept of "one health" is increasingly being used in the context of zoonotic disease.

The first use of the term "one health" can be traced to William Karesh, the head of the field veterinary program of the Wildlife Conservation Society, in a 2003 *Washington Post* article (Weiss 2003). He was commenting on the decline by half in less than two decades of the gorilla and chimpanzee populations in Gabon and the Republic of Congo due to bushmeat hunting and infection with the Ebola virus. He stated, "human or livestock or wildlife health can't be discussed in isolation anymore . . . there is just one health. And the solutions require everyone working together on all the different levels." Karesh's term one health has now come into broader use as a paradigm for approaching the intersection between animal health, human health, and the ecosystem at local, national, and global levels (Webster et al. 2015).

The problems and solutions are complex and include medical treatments, sanitation, vector control, food safety, and environmental protection. In some cases, the solutions may create new problems, such as the development of antibiotics and the consequent evolution of antibiotic-resistant bacteria. As previously described, wildlife reserves intended to protect wild primates and other species when coupled with ecotourism may facilitate parasite transfer. But what is clear is that public health strategies that only target human populations are not sufficient to address the recently emerging zoonotic infections today. If wild animal reservoirs are not addressed, interventions against zoonotic diseases will be inadequate. Further, we will not be adequately prepared for the next emerging zoonotic pandemic that will inevitably come.

References

Abubakar I, Zignol M, Falzon D et al. 2013. *Lancet Inf Dis* 13(6):529–39.

Abubakar S, Teoh BT, Sam SS et al. 2012. *Emerg Infec Dis* 19(12):1989–91.

Acardi SA, Rago MV, Liotta DJ et al. 2013. *Vet Parasitol* 193(1):256–9.

Adouchief S, Smura T, Sane K et al. 2016. *Rev Med Virol* 26(4):221–41.

Ahuka-Mundeke S, Liegéois F, Lunguya O et al. 2011. *Retrovirology* 8(1):A92.

Ahuka-Mundeke S, Mbala-Kingebeni P, Liegeois F et al. 2012. *AIDS Res Hum Retrov AIDS* 28(6):628–35.

Alexander KA, Sanderson CE, Marathe M et al. 2015. *PLoS Negl Trop Dis* 9(6):e0003652.

Alfonso R, Romero RE, Diaz A et al. 2004. *Vet Microbiol* 98(3):285–95.

Allen JE and Maizels RM. 2011. *Nat Rev Immunol* 11(6):375–88.

Almeida MA, Santos ED, Cardoso JD et al. 2012. *Am J Primatol* 74(1):68–76.

Anderson RM and May RM. 1991. In Anderson RM and May RM eds. *Infectious Diseases of Humans: Dynamics and Control*. Vol. 28. Oxford, UK: Oxford.

Apetrei C, Metzger MJ, Richardson D et al. 2005. *J Virol* (4):2631–6.

Appleton CC and Boinski S. 1991. *J Med Primatol* 20(8):402–3.

Appleton CC and Brain C. 1995. *Afr J Ecol* 33(3):257–65.

Araújo MS, Messias MR, Figueiró MR et al. 2013. *Malaria J* 12(1):180.

Arias CA and Murray B. 2015. In *Mandell, Douglas, and Bennett's Principles and Practice of Infectious Diseases* 202:2328–39.

Arricau-Bouvery N and Rodolakis A. 2005. *Vet Res* 36(3):327–49.

Ashford RW. 2000. *Int J Parasitol* 30(12):1269–81.

Ashford, RW, Reid GD, and RW Wrangham. 2000. *Ann Trop Med Parasitol* 94(2):173–179.

Attoui H and Mohd JF. 2015. *Revue scientifique et technique (International Office of Epizootics)* 34(2):353–61.

Auguste AJ, Liria J, Forrester NL et al. 2010. *Emerg Infect Dis* 21(10):1742–50.

Awang A and Yap KL. 1990. *J Diarrhoeal Dis Res* 1:82–6.

Ayouba A and Peeters M. 2015. In Morand S, Krasnov BR and Littlewood DT eds. *Parasite Diversity and Diversification*. Cambridge: Cambridge University Press, pp. 117–49.

Ayouba A, Duval L, Liégeois F et al. 2013. *Infect Genet Evol* 18:324–34.

Bailey LL, Nehlsen-Cannarella SL, Concepcion W et al. *JAMA* 254(23):3321–29.

Bain O, Moisson P, Huerre M et al. 1995. *Parasite* (3):315–22.
Bandeira AC, Campos GS, Sardi SI et al. 2016. *IDCases* 5:57–9.
Banish LD, Sims R, Sack D et al. 1993. *JAVMA* 203(1):126–32.
Banish LD, Bush M, Montali RJ et al. 1990. *J Wildlife Med* 12(3):302–9.
Barré-Sinoussi F, Chermann JC, Rey F et al. 2004. *(AIDS). Rev Invest Clin* 56(2):126–9.
Basak S, Rajurkar MN and Mallick SK. 2014. *Parasitol Res* 113(1):261–5.
Baxter R, Ray P, Tran TN et al. 2013. *Pediatrics* 131(5):e1389–96.
Baylet R, Thivolet J, Sepetjian M et al. 1970. *B Soc Pathol Exot* 64(6):842–6.
Beck R, Sprong H, Bata I et al. 2011. *Vet Parasitol* 175(1):40–6.
Béland K, Dore-Nguyen M, Gagné MJ et al. 2014. *J Infect Dis* 209(2):247–54.
Bellinger DA and Bullock BC. 1988. *Lab Anim Sci* 38(1):85.
Benavides JA, Huchard E, Pettorelli N et al. 2012. *Am J Phys Anthropol* 147(1):52–63.
Bengis RG, Kock RA and Fischer J. 2002. *Rev Sci Tech OIE* 21(1):53–66.
Bennett JE, Dolin R, and Blaser MJ. 2014. *Principles and Practice of Infectious Disease*. Philadelphia: Elsevier.
Bente DA. 2015. In *Mandell, Douglas, and Bennett's Principles and Practice of Infectious Diseases* 168:2025–30.
Bente DA, Forrester NL, Watts DM et al. 2013. *Antivir Res* 100(1):159–89.
Bentley R and Meganathan R. 1982. *Microbiol Rev* 46(3):241–80.
Berghe L, Chardome M and Peel E. 1963. *J Protozool* 10(2):133–5.
Betsem E, Rua R, Tortevoye P et al. 2011. *PLoS Pathog* 7(10):e1002306.
Bharti AR, Nally JE, Ricaldi JN et al. 2003. *Lancet Inf Dis* 3(12):757–71.
Bhatt PN, Brandt CD, Weiss RA et al. 1966. *Am J Trop Med Hyg* 15(4):561–6.
Bhatt S, Gething PW, Brady OJ et al. 2013. The global distribution and burden of dengue. *Nature* 496(7446):504–7.
Bittar F, Keita MB, Lagier JC et al. 2014. *ci Rep* 4:7174.
Bommineni YR, Dick EJ, Estep JS et al. 2009. *J Med Primatol* (4):247–51.
Brack M. 1987. *Agents Transmissible From Simians to Man*. Heidelburg, Germany: Springer-Verlag.
Brashares JS, Arcese P, Sam MK et al. 2004. *Science* 306(5699):1180–3.
Brede HD. 1972. *Med Primatol* 3:35–8.
Breitschwerdt EB. 2014. *ILAR J* 55(1):46–58.
Bronson RT, May BD, Ruebner BH. 1972. *Amer J Pathol* 69(2):289–304.
Broutet N, Krauer F, Riesen M et al. 2016. *New Engl J Med* 374(16):1506–9.
Brown-Elliot BA and Wallace RJ. 2015. In *Mandell, Douglas, and Bennett's Principles and Practice of Infectious Diseases* 254:2844–52.
Bryant AE and Stevens DL. 2015. In *Mandell, Douglas, and Bennett's Principles and Practice of Infectious Diseases* 199:2285–99.
Bublitz DC, Wright PC, Rasambainarivo FT et al. 2015. *Am J Primatol* 77(3):330–7.
Bueno MG, Iovine RO, Torres LN et al. 2015. *J Vet Diagn Invest* 27(3):387–91.
Bueno MG, Rohe F, Kirchgatter K et al. 2013. *Eco Health* 10(1):48–53.
Buhles WC, Vanderlip JE, Russell SW et al. 1981. *J Clin Microbiol* 13(3):519–25.
Burke RL, Whitehouse CA, Taylor JK et al. 2009. *Comparative Med* 59(6):589–97.
Butynski TM. 2003. In *Status Survey and Conservation Action Plan: West African Chimpanzees*, pp. 5–12. Gland, Switzerland: IUCN/SSC Primate Specialist Group.

Calik ZZ, Karamese M, Aktas O. 2016. *Dicle Med J* 43(2):205–11.
Calvignac-Spencer S, Leendertz SA, Gillespie TR et al. 2012. *Clin Microbiol Infect* 18(6):521–7.
Campos GS, Bandeira AC and Sardi SI. 2015. *Emerg Infect Dis* 21(10):1885.
Cao-Lormeau V, Roche C, Teissier A et al. 2014. *Emerg Infect Dis* 20(11):1960.
Cárdenas WB and Basler CF. 2013. In Munir M ed. *Mononegaviruses of Veterinary Importance, Volume 1: Pathobiology and Molecular Diagnosis*. Oxfordshire, UK: CABI, pp. 248–60.
Carey DE. 1971. *J History Med All Sci* 26(3):243–62.
Carme B, Aznar C, Motard A et al. 2002. *Vector-Borne Zoonot* 2(1):11–17.
Carmeli Y. 2014. *Int J Infect Dis* 21:14.
Carmona MC, Bermúdez OG, Gutiérrez-Espeleta GA et al. 2005. *Int J Trop Biol Conserv* 53(3–4):437–45.
Carod-Artal FJ. 2016. *Rev Neurologia* 62(7):317.
Carter R and Mendis KN. 2002. *Clin Microbiol Rev* 15:564–94.
CDC. 2013. Parasites – Cyclosporiasis. Accessed on 11/06/2015. www.cdc.gov/parasites/cyclosporiasis/gen_info/faqs.html
CDC. 2014. B Virus. Accessed on 11/06/2016. www.cdc.gov/herpesbvirus/.
CDC. 2015a. Parasites – Amebiasis – *Entamoeba histolytica* Infection. Accessed on 6/30/2016. www.cdc.gov/parasites/amebiasis/
CDC. 2015b. Parasites – *Giardia*. Accessed on 6/30/2016. www.cdc.gov/parasites/giardia/.
CDC. 2015c. Parasites – Toxoplasmosis. Accessed on 11/11/2015. www.cdc.gov/parasites/toxoplasmosis/epi.html
CDC. 2017. HIV/AIDS. Accessed on 5/29/2017. www.cdc.gov/hiv/library/factsheets/index.html
Cedillo-Peláez C, Rico-Torres CP, Salas-Garrido CG et al. 2011. *Vet Parasitol* 180(3):368–71.
Chaber AL, Allebone-Webb S, Lignereux Y et al. 2010. *Conserv Lett* 3(5):317–21.
Chapman CA, Bowman DD, Ghai RR et al. 2012. *Am J Primatol* 74(6):510–7.
Checkley W, White AC, Jaganath D et al. 2015. *Lancet* 15(1):85–94.
Chen YM, Jang YJ, Kanki PJ et al. 1994. Isolation and characterization of simian T-cell leukemia virus type II from New World monkeys. *J Virol* 68(2):1149–57.
Chen Z, Telfier P, Gettie A et al. 1996. *J Virol* 70(6):3617–27.
Chikweto A, Hariharan H, Bhaiyat MI et al. 2013. *Int J Vet Med* 264913:1–4.
Chin W, Contacos PG, Coatney GR et al. 1965. *Science* 149(3686):865.
Chou HH, Takematsu H, Diaz S et al. 1998. *P Natl A Sci USA* 95(20):11751–6.
Chu DM, Sherchand JB, Cross JH et al. 2004. *Am J Trop Med Hyg* 71(4):373–9.
Clark HC, Dunn LH, Benavides J. 1931. *Am J Trop Med Hyg* 1(4):243–57.
Cleaveland S, Haydon DT and Taylor L. 2007. In Child JE, Richt JA, Mackenzie JS eds. *Wildlife and Emerging Zoonotic Diseases: The Biology, Circumstances and Consequences of Cross-Species Transmission*. Heidelberg, Germany: Springer-Verlag, pp. 85–111.
Clements AN. 2012. *The Biology of Mosquitoes, Volume 3 Transmission of Viruses and Interactions With Bacteria*. Vol. 3. Oxfordshire, UK: CABI.
Clough D. 2010. *J Parasitol* 96(2):245–51.
Coatney GR. 1968. *Am J Trop Med Hyg* 17(2):147–55.

Coatney GR. 1971. *Am J Trop Med Hyg* 20(6):795–803.

Coatney GR, Collins WE, Warren M et al. 1971. *The Primate Malarias*. Bethesda, MD: NIAID.

Cogswell, FB. 2000. In Bowman DD ed. *Companion and Exotic Animal Parasitology*. Ithaca, New York: International Veterinary Information Service.

Collins WE, Skinner JC, Huong AY et al. 1985. *J Parasitol* 1:767–70.

Cook N, Bridger J, Kendall K et al. 2004. *J Infect* 48(4):289–302.

Cooper DK, Ekser B, and Tector AJ. 2015. *Int J Surg* 23:3321–9.

Cooper JE and Needham JR. 1976. *J Hyg-Cambridge* 76(3):415–24.

Cordon-Obras C, Rodriguez YF, Fernandez-Martinez A et al. 2015. *Front Microbiol* 6:765.

Corlett RT. 2007. *Biotropica* 39(3):292–303.

Cormier LA. 2003. *Kinship With Monkeys: The Guajá Foragers of Eastern Amazonia*. New York: Columbia University Press.

Cormier LA. 2006. *Ecol Environ Anthropol* 2(1):14–32.

Cormier LA. 2011. *The Ten-Thousand Year Fever: Rethinking Human and Wild Primate Malarias*. Walnut Creek, CA: Left Coast Press.

Costa DC, Cunha VP, Assis GM et al. 2014. *Mem I Oswaldo Cruz* 109(5):641–53.

Cotruvo JA, Dufour A, Rees G et al. eds. 2004. *Waterborne Zoonoses*. London: IWA Publishing.

Coughlin MM, Beck AS, Bankamp B et al. 2017. *Viruses* 9(1):11.

Courngaud V, Van Dooren S, Liegeois F et al. 2004. *J Virol* 78(9):4700–9.

Cox-Singh J, Davis TM, Lee KS et al. 2008. *Clin Infect Dis* 46(2):165–71.

Cross JH, Hsu MY and Hung CK. 1983. *SE Asia J Trop Med Public Health* 14(4):536–42.

Croxen MA, Law RJ, Scholz R et al. 2013. *Clin Microbiol Rev* 26(4):822–80.

Crumpacker CS. 2015. Cytomegalovirus (CMV). In *Mandell, Douglas, and Bennett's Principles and Practice of Infectious Diseases* 140:1738–53.

D'Agata E. 2015. In *Mandell, Douglas, and Bennett's Principles and Practice of Infectious Diseases* 221:2518–31.

da Fonseca F. 1951. *Mem I Oswaldo Cruz* 49:543–51.

da Rocha EM, Fontes G and Ehrenberg JP. 2017. In Marcondes CB ed. *Arthropod Borne Diseases*. Basel: Springer, pp. 369–81.

da Silva AS, Gressler LT, Lara VM et al. 2009. *Cienc Anim Brasil* 10(2):669–72.

da Silva Barbosa A, Bastos OM, Uchôa CM et al. 2015. *Vet Parasitol* 210(3):240–5.

Da Silva FM, Rodrigues AC, Campaner M et al. 2004. *Parasitology* 128(3):283–94.

Dagci H, Özgür KU, Demirel M et al. 2014. *Iran J Parasitol* 9(4):519.

Davies CR, Ayres JM, Dye C et al. 1991. *Funct Ecol* 5:655–62.

De Arruda M, Nardin EH, Nussenzweig RS et al. 1989. *Am J Trop Med Hyg* 41(4):379–85.

de Castro Duarte AM, dos Santos Malafronte R, Cerutti C et al. 2008. *Acta Trop* 107(2):179–85.

de Lima VM, Santiago ME, da Cruz Sanches L et al. 2012. *J Zoo Wildlife Med* 43(4):943–5.

De Silva AM, Dittus WP, Amerasinghe PH et al. 1999. *Am J Trop Med Hyg* 60(2):300–6.

De Silva TI, Cotten M, and Rowland-Jones SL. 2008. *Trends Microbiol* 16(12):588–95.
de Thoisy B, Demar M, Aznar C et al. 2003. *J Wildlife Dis* 39(2):456–9.
de Thoisy B, Dussart P and Kazanji M. 2004. *Trans Roy Soc Trop Med Hyg* 98:409–12.
de Thoisy B, Vogel I, Reynes J et al. 2001. *Am J Primatol* 54(1):1–16.
de Vos V, van Niekerk GA and McConell EE. 1973. *Koedoe* 16(1):1–0.
Deane LM. 1964. *B World Health Organ* 31(5):752–3.
Deane LM. 1972. *Simian Malaria Survey in Brazil: A Brief Summary of Data Obtained in 1964-1971*. Geneva: World Health Organization.
Deane LM. 1992. *Mem I Oswaldo Cruz* 87:1–20.
Deane LM, Ferrerira N, Okumura M et al. 1969. *Revista Inst Med Trop SP* 11(2): 71–86.
Deane LM, Lourenço-de-Oliveira R, Ziccardi MCB and Luz SLB. 1989. *Mem I Oswaldo Cruz* 84(s2):143.
DeBiasi RL and Tyler KL. 2015. In *Mandell, Douglas, and Bennett's Principles and Practice of Infectious Diseases* 150:1848–50.
DelVecchio VG, Connolly JP, Alefantis TG et al. 2006. *App Environ Microb* 72(9):6355–63.
den Bakker HC, Warchocki S, Wright EM et al. 2014. *Int J Syst Evol Micr* 64(6):1882–9.
Diallo M, Thonnon J, Traore-Lamizana M et al. 1999. *Am J Trop Med Hyg* 60(2):281–6.
Díaz LA, del Pilar Díaz M, Almirón WR et al. 2007. *Trans Roy Soc Trop Med Hyg* 101(10):1039–41.
Diaz LA, Flores FS, Beranek M et al. 2013. *Trans Roy Soc Trop Med Hyg* 107(5):332–4.
Dick GW, Kitchen SF and Haddow AJ. 1952. *Trans Roy Soc Trop Med Hyg* 46(5):509–20.
Dienstag JL and Delmos AS. 2015. In *Mandell, Douglas, and Bennett's Principles and Practice of Infectious Diseases* 119:1439–68.
Dobyns HF. 1993. *Ann Rev Anthropol* 22(1):273–91.
Donnenberg MS. 2015. In *Mandell, Douglas, and Bennett's Principles and Practice of Infectious Diseases* 220:2503–17.
Dormitzer PR. 2015. Rotaviruses. In *Mandell, Douglas, and Bennett's Principles and Practice of Infectious Diseases* 152:1854–64.
Drewe JA and O'Riain MJ. 2012. *Emerg Infect Dis* 18(2):298–301.
Drummond N, Murphy BP, Ringwood T et al. 2012. *Foodborne Pathog Dis* 9(3):179–89.
Drzewiecka D. 2016. *Microb Ecol* 72(4):1–18.
Dubey JP, Calero-Bernal R, Rosenthal BM et al. 2015. In Dubey JP et al. eds. *Sarcocystosis of Animals and Humans*. Boca Raton, FL: CRC Press.
Duffy MR, Chen TH, Hancock WT et al. 2009. *N Engl J Med* 360:2536–43.
Duke BO. 1972. Behavioural aspects of the life cycle of Loa. In Canning EU and Wright CA eds. *Behavioural Aspects of Parasite Transmission*. London: Academic Press.
Duncan M, Cranfield MR, Torano H et al. 2013. *Virology* 444(1):119–23.
Dunn FL, Lambrecht FL and Du Plessis R. 1963. *Am J Trop Med Hyg* 12(4):524–34.

Dupont HL. 2015. In *Mandell, Douglas, and Bennett's Principles and Practice of Infectious Diseases* 226:2569–74.
Dutton CJ, Junge RE and Louis EE. 2003. *J Zoo Wildlife Med* 34(1):16–24.
Duval L, Fourment M, Nerrienet E et al. 2010. *P Natl A Sci USA* 107(23):10561–6.
Eberhard ML and D'Alessandro A. 1982. *Am J Trop Med Hyg* 31(5):931–3.
Eberhard ML, da Silva AJ, Lilley BG et al. 1999. *Emerg Infec Dis* 5(5):651–8.
Eberhard ML, Njenga MN, DaSilva AJ et al. 2001. *J Parasitol* 87(6):1394–7.
Eberhard ML, Owens JR, Bishop HS et al. 2014. *Emerg Infec Dis* 20(3):510–11.
Edeson JF and Wilson T. 1964. *Annu Rev Entomol* 9(1):245–68.
Ekanayake DK, Arulkanthan A, Horadagoda NU et al. 2006. *Am J Trop Med Hyg* 74(2):322–9.
Ekanayake DK, Rajapakse RP, Dubey JP et al. 2004. *J Parasitol* 90(4):870–1.
Else JG, Satzger M and Sturrock RF. 1982. *Ann Trop Med Parasitol* 76(1):111–2.
Emmanuel FX, Seagar AL, Doig C et al. 2007. *Emerg Infect Dis* 13(12):1924.
Engel GA, Wilbur AK, Westmark A et al. 2012. *Emerg Microb Infect* 1(10):e30.
Escalante AA, Barrio E and Ayala FJ. 1995. *Mol Biol Evol* 12(4):616–26.
Esposito DH, Freedman DO, Neumayr A et al. 2012. *Eur Communic Dis Bull* 17(45):20310.
Estrada A, Garber PA, Rylands AB et al. 2017. *Science Advances* 3(1):e1600946.
Ewald PW. 1983. *Ann Rev Ecol Syst* 14:465–85.
Ewald PW. 1994. *The Evolution of Infectious Disease*. Oxford.
Eyles DE. 1963. *J Parasitol* 49(6):866–87.
Eyles DE, Coatney GR and Getz ME. 1960. *Science* 131(3416):1812–13.
Fa JE, Peres CA and Meeuwig J. 2002. *Conserv Biol* 16(1):232–7.
Fairhurst RM and Wellems TE. 2015. In *Mandell, Douglas, and Bennett's Principles and Practice of Infectious Diseases* 276:3070–90.
Falsey AR. 2015. In *Mandell, Douglas, and Bennett's Principles and Practice of Infectious Diseases* 161:1961–6.
Fandeur TB, Volney B, Peneau C et al. 2000. *Parasitology* 120(1):11–21.
Fauci AS and Morens DM. 2016. *New Engl J Med* 374(7):601–4.
Favoretto S, Araujo D, Oliveira D et al. 2016. *bioRxiv*:049395.
Fayer R. 2004. *Vet Parasitol* 126(1):37–56.
Fayer R, Dubey JP and Lindsay DS. 2004. *Trends Parasitol* 20(11):531–6.
Feasey NA, Dougan G, Kingsley RA et al. 2012. *Lancet* 379(9835):2489–99.
Felsenfeld O and Wolf RH. 1971. *Folia Primatol* 16(3/4):294–305.
Fenwick A. 1969. *Trans Roy Soc Trop Med Hyg* 63(5):557–67.
Ferber D. 2000. *Science* 289(5483):1277–8.
Fitzgerald DW, Sterling TR and Haas DW. 2015. In *Mandell, Douglas, and Bennett's Principles and Practice of Infectious Diseases* 251:2787–818.
Fleagle JG. 1999. *Primate Adaptation and Evolution.* 2nd edition. New York: Academic Press.
Fooden J. 1963. *J Mammol* 44(2):213–47.
Formenty P, Boesch C, Wyers M et al. 1999. *J Infect Dis* 179(S1):S120–6.
Franco J, Ferreira RC, Ienne S et al. 2015. *Infect Genet Evol* 31:198–208.
Fribourg-Blanc A and Mollaret HH. 1969. *Primates Med* 3:113–21.

Fribourg-Blanc A, Neil G and Mollaret HH. 1963. *B Soc Pathol Exot* 56(3):474–85.
Fricker J. 1996. *Lancet* 347(8999):457.
Fuller GK, Lemma A and Haile T. 1979. *Am J Trop Med Hyg* 28(3):526–30.
Funk S, Nishiura H, Heesterbeek H et al. 2013. *PLoS Comput Biol* 9(1):e1002855.
Galindo P and Srihongse S. 1967. *B World Health Organ* 36(1):151–61.
Galton MM, Mitchell RB, Clark G et al. 1948. *J Infect Dis* 83(2):147–54.
Gandhi T, Slater LN, Welch DF et al. 2015. In *Mandell, Douglas, and Bennett's Principles and Practice of Infectious Diseases* 236:2649–63.
Gao F, Yue L, White AT et al. 1992. *Nature* 358(6386):495–9.
Garcea RL and Imperiale MJ. 2003. *J Virol* 77(9):5039–45.
Garcia JL, Svoboda WK, Chryssafidis AL et al. 2005. *Vet Parasitol* 133(4):307–11.
Garnham PC. 1963. *J Parasitol* 49(6):905–11.
Geisbert TW. 2015. In *Mandell, Douglas, and Bennett's Principles and Practice of Infectious Diseases* 166:1995–9.
Gérardin P, Couderc T, Bintner M et al. 2016. *Neurology* 86(1):94–102.
Gerrard SR, Li L, Barrett AD and Nichol ST. 2004. *J Virol* 78(16):8922–6.
Gershon AA. 2015. In *Mandell, Douglas, and Bennett's Principles and Practice of Infectious Diseases* 162:1967–73.
Ghandour AM, Zahid NZ, Banaja AA et al. 1995. *J Trop Med H* 98(6):431–9.
Gibrail MM, Fiaccadori FS, Souza M et al. 2016. *Rev Soc Bras Med Trop* 49(3): 357–60.
Gicheru MM, Jeneby MM, Macharia JC et al. 2009. *Acta Trop* 109(2):136–40.
Gilardi KV, Oxford KL, Gardner-Roberts D et al. 2014. *Emerg Infect Dis* 20(11): 1883–6.
Gillespie TR, Greiner EC and Chapman CA. 2005. *J Parasitol* 91(3):569–73.
Gillespie TR, Lonsdorf EV, Canfield EP et al. 2010. *Am J Phys Anthropol* 143(4):534–44.
Go YY, Balasuriya UR and Lee C. 2014. *Clin Exp Vaccine Res* 3(1):58–77.
Goldberg TL, Sintasath DM, Chapman CA et al. 2009. *J Virol* 83(21):11318–29.
Goldsmid JM. 1974. *Ann Soc Belge Med Trop* 54:87–101.
Gómez MS, Gracenea M, Montoliu I et al. 1996. *J Med Primatol* 25(6):419–23.
Gonin P and Trudel L. 2003. *J Clin Microbiol* 41(1):237–41.
Gonzalo A and Tantaleán M. 1996. *Lab Primate News* 35:1–6.
Gordin FM and Horsburgh CR. 2015. In *Mandell, Douglas, and Bennett's Principles and Practice of Infectious Diseases* 253:2832–43.
Gormus BJ, Wolf RH, Baskin GB et al. 1988. *Int J Leprosy* 56(1):61–5.
Gottdenker NL, Streicker DG, Faust CL et al. 2014. *Ecohealth* 11(4):619–32.
Goyette-Desjardins G, Auger JP, Xu J et al. 2014. *Emerg Microbe Infect* 3(6):e45.
Graczyk T, DaSilva A, Cranfield M et al. 2001. *Parasitol Res* 87(5):368–70.
Graczyk R, Lowenstine M, and Cranfield M. 1999. *J Parasitol* 85(6):1168–70.
Gramiccia M and Gradoni L. 2005. *Int J Parasitol* 35(11):1169–80.
Gray J, Zintl A, Hildebrandt A et al. 2010. *Ticks Tick-borne Dis* 1(1):3–10.
Gray WL. 2003. *J Med Virol* 70(S1):S4–8.
Grinde B. 2013. *J Oral Microbiol* 5:1–9.
Gubler DJ. 2004. *Comp Immunol Microb* 27(5):319–30.

Guebler DF. 2014. In Guebler DF, Ooi EE, Vasudevan S, Farrar J eds. *Dengue and Dengue Hemorrhagic Fever*. 2nd edition. Boston: CABI, pp. 1–29.

Gul HC and Erdem H. 2015. In *Mandell, Douglas, and Bennett's Principles and Practice of Infectious Diseases* 228:2584–9.

Haddow AD, Schuh AJ, Yasuda CY et al. 2012. *PLoS Negl Trop Dis* 6(2):e1477.

Haddow AJ. 1952. *Proc Zool Soc Lond* 122(2):297–394. Blackwell Publishing Ltd.

Hadush A and Pal M. 2013. *Int J Livest Res* 3(1):28–34.

Hahn NE, Capuano II and Saverio V. 2010. *J Am Assoc Lab Anim* 49(6):873–5.

Hahn NE, Proulx D, Muruthi PM et al. 2003. *Int J Primatol* 24(2):271–9.

Hall CA, Polizzi C, Yabsley MJ et al. 2007. *J Parasitol* 93(1):93–6.

Halliez MC and Buret AG. 2013. *World J Gastroenterol* 19(47):8974–85.

Hamad I, Forestier CL, Peeters M et al. 2015. *J Infect Dis* 211(2):267–73.

Hamilton CM, Katzer F, Beierschmitt A et al. 2014. *Parasit Vectors* 10;7(1):571.

Hanley PW, Barnhart KF, Abee CR et al. 2015. *Emerg Infec Dis* 21(12):2158–60.

Hansen MC, Potapov PV, Moore R et al. 2013. *Science* 342(6160):850–3.

Harper DR. 2011. *Viruses: Biology, Applications, and Control*. New York: Garland Science.

Harper KN, Fyumagwa RD, Hoare RH et al. 2012. *PLoS ONE* 7(12):e50882.

Harris LG, Foster SJ and Richards RG. 2002. *Eur Cell Mater* 4(3):39–60.

Harrison VR, Marshall JD and Guilloud NB. 1967. *J Immunol* 98(5):979–81.

Hassell JM, Blake DP, Cranfield MR et al. 2013. *J Wildlife Dis* 49(4):1063–5.

Heldstab A and Rüedi D. 1982. *J Comp Pathol* 92(4):609–12.

Helenbrook WD, Wade SE, Shields WM et al. 2015. *J Parasitol* 101(3):341–50.

Hensgens MP and Kuijper EJ. 2013. *Clin Infect Dis* 19(9):1540–1.

Herder S, Simo G, Nkinin S and Njiokou F. 2002. *Parasite* 9(4):345–9.

Herrer A, Christensen HA, and Beumer RJ. 1973. *Am J Trop Med Hyg* 22(5):585–91.

Herrer A and Christensen HA. 1976. *Am J Trop Med Hyg* 25(1):54–8.

Higgs S and Beaty BJ. 2005. In Marquardt WC et al. eds. *The Biology of Disease Vectors*. Burlington: Elsevier, pp. 167–86.

Hill DR and Nash TE. 2015. In *Mandell, Douglas, and Bennetts's Principles and Practice of Infectious Diseases* 281:3154–60.

Hoch AL, Peterson NE, LeDuc JW et al. 1981. *Am J Trop Med Hyg* 30(3):689–98.

Hogan JN, Miller WA, Cranfield MR et al. 2014. *J Wildlife Dis* 50(1):21–30.

Holzmann I, Agostini I, Areta JI et al. 2010. *Am J Primatol* 72(6):475–80.

Homer MJ, Aguilar-Delfin I, Telford SR et al. 2000. *Clin Microbiol Rev* 13(3): 451–69.

Hope K, Goldsmith ML and Graczyk T. 2004. *Vet Parasitol* 122(2):165–70.

Hoppe E, Pauly M, Gillespie TR et al. 2015b. *Mol Biol Evol* 32(8):2072–84.

Hoppe E, Pauly M, Robbins M et al. 2015a. *J Gen Virol* 96(10):3090–8.

Howells ME, Pruetz J and Gillespie TR. 2011. *Am J Primatol* 73(2):173–9.

Hrdy DB. 1981. *J Med Primatol* 11(1):35–8.

HRSA. 2016. Accessed on 03/21/2016 from http://optn.transplant.hrsa.gov/data/.

Hubálek Z and Rudolf I eds. 2010. Vertebrates as hosts and reservoirs of zoonotic microbial agents. In *Microbial Zoonoses and Sapronoses*. Netherlands: Springer, pp. 83–128.

Huffman MA, Gotoh S, Turner LA et al. 1997. *Primates* 38(2):111–25.

Ildstad, ST. 1996. *Lancet* 347(9003):761.

Imura K, Chambers JK, Uchida K et al. 2014. *J Vet Med Sci* 76(12):1667–70.

Inglis FM, Lee KM, Chiu KB et al. 2016. *J Neurovirol* 22(2):140–8.

Inoue S, Morita K, Matias RR et al. 2003. *J Med Primatol* 32(2):89–94.

Irie A, Koyama S, Kozutsumi Y et al. 1998. *J Biol Chem* 272(25):15866–71.

Irwin MT, Junge RE, Raharison J et al. 2010. *Am J Primatol* 72(11):1013–25.

Iscovich J, Boffetta P, Franceschi S et al. 2000. *Cancer* 88(3):500–17.

Ison MG. 2015. In *Mandell, Douglas, and Bennett's Principles and Practice of Infectious Diseases* 158:1937–41.

Iwata T, Une Y, Okatani AT et al. 2005. *Microbiol Immun* 49(1):1–7.

Jagielski T, Van Ingen J, Rastogi N et al. 2014. *BioMed Res Int* 645802.

Janoff EN and Musher DM. 2015. In *Mandell, Douglas, and Bennett's Principles and Practice of Infectious Diseases* 201:2310–27.

Jeneby M[1]. 2011. *Haemoprotozoan Parasites of Non-Human Primates in Kenya.* Upsala University (diss).

Jeneby MM, Suleman MA and Gichuki C. 2002. *J Zoo Wildlife Med* 33(4):337–41.

Jiram AI, Vythilingam I, NoorAzian YM et al. 2012. *Malar J* 11(1):213.

Jirků M, Votýpka J, Petrželková KJ et al. 2015. *Int J Parasitol* 4(3):277–82.

Jobbins SE and Alexander KA. 2015. *Trans Roy Soc Trop Med Hyg* 109(5):349–51.

Johannsen EC and Kaye KM. 2015. In *Mandell, Douglas, and Bennett's Principles and Practice of Infectious Diseases* 141:1754–71.

Johnson JM, Harrod R and Franchini G. 2001. *Int J Exp Pathol* 82(3):135–47.

Johnston AR, Gillespie TR, Rwego IB et al. 2010. *PLoS Negl Trop Dis* 4(5):e683.

Jones-Engel L, Engel GA, Schillaci MA et al. 2004. *Am J Primatol* 62(2):71–82.

Jongwutiwes S, Putaporntip C, Iwasaki T et al. 2004. *Emerg Infec Dis* 10(12): 2211–13.

Julian TR. 2016. *Environ Sci* 18(8):944–55.

Jun SR, Wassenaar TM, Nookaew I et al. 2016. *Appl Environ Microb* 82(1):375–83.

Junge RE, Barrett MA and Yoder AD. 2011. *Am J Primatol* 73(7):632–42.

Junge RE and Louis EE. 2002. *Lemur News* 7:23–5.

Junge RE and Louis EE. 2005. *J Zoo Wildlife Med* 36(4):581–9.

Junge RE and Louis EE. 2007. *J Zoo Wildlife Med* 38(1):67–76.

Kaakoush NO, Castaño-Rodríguez N, Mitchell HM et al. 2015. *Clin Microbiol Rev* 28(3):687–720.

Kadariya J, Smith TC and Thapaliya D. 2014. Staphylococcus aureus and staphylococcal food-borne disease: an ongoing challenge in public health. *BioMed Res Int* 827965.

Kading RC, Borland EM, Cranfield M et al. 2013. *J Wildlife Dis* 49(3):587–99.

Kageyama T, Ogasawara A, Fukuhara R et al. 2002. *J Med Primatol* 31(3):129–35.

Kaiser M, Löwa A, Ulrich M et al. 2010. *Emerg Infect Dis* 16(12):1956.

Kalema-Zikusoka G, Rothman JM and Fox MT. 2005. *Primates* 46(1):59–63.

Kalter SS, Kuntz RE, Al-Coory Y et al. 1966. *Lab Anim Care* 16(2):161–77.

Kalyanaraman VS, Sarngadharan MG, Robert-Guroff M et al. 1982. *Science* 218(4572):571–3.

Kan SP, Prathap K and Dissanaike AS. 1979. *Am J Trop Med Hyg* 28(4):634–2.

Karesh WB, Wallace RB, Painter RL et al. 1998. *Am J Primatol* 44(2):107–23.
Karim MR, Wang R, Yu F et al. 2015. *Infect Genet Evol* 30:82–8.
Karr SL and Wong MM. 1975. *Lab Anim Sci* 25(5):641–5.
Kasa TJ, Lathrop GD, Dupuy HJ et al. 1977. *JAVMA* 171(9):850–4.
Kaschula VR, Van Dellen AF, De Vos V. 1978. *J S Afr Vet Assoc* 49(3):223–7.
Kaur T, Singh J, Tong S et al. 2008. *Am J Primatol* 70(8):755–65.
Kazura JW. 2015. In *Mandell, Douglas, and Bennett's Principles and Practice of Infectious Diseases* 289:3208–15.
Keele BF, Van Heuverswyn F, Li Y et al. 2006. *Science* 313(5786):523–6.
Keesing F, Belden LK, Daszak P et al. 2010. *Nature* 468(7324):647–52.
Keet DF, Kriek NP, Bengis RG et al. 2000. *Onderstepoort J Vet* 67(2):115–22.
Keet DF, Kriek NP, Penrith M et al. 1996. *Onderstepoort J Vet* 63(3):239–44.
Kekarainen T and Segalés J. 2012. *Transboundary Emerg Dis* 59(s1):103–8.
Kennedy F, Astbury J, Needham JR et al. 1993. *Epidemiol Infect* 110(2):247–51.
Kesdangsakonwut S, Sommanustweechai A and Chaiprasert A. 2015. *Emerg Infect Dis* 21(3):534–5.
Keymer IF. 1971. *J Zool* 163(4):421–41.
Kilbourn AM, Karesh WB, Wolfe ND et al. 2003. *J Wildlife Dis* 39(1):73–83.
Kilonzo CT, Stopka TJ and Chomel B. 2013. *Viral Infect Global Change* 10:179–94.
Kiple KF, Higgins BT. 1992. In Verano JW, Ubelaker DH eds. *Disease and Demography in the Americas*. Washington, DC: Smithsonian Inst Press, pp. 237–48.
Kirchhoff LV. 2015. In *Mandell, Douglas, and Bennett's Principles and Practice of Infectious Diseases* 279:3116–21.
Kirya BG and Okia NO. 1972. *T Roy Soc Trop Med H* 71(4):300–3.
Klee SR, Özel M, Appel B et al. 2006. *J Bacteriol* 188(15):5333–44.
Kliks MM. 1983. *Hum Ecol Infect Dis* (1983):291–313.
Kliks MM. 1990. *Parasitol Today* 6(4):93–100.
Kluytmans J, Van Belkum A and Verbrugh H. 1997. *Clin Microbiol Rev* 10(3):505–20.
Knauf S, Barnett U, Maciej P et al. 2015. *PLoS ONE* 10(11):e0143100.
Knauf S, Batamuzi EK, Mlengeya T et al. 2012. *Vet Pathol Online* 49(2):292–303.
Knauf S, Liu H and Harper KN. 2013. *Emerg Infect Dis* 19(12):2058–60.
Kollien A and Schaub G. 2000. *Parasitol Today* 16(9):381–7.
Köndgen S, Kühl H, N'goran PK et al. 2008. *Curr Biol* 18(4):260–4.
Kooriyama T, Hasegawa H, Shimozuru M et al. 2012. *Primates* 53(4):365–75.
Kortlandt A. 1996. *Pan Afr News* 3(2):9–10.
Kourany M and Porter JA. 1969. *Lab Anim Care* 19(3):336–41.
Kowalewski MM, Salzer JS, Deutsch JC et al. 2011. *Am J Primatol* 73(1):75–83.
Krief S, Escalante AA, Pacheco MA et al. 2010. *PLoS Pathog* 6(2):e1000765.
Kumar CN and Gopal DS. 2010. *Indian J Virol* 21(1):8–17.
Kuncl RW and Richter W. 1988. *Jpn J Vet Med Sci* 50(2):519–27.
Kuntz RE. 1978. *Am J Trop Med Hyg* 27(1):208–9.
Kurpiers LA, Schulte-Herbrüggen B, Ejotre I et al. 2016. In Angelici, FM ed. *Problematic Wildlife.* Basel: Springer, pp. 507–51.
Laemmert HW and de Castro Ferreira L. 1945. *Am J Trop Med Hyg* 25(3):231–2.
Laing AB, Edeson JF and Wharton RH. 1960. *Ann Trop Med Parasit* 54(1):92–9.
Lainson R, Braga RR, De Souza AA et al. 1988. *Ann Parasit Hum Comp* 64(3):200–7.

Lal AA, De La Cruz VF, Collins WE et al. 1988. *J Biol Chem* 263(12):5495–8.
Laroque PO, Valença-Montenegro MM, Ferreira DR et al. 2014. *Pesquis Vet Brasil* 34(5):462–8.
Larsen PA, Hayes CE, Williams CV et al. 2016. *Biol Letters* 12(1):20150829.
Le Guenno B, Formenty P, Wyers M et al. 1995. *Lancet* 345(8960):1271–4.
Le Tourneau F. 2015. *Curr Opin Enviro Sustain* 14:213–20.
Leather SR, Walters KF and Bale JS. 1995. *The Ecology of Insect Overwintering.* Cambridge: Cambridge University Press.
Lebreton F, Willems RJ and Gilmore MS. 2014. *Enterococcus Diversity, Origins in Nature, and Gut Colonization.* Creative Commons.
LeBreton M, Yang O, Tamoufe U et al. 2007. *Emerg Infect Dis* 13(10):1579–82.
LeBreton M, Switzer WM, Djoko CF et al. 2014. *Emerg Microbe Infect* 3(1):e7.
LeClerc MC, Hugot JP, Durand P et al. 2004. *Parasitol* 129:677–84.
Lee H, Park HJ, Cho SN et al. 2000. *J Clin Microbiol* 38(8):2966–71.
Lee KA, Wikelski M, Robinson WD et al. 2008. *J Anim Ecol* 77(2):356–63.
Lee PC and Priston NE. 2005. In Paterson JD and Wallis J eds. *Commensalism and Conflict: The Human-Primate Interface.* Vol. 4. American Society of Primatologists.
Lee TM, Sigouin A, Pinedo-Vasquez M et al. 2014. *The Harvest of Wildlife for Bushmeat and Traditional Medicine in East, South and Southeast Asia: Current Knowledge Base, Challenges, Opportunities and Areas for Future Research.* Vol. 115. CIFOR.
Leendertz FH, Ellerbrok H, Boesch C et al. 2004. *Nature* 430(6998):451–2.
Leendertz FH, Yumlu S, Pauli G et al. 2006. *PLoS Pathog* 2(1):e8.
Leendertz SA, Gogarten JF, Düx A et al. 2016. *EcoHealth* 13(1):18–25.
Leendertz SA, Junglen S, Hedemann C et al. 2010. *J Virol* 84(15):7427–36.
Legesse M and Erko B. 2004. *Acta Trop* 90(3):231–6.
Leininger JR, Donham KJ and Meyers WM. 1980. *Int J Leprosy* 48(4):414–21.
Lemoy MJ, Lopes DA, Reader JR et al. 2012. *Comparative Med* 62(5):443–7.
Leroy EM, Rouquet P, Formenty P et al. 2004a. *Science* 303(5656):387–90.
Leroy EM, Tefler B, Kumulungui B et al. 2004b. *J Infect Dis* 190(11):1895–9.
Leroy EM, Kumulungui B, Pourrut X et al. 2005. *Nature* 438(7068):575–6.
Levréro F, Gatti S, Gautier-Hion A et al. 2007. *Am J Phys Anthropol* 132(4):568–75.
Levy JA, Levy SB, Hirshaut Y et al. 1971. *Nature* 233:559–60.
Liégeois F, Boué V, Mouacha F et al. 2012. *Retrovirology* 9(1):28.
Liégeois F, Lafay B, Switzer WM et al. 2008. *Virology* 371(2):405–17.
Lilenbaum WR, Varges R, Moraes IA et al. 2005. *Vet J* 169(3):462–4.
Lilly AA, Mehlman PT and Doran D. 2002. *Int J Primatol* 23(3):555–73.
Lion T. 2014. *Clin Microbiol Rev* 27(3):441–62.
Lisboa CV, Mangia RH, De Lima NR et al. 2004. *Parasitology* 129(6):703–11.
Lisboa CV, Mangia RH, Luz SL et al. 2006. *Parasitology* 133(5):603–11.
Lisboa CV, Mangia RH, Rubião E et al. 2004. *Acta Trop* 31;90(1):97–106.
Litman N and Baum SG. 2015. In *Mandell, Douglas, and Bennett's Principles and Practice of Infectious Diseases* 159:1942–7.
Liu W, Li Y, Learn GH et al. 2010. *Nature* 467(7314):420–5.
Livi-Bacci M. 2012. *A Concise History of World Population.* Malden, MA: John Wiley & Sons.

Locatelli S and Peeters M. 2012. *Aids* 26(6):659–73.
Lombardi MC, Turchetti AP, Tinoco HP et al. 2014. *Pesquis Vet Brasil* 34(12):1243–6.
Lorber B. 2015. In *Mandell, Douglas, and Bennett's Principles and Practice of Infectious Diseases* 208:2383–90.
Lourenço-de-Oliveira R and Deane LM. 1995. *Mem I Oswaldo Cruz* 90(3):331–9.
Luchavez J, Espino FE, Curameng P et al. 2008. *Emerg Infect Dis*14(5):811–3.
Lugli EB, Pouliot M, Portela MD et al. 2004. *Mol Biochem Parasit* 138(1):9–20.
Lum LC, Chua KB, McMinn PC et al. 2002. *J Clin Virol* 23(3):153–60.
Maamun JM, Suleman MA, Akinyi M et al. 2011. *J Parasitol* 97(1):63–7.
MacArthur RH and Wilson EO. 1967. *The Theory of Island Biogeography*. Princton, NJ: Princeton University Press.
MacLennan CA and Levine MM. 2013. *Expert Rev Anti-infect Therapy* 11(5): 443–6.
Maesano G, Capasso M, Ianniello D et al. 2014. *Acta Parasitol* 59(2):343–53.
Mafuyai HB, Barshep Y, Audu BS et al. 2013. *Afri Health Sci* 13(2):252–4.
Maganga GD, Bourgarel M, Vallo P et al. 2014. *PLoS ONE* 9(6):e100172.
Magill AJ. 2015. In *Mandell, Douglas, and Bennett's Principles and Practice of Infectious Disease* 277:3091–107.
Maguire JH. 2015. In *Mandell, Douglas, and Bennett's Principles and Practice of Infectious Diseases* 290:3216–26.
Magwedere K, Hemberger MY, Hoffman LC et al. 2012. *Infect Ecol Epidemiol* 2.
Mahieux R, Pecon-Slattery J, Chen GM et al. 1998. *Virology* 251(1):71–84.
Majowicz SE, Musto J, Scallan E et al. 2010. *Clin Infect Dis* 50(6):882–9.
Mak JW, Cheong WH, Yen PK et al. 1982. *Acta Trop* 39(3):237–45.
Malta MC, Tinoco HP, Xavier MN et al. 2010. *Vet Parasitol* 169(1):193–7.
Man SM. 2011. *Nat Rev Gastroentero* 8(12):669–85.
Mapua MI, Qablan MA, Pomajbãkovã K et al. 2015. *Parasitology* 142(7):890.
Marangi M, Koehler AV, Zanzani SA et al. 2015. *Parasit Vectors* 8(1):274.
Marcili A, Lima L, Valente VC et al. 2009. *Infect Genet Evol* 9(6):265–74.
Marcili A, Valente VC, Valente SA et al. 2009. *Int J Parasitol* 39(5):615–23.
Markoff L. 2015. In *Mandell, Douglas, and Bennett's Principles and Practice of Infectious Diseases* 153:1865–74.
Maroli M, Feliciangeli MD, Bichaud L et al. 2013. *Med Vet Entomol* 27(2):123–47.
Marrie TJ. and Didier R. 2015. In *Mandell, Douglas, and Bennett's Principles and Practice of Infectious Diseases* 190:2208–16.
Marsh, K. 2002. In Warrell DA and Giles H eds. *Essential Malariology.* 4th edition. London: Arnold, pp. 252–67.
Martin LB, Hasselquist D and Wikelski M. 2006. *Oecologia* 147(4):565–75.
Martin LB, Weil ZM and Nelson RJ. 2007. *Ecology* 88(10):2516–28.
Martini GA. 1973. *Postgrad Med J* 49(574):542–6.
Martino M, Hubbard GB and Schlabritz-Loutsevitch N. 2007. *J Med Primatol* 36(2):108–12.
Marx PA, Li Y, Lerche NW et al. 1991. *J Virol* 65(8):4480–5.
Masbar S, Palmieri JR, Marwoto HA et al. 1981. *SE Asia J Trop Med Public Health* 12(1):42–6.
Masters N, Niphuis H, Verschoor E et al. 2010. *J Zoo Wildlife Med* 41(4):713–6.

Mauricio IL, Stothard JR and Miles MA. 2000. *Hum Mol Genet* 9:549–59.
Mavalankar D, Shastri P, Raman P. 2007. *Lancet* 7(5):306–7.
Mayer K, Pizer HF and Venkatesh KK. 2008. *Med Clin N Am* 92(6):1363–75.
Mbora DM and McPeek MA. 2009. *J Anim Ecol* 78(1):210–8.
Mbora DM, Wieczkowski J and Munene E. 2009. *Am J Phy Anthropol* 140(3): 562–71.
McClure HM, Chiodini RJ, Anderson DC et al. 1987. *J Infect Dis* 155(5):1011–9.
McConnell EE, Basson PA, De Vos V et al. 1974. *Onderstepoort J Vet* 41(3):97–167.
McConnell EE, Basson PA, Wolstenholme B et al. 1973. *Trans Roy Soc Trop Med Hyg* 67(6):851–5.
McCrae AW and Kirya BG. 1982. *Trans Roy Soc Trop Med Hyg* 76(4):552–62.
McCutchen TF. 2008. Is monkey malaria from Borneo an emerging human disease? *Future Microbiol* 3(2):115–8.
McGrew WC, Tutin CE, Collins DA et al. 1989. *Am J Primatol* 17(2):147–55.
McIntosh BM, Harwin RM, Paterson HE et al. 1963. *Cent Afr J Med* 9(9):351–9.
McNeill WH. 1976. *Plagues and People*. Garden City, NJ: Anchor.
Mead PS. 2015. In *Mandell, Douglas, and Bennett's Principles and Practice of Infectious Diseases* 231:2607–18.
Mehlhorn H, Heydorn AO and Janitschke K. 1977. *Parasitol Res* 51(2):165–78.
Menezes-Costa A, Machado-Ferreira E, Voloch CM et al. 2013. *Microb Ecol* 66(2):471–8.
Messina JP, Brady OJ, Scott TW et al. 2014. *Trends Microbiol* 22(3):38–46.
Michel AL and Huchzermeyer HF. 1998. *J S Afr Vet Assoc* 69(2):64–5.
Michel AL, Venter L, Espie IW et al. 2003. *J Zoo Wildlife Med* 34(4):364–70.
Miller JH. 1960. *T Roy Soc Trop Med H* 54(1):45–6.
Minette HP. 1966. *Am J Trop Med Hyg* 15(2):190–8.
Minuzzi-Souza TT, Nitz N, Knox MB et al. 2016. *Parasit Vectors* 9(1):39.
Molina CV, Catão-Dias JL, Ferreira Neto JS et al. 2014. *J Med Primatol* 43(3): 197–201.
Monath TP, Craven RB, Adjukiewicz A. 1980. *Am J Trop Med Hyg* 29(5):912–28.
Monath TP, Lee VH, Wilson DC et al. 1974. *Trans Roy Soc Trop Med Hyg* 68(1):30–8.
Monteiro RV, Baldez J, Dietz J et al. 2006. *J Med Primatol* 35(1):48–55.
Monteiro RV, Dietz JM, Raboy B et al. 2007. *Parasitol Res* 101(6):1689–98.
Montoya C, Oyola N, Ocampo M et al. 2013. *Rev Lasallista Invest* 10(2):25–34.
Montoya JG, Boothroyd JC and Kovacs JA. 2015. In *Mandell, Douglas, and Bennett's Principles and Practice of Infectious Diseases* 280:3122–53.
Morgan M. 2008. *J Antimicrob Chemoth* 62(6):1181–7.
Morozova V, Kozlova Y, Shedko E et al. 2016. *Arch Virol* 161(9):2457–72.
Mourão MP, Bastos MS, Gimaque JB et al. 2009. *Emerg Infect Dis* 15(12):2063–4.
Mourya DT, Yadav PD and Patil DY. 2014. *Who S Asia J Public Health* 3(1):8–21.
Muchmore EA, Diaz S and Varki A. 1998. *Am J Phys Anthropol* 107(2):187–98.
Muehlenbein MP. 2005. *Am J Primatol* 65(2):167–79.
Mugisha L, Köndgen S, Kaddu-Mulindwa D et al. 2014. *Am J Primatol* 76(2):103–10.
Müller-Graf CD, Collins DA, Packer C et al. 1997. *Parasitology* 115(6):621–7.
Muniz CP, Troncoso LL, Moreira MA et al. 2013. *PLoS ONE* 8(7):e67568.
Munune E, Otsyula M, Mbaabu DA et al. 1998. *Vet Parasitol* 78:195–201.

Muriuki SM, Murugu RK, Munene E et al. 1998. *Acta Trop* 71(1):73–82.
Murray S, Stem C, Boudreau B et al. 2000. *J Zoo Wildlife Med* 31(2):176–8.
Murray SM and Linial ML. 2006. *J Med Primatol* 35(4/5):225–35.
Myers BJ and Kuntz RE. 1968. *J Eukaryot Microbiol* 15(2):363–5.
Myers MG, Kramer LW and Stanberry LR. 1987. *J Med Virol* 23(4):317–22.
Nackoney J, Molinario G, Potapov P et al. 2014. *Biol Conserv* 170:321–8.
Nagel M, Dischinger J, Türck M et al. 2013. *Clin Microbiol Infect* 19(11):1072–7.
Nakgoi K, Nitatpattana N, Wajjwalku W et al. 2014. *Am J Primatol* 76(1):97–102.
Nahar A, Siddiquee M, Nahar S et al. 2014. *J Biosafety Health Educ* 2:120.
Nakauchi K. 1999. *J Vet Med Sci* 61(1):63–5.
Nakayima J, Hayashida K, Nakao R et al. 2014. *Parasit Vectors* 7(1):490.
Nasher AK. 1988. *Ann Parasit Hum Comp* 63(6):448–54.
Navarro JC, Giambalvo D, Hernandez R et al. 2016. *Am J Trop Med Hyg* 95(2): 328–38.
Neel C, Etienne L, Li Y et al. 2010. *J Virol* 84(3):1464–76.
Nelleman C, Redmond I, and Refisch J. 2010. *The Last Stand of the Gorilla*. Arendal, Norway: UNEP.
Nelson GS. 1960. *T Roy Soc Trop Med H* 54(4):301–16.
Nerrienet E, Meertens L, Kfutwah A et al. 2004. *J Gen Virol* 85(1):25–9.
Ng OT, Ooi EE, Lee CC et al. 2008. *Emerg Infect Dis* 14(5):814.
Nidom CA, Nakayama E, Nidom RV et al. 2012. *PLoS ONE* 7(7):e40740.
Ninomiya M, Takahashi M, Hoshino Y et al. 2009. *J Gen Virol* 90(2):347–58.
Ninomiya M, Takahashi M, Nishizawa T et al. 2008. *J Clin Microbiol* 46(2):507–14.
Nizeyi JB, Innocent RB, Erume J et al. 2001. *J Wildlife Dis* 37(2):239–44.
Nizeyi JB, Mwebe R, Nanteza A et al. 1999. *J Parasitol* 1:84–8.
Njiokou F, Laveissière C, Simo G et al. 2006. *Infect Genet Evol* 6(2):147–53.
Njiokou F, Simo G, Nkinin SW et al. 2004. *Acta Trop* 92(2):139–46.
Nkogue CN, Horie M, Fujita S et al. 2016. *Virus Genes* 52(5):671–8.
Noah DL, Noah DL and Crowder HR. 2002. *JAVMA* 221(1):40–3.
Nunn CL and Altizer S. 2006. *Infectious Diseases in Primates: Behavior, Ecology and Evolution*. Oxford, UK: Oxford University Press.
Odhiambo C, Venter M, Limbaso K et al. 2014. *PLoS ONE* 9(8):e105446.
Ogden SC, Hammack C and Tang H. 2016. *Sci China Life Sci* 59(5):536.
Olson LC, Skinner SF, Palotay JL et al. 1986. *Lab Anim Sci* 36(6):667–70.
Oyer RJ, Beckham JD and Tyler KL. 2014. *Handb Clin Neurol* 123:433–47.
PAHO (Pan American Health Organization). 2003. *Zoonoses and Communicable Diseases Common to Man and Animals: Bacteria and Mycoses*. Vol. 3.
Palacios G, Lowenstine LJ, Cranfield MR et al. 2011. *Emerg Infect Dis* 17(4):711.
Panteix G, Gutierrez MC, Boschiroli ML et al. 2010. *J Med Microbiol* 59(8):984–9.
Paquet C, Yudin MH, Allen VM et al. 2013. *J Obstet Gynaecol* 35(1):78–9.
Parks T, Barrett L and Jones N. 2015. *Brit Med Bull* 115(1):77–89.
Parr NA, Fedigan LM and Kutz SJ. 2013. *Folia Primatol* 84(2):102–14.
Pattnaik P. 2006. *Rev Medical Virol* 16(3):151–65.
Peel E and Chardome M. 1946. *Ann Soc Belge de Med Trop* 26(2):117–56.
Pegues DA. 2015. In *Mandell, Douglas, and Bennett's Principles and Practice of Infectious Diseases* 225:2559–68.

Peiris JS, Dittus WP and Ratnayake CB. 1993. *J Med Primatol* 22(4):240–5.
Perea-Rodriguez JP, Milano AM, Osherov BE et al. 2010. *Neotrop Prim* 17(1):7–11.
Petersen LR, Brault AC and Nasci RS. 2013. *JAMA* 310(3):308–15.
Petersen LR, Jamieson DJ, Powers AM et al. 2016. *New Engl J Med* 374:1552–63.
Petrášová J, Modrý D, Huffman MA et al. 2010. *Int J Primatol* 31(5):920–36.
Petri WA and Rashidul H. 2015. In *Mandell, Douglass, and Bennett's Principals and Practice of Infectious Diseases* 271:3047–58.
Pettersson JH, Aspán A, Krützen M et al. 2013. *International Meeting on Microbial Epidemiological Markers*. Paris, France: Institut Pasteur.
Pfeffer M. 2001. Semliki Forest virus. In Service MW ed. *Encyclopedia of Arthropod- Transmitted Infections of Man and Domesticated Animals*. Oxon, UK: CABI.
Phillips KA, Haas ME, Grafton BW et al. 2004. *J Zool* 264(2):149–51.
Pigott DM, Golding N, Mylne A et al. 2015. *Trans Roy Soc Trop Med Hyg* 109(6):366–79.
Pinkerton ME. 1972. Miscellaneous organisms. In Riennes RN ed. *Pathology of Simian Parasites*. Basel: Karger Publishers, pp. 283–313.
Pisharath HR, Cooper TK, Brice AK et al. 2005. *Lab Anim Sci* 44(1):35–7.
Pitchford E and Pienaar PS. 1974. *J S Afr Vet Assoc* 45(3):211–8.
Plantier JC, Leoz M, Dickerson JE et al. 2009. *Nat Med* 15(8):871.
Podschun R and Ullmann U. 1998. *Clin Microbiol Rev* 11(4):589–603.
Poelma FG, Borst GH and Zwart P. 1977. *Acta Zool Pathol Ant* 69:3–9.
Poiesz BJ, Ruscetti FW, Gazdar AF et al. 1980. *Proc Natl Acad Sci USA* 77(12):7415–9.
Poirier P, Wawrzyniak I, Vivarès CP et al. 2012. *PLoS Pathog* 8(3):e1002545.
Poirotte C, Basset D, Willaume E et al. 2016. *Am J Phys Anthropol* 159(3):442–56.
Pons-Salort M, Parker EP and Grassly NC. 2015. *Curr Opion Infect Dis* 28(5): 479–87.
Poulsen CS and Stensvold CR. 2014. *J Clin Microbiol* 52(10):3524–30.
Pourrut X, Diffo JL, Somo RM et al. 2011. *Vet Parasitol* 175(1):187–91.
Powers AM, Brault AC, Shirako Y et al. 2001. *J Virol* 75(21):10118–31.
Prathap K. 1973. *Trans Roy Soc Trop Med Hyg* 67(4):615.
Prugnolle F, Durand P, Neel C et al. 2010. *Proc Natl Acad Sci USA* 107(4):1458–63.
Pung OJ, Spratt J, Clark CG et al. 1998. *J Zoo Wildlife Med* 29(1):25–30.
Purvis AJ, Ellison IR and Husting EL. 1965. *Cent Afr J Med* 11(12):368.
Putaporntip C, Hongsrimuang T, Seethamchai S et al. 2009. *J Infect Dis* 199(8): 1143–50.
Quammen D. 2012. *Spillover: Animal Infections and the Next Human Pandemic*. New York: WW Norton.
Que Y. 2015. In *Mandell, Douglas, and Bennett's Principles and Practice of Infectious Diseases* 196:2237–71.
Quevedo M and Lescano J. 2014. *Rev Invest Vet Peru* 25(2):317–23.
Ramos da Silva S and Gao S. 2016. *J Med Virol* 88(8):1291–6.
Rasambainarivo FT, Gillespie TR, Wright PC et al. 2013. *J Wildlife Dis* 49(3):741–3.
Reemtsma K, McCracken BH, Schlegel JU et al. 1964. *Ann Surg* 160(3):384.
Reid G, Howard J and Gan BS. 2001. *Trends Microbiol* 9(9):424–8.
Reid SR. 2009. *Harm Reduct J* 6(1):24.

Reitz MS and Gallo RC. 2015. In *Mandell, Douglas, and Bennett's Principles and Practice of Infectious Diseases* 171:2045–65.
Renault CA and Ernst JD. 2015. In *Mandell, Douglas, and Bennett's Principles and Practice of Infectious Diseases* 252:2819–31.
Rhee EG and Barouch DH. 2015. In *Mandell, Douglas, and Bennett's Principles and Practice of Infectious Diseases* 145:1787–93.
Rich SM and Ayala FJ. 2000. *Proc Natl Acad Sci USA* 97(13):6994–7001.
Richard L, Betsem E, Filippone C et al. 2015. *Retrovirology* 12(S1):P83.
Rios-González CM. 2017 (in press). O'nyong'nyong virus: Next arbovirus in Latin America? *J Infect Public Health.*
Roberts DR, Pinheiro FP, Hoch AL et al. 1977. *Vectors and Natural Reservoirs of Oropouche Virus in the Amazon Region*. Washington, DC: Pan American Health Organization.
Robinson CM, Singh G, Lee JY et al. 2013. *Sci Rep* 3:1812.
Rocha TC, Batista PM, Andreotti R et al. 2015. *Rev Soc Brasil Med Trop* 48(2): 143–8.
Rocha VC, Ikuta CY, Gomes MS et al. 2011. *Vector-Borne Zoonotic Dis* 11(5): 593–4.
Romero JR and Modlin JF. 2015. In *Mandell, Douglas, and Bennett's Principles and Practice of Infectious Diseases* 173:2073–9.
Roncancio-Duque N and Benavides Montaño JA. 2013. *Vet Y Zootec* 7:71–89.
Rosadas C, Vicente AC, Zanella L et al. 2014. *J Neurovirol* 20:636–9.
Rosenbaum A, Papaliodis D, Alley M et al. 2013. *Am J Orthop* 42:37–9.
Rougeron V, Feldmann H, Grard G et al. 2015. *J Clin Virol* 64:111–9.
Rovirosa-Hernández MD, Cortes-Ortíz L, García-Orduña F et al. 2013. *Am J Primatol* 75(2):161–9.
Ryan SJ, Brashares JS, Walsh C et al. 2012. *J Parasitol* 98(4):885–8.
Sá RM, Petrášová J, Pomajbíková K et al. 2013. *Am J Primatol* 75(10):1032–41.
Sachan D. 2015. *Lancet* 14(6):568.
Saha M, Debnath C and Pramanik AK. 2015. *Int J Curr Microbiol App Sci* 4:52–72.
Sak B, Petrzelkova KJ, Kvetonova D et al. 2013. *PLoS ONE* 8(8):e71840.
Saksena NK, Herve V, Durand JP et al. 1994. *Virology* 198(1):297–310.
Salfelder K, de Liscano TR and Sauerteig E. 1992. *Atlas of Parasitic Pathology*. Netherlands: Springer.
Sallis ES, de Barros VL, Garmatz SL et al. 2003. *J Vet Diagn Invest* 15(6):574–6.
Salzer JS, Rwego IB, Goldberg TL et al. 2007. *J Parasitol* 93(2):439–40.
Sandstrom PA, Phan KO, Switzer WM et al. 2000. *Lancet* 355(9203):551–2.
Santiago ML, Range F, Keele BF et al. 2005. *J Virol* 79(19):12515–27.
Santiago ML, Rodenburg CM, Kamenya S et al. 2002. *Science* 295(5554):465.
Sapolsky RM and Else JG. 1986. *J Med Primatol* 16(4):229–35.
Schaumburg F, Alabi AS, Köck R et al. 2012. *Enviro Microbiol Rep* 4(1):141–6.
Schaumburg F, Mugisha L, Kappeller P et al. 2013. *PLoS ONE* 8(10):e78046.
Schaumburg F, Mugisha L, Peck B et al. 2012. *Am J Primatol* 74(12):1071–5.
Schielke JE, Selvarangan R, Kyes KB et al. 2002. *Lab Anim Sci* 41(4):42–5.
Schiffer JT and Corey L. 2015. In *Mandell, Douglas, and Bennett's Principles and Practice of Infectious Diseases* 138:1713–30.

Schuster FL and Ramirez-Avila L. 2008. *Clin Microbiol Rev* 21(4):626–38.
Seed JR, Sechelski JB and Loomis MR. 1990. *J Protozool* 37(5):393–400.
Seed JR, Sechelski JB, Ortiz JC et al. 1993. *J Parasitol* 79(2):226–32.
Seimon TA, Olson SH, Lee KJ et al. 2015. *PLoS ONE* 10(3):e0118543.
Sejvar JJ. 2014. *Viruses* 6(2):606–23.
Setchell JM, Bedjabaga IB, Goossens B et al. 2007. *Int J Primatol* 28(6):1345–62.
Seymour C, Peralta PH and Montgomery GG. 1983. *Am J Trop Med Hyg* 32(4): 854–61.
Shagari H, Rossman JS, Wass MN et al. 2016. *J Emerg Dis Virol* 2(4):1–4.
Shah KV. 2007. *Intl J Cancer* 120(2):215–23.
Sharma A, Bloss E, Heilig CM et al. 2016. *Emerg Infect Dis* 22(3):396.
Shields JM and Olson BH. 2003. *Int J Parasitol* 33(4):371–91.
Shimoda H, Saito A, Noguchi K et al. 2014. *Primates* 55(3):441–5.
Shon AS, Bajwa RP and Russo TA. 2013. *Virulence* 4(2):107–18.
Siegal-Willott J, Isaza R, Fiorello C et al. 2006. *J Zoo Wildlife Med* 37(3):413–5.
Silva RC, Machado GP, Cruvinel TM et al. 2013. *Pesquis Vet Brasil* 33(2):251–3.
Simpson DI, Haddow AJ, Williams MC. 1965. *T Roy Soc Trop Med H* 59(4):449–58.
Sinden RE and Gilles HM. 2002. In Warrell DA and Giles H eds. *Essential Malariology*. 4th edition. London: Arnold, pp. 8–34.
Singh B, Sung LK, Matusop A et al. 2004. *Lancet* 363(9414):1017–24.
Singh BR and Sharma VD. 1999. *Indian J Comp Microbiol Immunol Infect Dis* 20(2):79–90.
Sintasath DM, Wolfe ND, LeBreton M et al. 2009. *Emerg Infect Dis* 15(2):175.
Sleeman JM, Meader LL, Mudakikwa AB et al. 2000. *J Zoo Wildlife Med* 31(3): 322–8.
Smith DR, Bird BH, Lewis B et al. 2012. *J Virol* 86(4):2109–20.
Smith EK, Hunt RD, Garcia FG et al. 1973. *Am Rev Respir Dis*107(3):469–71.
Smith HV, Paton CA, Girdwood RW et al. 1996. *Vet Rec* 138(21):528.
Smith JL, David NJ, Indgin S et al. 1971. *Brit J Vener Dis* 47(4):226.
Smithburn KC and Haddow AJ. 1944. *J Immunol* 49(3):141–57.
Smithburn KC, Mahaffy AF and Haddow AJ. 1944. *J Immunol* 49(3):159–73.
Soloman N, Ukibe I, Mbanugo J et al. 2015. *Annu Res Rev Biol* 5(5):372–84.
Sousa OE, Rossan RN and Baerg DC. 1974. *Am J Trop Med Hyg* 23(5):862–8.
Spengler JR, Bergeron E and Rollin PE. 2016. *PLoS Negl Trop Dis* 10(1):e0004210.
Sprent JF. 1969. *Helminthol Abstr* 38:333–51.
Springer A, Fichtel C, Calvignac-Spencer S et al. 2015. *Int J Parasitol* 4(3):385–95.
Srivathsan A, Ang A, Vogler AP et al. 2016. *Front Zool* 13(1):1.
Ssemadaali MA, Effertz K, Singh P et al. 2016. *Sci Rep* 6:26655.
Starzl TE, Fung J, Tzakis A et al. 1993. *Lancet* 341(8837):65–71.
Stetter MD, Mikota SK, Gutter AF et al. 1995. *JAVMA* 207(12):1618–21.
Stothard JR, Mugisha L and Standley CJ. 2012. *Trends Parasitol* 28(8):320–6.
Strier KB. 2011. *Primate Behavioral Ecology*. 4th Edition. Upper Saddle River, NJ: Prentice Hall.
Stuart M, Pendergast V, Rumfelt S et al. 1998. *Int J Primatol* 19(3):493–512.
Suh KN, Kozarsky P and Keystone JS. 2015. In *Mandell, Douglas, and Bennett's Principles and Practice of Infectious Diseases* 285:3184–91.

Suthar MS, Diamond MS and Gale M. 2013. *Nat Rev Microbiol* 11(2):115–28.
Switzer WM, Bhullar V, Shanmugam V et al. 2004. *J Virol* 78(6):2780–9.
Switzer WM, Tang S, Ahuka-Mundeke S et al. 2012. *Retrovirology* 9(1):100.
Sylla M, Dubot-Peres A, Sylla ED. 2014. *Afr J Microbiol Res* 8(24):2368–75.
Ta TH, Hisam S, Lanza M et al. 2014. *Malaria J* 13(1):1.
Taffs LF and Dunn G. 1983. *Lab Anim* 17(4):311–20.
Takehisa J, Kraus MH, Ayouba A et al. 2009. *J Virol* 83(4):1635–48.
Takemura T, Yamashita M, Shimada MK et al. 2002. *J Virol* 76(4):1642–8.
Talarmin A, Chandler LJ, Kazanji M et al. 1998. *Am J Trop Med Hyg* 59(3):452–6.
Tappe D, Kapaun A, Emmerich P et al. 2014. *Emerg Infect Dis* 20(10):1766.
Tappe D, Stich A, Langeheinecke A et al. 2014. *Euro Surveill* 19(21):pii–20816.
Tarara R, Suleman MA, Sapolsky R et al. 1985. *J Wildlife Dis* 21(2):137–40.
Taylor LH, Latham SM and Mark EJ. 2001. *Philos T Roy Soc B* 356(1411):983–9.
Teichroeb JA, Kutz SJ, Parkar U et al. 2009. *Am J Phys Anthropol* 140(3):498–507.
Thomas SJ, Endy TP, Rothman AL et al. 2015. In *Mandell, Douglas, and Bennett's Principles and Practice of Infectious Diseases* 155:1881–903.
Thomson R, Genovese G, Canon C et al. 2014. *P Natl A Sci USA* 111(20):E2130–9.
Tischer BK and Osterrieder N. 2010. *Vet Microbiol* 140(3):266–70.
Toledo LF, Asmüssen MV and Rodríguez JP. 2012. *Nature* 483(7387):36.
Tomori O and Fabiyi A. 1976. *Trop Geogr Med* 28(3):233–8.
Traina-Dorge VL, Lorino R, Gormus BJ et al. 2005. *J Virol* 79(4):2541–8.
Tseng C and Chan Y. 2015. Overview of Ebola virus disease in 2014. *J Chin Medi Assoc* 78(1):51–5.
Twenhafel NA, Whitehouse CA, Stevens EL et al. 2008. *Vet Pathol* 45(2):226–31.
UNAIDS Fact Sheet. 2016. Accessed on 5/17/2017. www.unaids.org/sites/default/files/media_asset/UNAIDS_FactSheet_en.pdf
Valverde CR, Canfield D, Tarara R et al. 1998. *Int J Leprosy* 66(2):140.
Van Damme LR, Vandepitte J, Piot P et al. 1978. *Ann Soc Belg Med Trop* 58(4):341–5.
Van Den Berg S, Van Wamel WJ, Snijders SV et al. 2011. *PLoS ONE* 6(10):e26170.
Van den Berghe L, Chardome M and Peel E. 1964. *J Helminthol* 38(3/4):349–68.
Van Dooren S, Salemi M and Vandamme AM. 2001. *Mol Biol Evol* 18(4):661–71.
Van Heuverswyn F, Li Y, Bailes E et al. 2007. *Virology* 368(1):155–71.
Van Heuverswyn F, Li Y, Neel C et al. 2006. *Nature* 444(7116):164.
Vandamme A, Salemi M and Desmyter J. 1998. *Trends Microbiol* 6(12):477–83.
Vassalos CM, Papadopoulou C and Vakalis NC. 2008. *Vet Ital* 44(4):679–84.
Verdonck K, González E, Van Dooren S et al. 2007. *Lancet* 7(4):266–81.
Vetesi F, Balsai A and Kemenes F. 1971. *Acta Microbiol Hung* 19(4):441–3.
Vitazkova SK and Wade SE. 2006. *Am J Primatol* 68(11):1089–97.
Voevodin A, Samilchuk E, Allan J et al. 1997. *Virology* 228(2):350–9.
Volk SM, Chen R, Tsetsarkin KA et al. 2010. *J Virol* 84(13):6497–504.
Volney B, Pouliquen J, De Thoisy B et al. 2002. *Acta Trop* 82(1):11–23.
Vourc'h G, Desvars A, Boué F. 2014. *Vet Res* 45(1):52.
Vythilingam I, NoorAzian YM, Huat TC et al. 2008. *Parasit Vectors* 1(1):26.
Wallis J, Rick Lee D. 1999. *Int J Primatol* 20(6):803–26.
Walsh EE and Hall CB. 2015. In *Mandell, Douglas, and Bennett's Principles and Practice of Infectious Diseases* 160:1948–60.

Walsh GP, Meyers WM, Binford CH et al. 1981. *Lepr Rev* 52(S1):77–83.
Wammes LJ, Mpairwe H, Elliott AM et al. 2014. *Lancet* 14(11):1150–62.
Warren M and Wharton RH. 1963. *J Parasitol* 49(6):892–904.
Warren M, Cheong WH, Fredericks HK et al. 1970. *Am J Trop Med Hyg* 19(3): 383–93.
Weaver SC. 2014. *PLoS Negl Trop Dis* 6:e2921.
Weaver SC and Lecuit M. 2015. *New Engl J Med* 372(13):1231–9.
Weaver SC. 2005. In Peter CJ and Calisher CH eds. *Infectious Diseases From Nature: Mechanisms of Viral Emergence and Persistence.* Vienna: Springer, pp. 33–44.
Webster JP, Gower CM, Knowles SC et al. 2015. *Evol App* 9(2):313.
Weinman D. 1972. *Trans Roy Soc Trop Med Hyg* 66(4):628–36.
Weiss R. 2003. *Washington Post*, April 7, 2003.
Wenz A, Heymann W, Petney TN et al. 2010. *Parsitol* 137(4):675–84.
West KA, Heymann EW, Mueller B et al. 2013. *Int J Primatol* 34(5):939–45.
Wevers D, Metzger S, Babweteera F et al. 2011. *J Virol* 85(20):10774–84.
Weyher AH, Ross C and Semple S. 2006. *Int J Primatol* 27(6):1519.
White AC. 2015. In *Mandell, Douglas, and Bennett's Principles and Practice of Infectious Diseases* 284:3173–83.
White NJ. 2008. *Clin Infect Dis* 46(2):172–3.
Whitehouse CA, Keirstead N, Taylor J et al. 2010. *J Wildlife Dis* 46(3):971–6.
Whitley RJ. 2015. In *Mandell, Douglas, and Bennett's Principles and Practice of Infectious Diseases* 139:1731–7.
Whittier CA, Cranfield MR and Stoskopf MK. 2010. *J Wildlife Dis* 46(3):791–802.
WHO. 2005. *Guidelines for the Control of Shigellosis.* Geneva: WHO.
WHO. 2008. *Anthrax in Humans and Animals*. Geneva: WHO.
WHO. 2012. Research priorities for Chagas disease, human African trypanosomiasis and leishmaniasis. In *World Health Organization Technical Report Series* 975. Geneva: WHO.
WHO. 2015a. *World Malaria Report 2015*. Geneva: WHO.
WHO. 2015b. Yaws. In *Control of Neglected Tropical Diseases World Health Organization* and *The Task Force for Global Health*. Geneva: WHO.
WHO. 2015c. *Wkly Epidemiol Rec* 90(2015):25–32.
WHO. 2016a. Zoonoses. Accessed on 3/23/2016. www.who.int/topics/zoonoses/en/.
WHO. 2016b. Xenotransplantation. Accessed on 3/21/2016. www.who.int/transplantation/xeno/en/
WHO. 2016c. Trypanosomiasis, human African. Accessed on 7/8/2016. www.who.int/mediacentre/factsheets/fs259/en/.
WHO. 2016d. Leishmaniasis. Accessed on 6/20/2016. www.who.int/mediacentre/factsheets/fs375/en/.
WHO. 2016e. Leprosy Fact Sheet. Accessed on 9/8/2016 www.who.int/mediacentre/factsheets/fs101/en/.
WHO. 2017a. Leprosy. Accessed on 5/29/2017. www.who.int/mediacentre/factsheets/fs101/en/
WHO. 2017b. Chagas disease. Accessed on 5/29/2017. www.who.int/mediacentre/factsheets/fs340/en/

WHO and International Office of Epizootics. 2008. *Anthrax in Humans and Animals*. Geneva: WHO.
Wilbur AK, Engel GA, Rompis A et al. 2012. *Am J Primatol* 74(7):676–86.
Williams JT, Dick EJ, VandeBerg JL et al. 2009. *J Med Primatol* 38(2):107–13.
Wilson P, Weavers E, West B et al. 1984. *Lab Anim* 18(4):383–7.
Wirsing RL. 1985. *Curr Anthropol* 26(3):303–22.
Wittmann TJ, Biek R, Hassanin A et al. 2007. *Proc Natl Acad Sci USA* 104(43): 17123–7.
Wolfe ND, Daszak P, Kilpatrick AM et al. 2005.*Emerg Infect Dis* 11(12):1822–7.
Wolfe ND, Kilbourn AM, Karesh WB et al. 2001. *Am J Trop Med Hyg* 64(5):310–6.
Wood CL, Lafferty KD, DeLeo G et al. 2014. *Ecology* 95(4):817–32.
Work TH and Trapido H. 1957. *Indian J Med Sci* 11(5):341–2.
Worobey M, Santiago ML, Keele BF et al. 2004. *Nature* 428(6985):820.
Wozniakowski G and Samorek-Salamonowicz E. 2015. *Ann Agr Environ Med* 22(2):191–4.
Wyers M, Formenty P, Cherel Y et al. 1999. *J Infect Dis* 179(S1):S54–9.
Xiao L and Feng Y. 2008. *FEMS Immunol Med Microbiol* 52(3):309–23.
Yamagiwa J. 2003. *J Sustain Forestry* 16(3/4):111–30.
Yang ZQ, Wei CG, Zen JS et al. 2005. *Parasitol Int* 54(1):75–81.
Yong TS, Park SJ, Hwang UW et al. 2000. *J Parasitol* 86(4):887–91.
Yoshida T, Takemoto H, Sakamaki T et al. 2016. *Front Microbiol* 7:1262.
Yoshikawa H. 2012. In Mehlhorn H, Tan KS, Yoshikawa H. *Blastocystis: Pathogen or Passenger?* Heidelberg, Berlin: Springer, pp. 37–49.
Yu WH, Zhao Y, Huang F et al. 2013. *Chin J Zoo* 3:016.
Zanluca C, Melo VC, Mosimann AL et al. 2015. *Mem I Oswaldo Cruz* 110(4):569–72.
Zavala RM, Devesa M, Loureiro CL et al. 2006. *Acta Cient Venez* 57(1):22–7.
Zeledon R, Beard CB, Dias JP et al. 2012. In Beard CB et al. eds. *An appraisal of the Status of Chagas Disease in the United States*. Boston, MA: Elsevier.
Ziccardi M and Lourenço-de-Oliveira R. 1997. *Mem I Oswaldo Cruz* 92:465–70.
Ziccardi M and Lourenço-de-Oliveira R. 1998. *Mem I Oswaldo Cruz* 93(1):301.
Ziccardi M, Lourenço-de-Oliveira R, Lainson R et al. 2000. *Mem I Oswaldo Cruz* 95(2):157–9.

Note

1. Publishes as both Maamun Jeneby and Jeneby Maamun.

Index

adaptive severity hypothesis 3
Adenoviridae 21–2
Aedes: *Ae. aegypti* 27, 30, 33, 43; *Ae.* species 7, 28, 30, 34, 39, 43, 44, 53–4; *see also* mosquitoes
Afrotropics 14, 33
agriculture 12
AIDS vii, 6, 40, 41, 57; *see also* HIV-AIDS
air-borne 6, 16
Alouatta: *A. belzebul* 46, 52, 74, 102; *A caraya* 18, 28, 45–6, 52, 63–4, 73–4, 79, 102; *A. clamitans* 74; *A. guariba* 28, 45–6, 73–4, 81; *A. palliata* 61, 63, 75, 79, 81; *A. pigra* 46, 63, 75, 79, 81; *A. seniculus* 46, 49, 52, 61–4, 73–5, 79; *Alouatta* species 45, 53, 55–7, 67, 72–4, 79, 89, 91; *A. villosa* 46, 52, 99–100; *see also* howler monkey
Alphatorquevirus 22
Alphavirus 43–4, 51–4
Amazonia, Amazon Basin 14–15, 68
American trypanosomiasis viii, 70–2, 79–80; *see also Trypanosoma cruzi*
amphibians 3, 56, 57
Anderson, R. 3
Anelloviridae 22, 26, 44
Anopheles: *An. cracens* 17; *An. gambiae* 27; *An.* species 7, 39; *see also* mosquitoes
Anthropoidea 9
anthroponosis, anthroponotic viii, 1–3, 17–19, 22, 24–5, 35–6, 40, 55–6, 67–8, 85, 90, 93, 98
Aotus: *A. azarae* 61, 63, 80–1; *A nigriceps* 75; *Aotus* species 24, 33, 56, 71, 72, 80, 89, 91; *A. trivirgatus* 36, 40, 46, 81, 99–100, 107; *A. vociferans* 75; *see also* owl monkey
apes 19, 21–2, 29, 37–8, 56, 59, 65–7, 69, 72, 95, 97–8, 104, 108, 110; *see also Gorilla*; *Hylobates*; *Nomascus*; *Pan*; *Pongo*
APOL1 gene 69
Arctocebus calabarensis 78–9
armadillo 92, 94
arthropods 3, 5, 7, 86, 96; *see also* mites; individual insects; ticks
Ateles: *A. belzebuth* 62, 75; *A. chamek* 46, 52, 75; *A. fusciceps* 40, 75, 80, 89, 99, 101; *A. geoffroyi* 46, 75; *A. hybridus* 63; *A. paniscus* 55, 61, 75; *Ateles* species 33, 54–7, 65, 72, 73, 75, 80, 90–1, 94; *see also* spider monkey
Awa Guajá 15

Babesia 72, 81
babesiosis 72
baboons 6, 10, 25, 36–7, 39, 58, 60, 69, 72, 83, 85–9, 91–3, 95–6, 98, 108, 110; *see also Papio*
Baby Fae 6
Bacillaceae 83–4, 99
Bacillus: *B. anthracis* 83, 99; *B. cereus* 83, 99
bacteria viii, 1, 3, 17–18, 35, 105, 109, 111

Balantidium species 55, 61
Bartonella: *B. auintana* 84; *B. bacilliformis* 84; *B. henselae* 84; *Bartonella* species 84, 99
Bartonellaceae 84, 99
bats vii, 4–5, 14, 27–30, 32, 84
beaver 90
biodiversity, loss 13–14
biological weapon 83, 85
birds 13–14, 23, 28, 31–2, 43, 56–7, 65, 86, 88, 90–2, 94
black market 15
Blastocystis 56, 61–2
bobcat 65; *see also* felids
bone marrow transplant 6
bonobos 24, 40, 68–9, 106, 110; *see also Pan paniscus*
Borrelia: *B. burgdorgeri* 96; *B. recurrentis* 96, 102; *B.* species 95–7, 102
bovids 69
Brachyteles: *B. arachnoides* 71, 74–5; *Brachyteles* species 55, 67
Bronze Age 12
Brucellaceae 85, 99
Brucella spp. 85
buffalo 27, 93
Bunyamwera virus 27–8, 45
Bunyaviridae 27–8, 45
bushmeat vii, 5, 10, 14–16, 19, 22, 29, 40, 42, 83, 85–6, 89, 95, 110; *see also* hunting
Bwamba virus 27

Cacajao: *C. calvus* 71, 75; *Cacajao* species 55
California encephalitis 27
Callibella 55; *see also* marmosets
Callicebus: *C. brunneus* 73, 76, 80; *C. caligatus* 76; *C. dubius* 76; *C. moloch* 76; *Callicebus personatus* 71; *Callicebus* species 55, 67, 72; *C. torquatus* 76
Callimico goeldii 55, 71
Callithrix: *C. emiliae* 80; *C. jacchus* 16, 26, 28, 35–6, 47, 102; *C. (Mico) argentata* 46, 52; *C. pencillata* 46, 64; *C. pygmaea* 26; *Callithrix* species 24, 33, 53, 55, 57, 71, 91; *see also* marmosets
Callithrix spp. *see* marmoset
camel 39, 86
Campylobacter: *C. fetus* 85; *C. jejuni* 85, 99; *Campylobacter* species 85–6, 99
Campylobacteriaceae 85–6, 99
Capillaria hepatica 18; *see also* Nematode
captive primates, exposure to parasites: laboratories primates viii, 2, 11, 29, 36, 70–1, 90, 93–4; research centers viii, 2, 11, 36, 41, 58, 70–1, 90, 94; zoos viii, 2, 11, 22, 40, 59, 65, 70–2, 90, 94, 97
capuchins 10, 16, 28, 35, 72; *see also Cebus*; *Sapajus*
cats, domesticated 22, 57, 65, 84, 86, 90, 94; *see also* felids
cat scratch fever 84; *see also Bartonella*
cattle 18, 39, 59, 84–5, 88, 90–4, 109
Cebuella pygmaea 55, 80; *see also* marmosets
Cebus: *C. albifrons* 76, 80; *C. capucinus* 63, 76, 80; *C. libidinosis* 28, 45 (*see also Sapajus libidinosis*); *C. olivaceus* 28, 45; *Cebus* species 45, 55, 64–5, 73, 76; *see also* capuchin
Cercocebus: *C. agilis* 49–50, 61; *C. albigena* 79; *C. atys* 16, 41, 49, 51, 69, 78, 93; *C. galeritis* 18; *Cercocebus* species 56, 70, 90–1, 94, 97; *C. torquatus* 49–50, 69, 79; *see also* mangabeys
cercopithecine monkey 58, 69
Cercopithecus: *C. ascanisus* 18, 35, 45–7, 49, 52, 62, 69, 79, 103; *C. cephus* 49–50, 78–9; *C. mitis* 52, 61–4, 72, 79, 81, 107; *C. mona* 46, 48, 50, 52, 78–9; *C. neglectus* 29, 49, 52, 61, 79; *C. nictitans* 49–50, 78–9, 103; *C. pogonias* 50; *Cercopithecus* species 53, 55–6, 60, 70, 91–2, 96; *C. torquatus* 51; *C. wolfi* 50; *see also* guenons
Cestodes 105
Chagas disease 2, 70; *see also Trypanosoma cruzi*
Changuinola virus 39
chicken pox 23; *see also* herpes viruses: human herpes viruses

chikungunya vii, 4, 7, 28, 43–4, 51–2
Chimpanzee Coryza Agent (CCA) 38
chimpanzees 2, 4–6, 12, 18–19, 22, 24, 29, 36–8, 40–1, 43, 44, 55–6, 58, 66–9, 71, 83, 87, 92–4, 96–8, 106, 110; *see also Pan troglodytes*
Chiropotes: *C. albinasus* 76; *C. chiropotes* 76; *C. satanas* 71–3, 76, 81; *Chiropotes* species 55, 76; *see also* sakis
Chlorocebus: *C. aethiops* 30, 47–8, 50, 52, 58, 61–4, 69, 72, 79, 81, 87, 107–8; *C. pygerythrus* 46, 64, 97, 99, 102; *C. sabaeus* 45, 47, 64–5, 87, 100; *Chlorocebus* species 10, 55–6, 97; *C. tantalus* 50
cladistic classification 9; *see also* gradistic classification
clear-cutting 12
co-evolution 3, 105
colobine monkeys 58, 69, 106
Colobus: *C. angolensis* 51, 58; *C. guereza* 35–6, 45–7, 50–2, 62, 64, 79; *C. polykomos* 103; *Colobus* species 53, 56, 70, 90, 94, 96; *C. vellerosus* 62
colobus monkeys 18, 37, 58; *see also Colobus*; *Piliocolobus*; *Procolobus*
Coltivirus 38
Congo Basin 14, 106
conservation, primate 17–20, 110
Coquillettidia 54 (mosquitoes)
Coxiella burnetii 86, 99
Coxiellaceae 86, 99
coxsackie virus 36–7, 48
Crimean-Congo hemorrhagic fever virus 27
crop-raiding 17, 108, 110
Cryptosporidium 18, 56–7; *C. andersoni* 57; *C. bovis* 57, 63; *C. canis* 57; *C. felis* 57; *C. hominis* 57; *C. melagridis* 57; *C. parvum* 57, 63; *Cryptosporidium* species 18, 56–7, 62–3
Culex 28, 31–2, 39, 43, 54; *see also* mosquitoes
Culicoides paraensis 28; *see also* midges
Culiseta 53–4; *see also* mosquitoes
Cyclospora: *C. cayentanensis* 57–8, 63; *C. colobi* 58; *C. papionis* 58; *Cyclospora* species 57–8, 63
Cytomegalovirus 23–6; *see also* herpes viruses: human herpes viruses

dams 11–12
deer 90
deforestation vii, 11–13, 15, 17, 109; *see also* forest fragmentation
Deltaretrovirus see HTLV; PTLV; STLV
Democratic Republic of Congo Wars 19; *see also* warfare
dengue 7–8, 28, 30–1, 45
disease ecology 19
dogs 22, 57, 69, 71, 84–6, 90, 94
domesticated animals 12, 17, 22, 27, 57, 59, 65, 68–9, 83, 85–6, 88, 90, 96, 108; *see also* livestock
domestic cycle *see* urban cycle
drug resistance 18, 88, 91, 93, 98, 104
drug use, IV 4, 39, 71

Eastern equine encephalitis 43, 52–3
Ebola virus vii, 4–5, 14, 28–30, 45, 109–10; *Budibugyo* 28–9; *Reston* 28–9; *Sudan* 28–9; *Taï Forest* 28–9, 45; *Zaire* 28–9
ECHO virus 37, 48
ecotourism viii, 2, 17–18, 36, 98, 111
elephantiasis 105
elephants 69
Entamoeba: *E. coli* 58; *E. dispar* 58–9; *E. hartmanni* 58; *E. histolytica* 58–9; *E. moshkoviskii* 58–9; *Entamoeba* species 58–9
enteric cytopathic human orphan virus *see* ECHO virus
Enterobacteriaceae 86–91, 99–101
Enterococcaceae 91–2, 101
Enterococcus: *E. faecalis* 91–2, 101; *E. faecium* 91–2
enteroviruses 36–7
enzootic cycle 7–8
epidemic 4, 7–8, 12, 16, 28–9, 33, 35, 37, 44, 56, 89, 98
epizootic outbreak 32, 90
Epstein Barr virus 23; *see also* herpes viruses: human herpes viruses

Erythocebus patas 47, 50, 56, 60, 65, 96–7, 103, 107
Escherichia coli: enteroaggregative (EAEC) 91; enterohemorrhagic (EHEC) 91; enteroinvasive (EIEC) 91; enteropathogenic (EPEC) 91; enterotoxogenic (ETEC) 91; Shiga toxin producing (STEC) 91
Eulemur: *E. fulvus* 51, 61, 100; *E. macacao* 65, 83, 99–100, 103; *E. rufifrons* 103; *Eulemur* species 55; *see also* lemurs; prosimians
Ewald, P. 3
experimental infections vii, 1–2, 11, 27, 33, 37–8, 95–6

felids 65; *see also* bobcats; cats (domesticated); jaguars; lions; tigers
filariasis 1, 105–6; lymphatic 105–6; subcutaneous 106
Filoviridae 28–30, 45; *see also* Ebola; Marburg
fish 23, 43, 57, 86, 92
Flaviviridae 30–5, 45–7
fleas 84, 90
flukes *see* trematodes
flying squirrels 84
food-borne parasites 7, 55–9, 65, 70, 83, 85–6, 88–90, 92, 97, 111
food security 15
forest fragmentation (fragmented forest) 12, 14, 18, 109; *see also* deforestation
fried rice syndrome 83

Galago senegalensis 51
garbage-raiding 60, 85, 89, 92
gastropods 5, 7
Giardia duodenalis see Giardia lamblia
Giardia: *G. lamblia* 59, 63–4; *Giardia* species 63
Giardia intestinalis see Giardia lamblia
gibbon 24, 59, 69, 94; *see also Hylobates*; *Nomascus*
giraffes 69
globalization vii, 4
Glossina spp. 68
goats 39, 85, 91–2
Gorilla: *G. beringei* 25–6, 46–8, 61, 63–4, 85, 99–101, 104; *G. gorilla* 25–6, 45, 50–1, 61, 63, 69, 72–4, 78, 81, 83, 89, 95, 99–103; *see also* gorillas
gorillas 5, 18–19, 22, 24–5, 29, 32, 36, 38, 40–1, 44, 55–7, 65–9, 72, 84, 86–9, 92, 95–8, 106, 110; *see also Gorilla*
gradistic classification 9; *see also* cladistic classification
ground hog 84
guenons 18, 35; *see also Ceropithecus*
Guillain-Barré syndrome 34, 57, 85

HAdV A-G 21–2, 25–6; *see also Mastadenovirus*
Haemagogus 53; *see also* mosquitoes
hand-foot-and-mouth disease 37
Hansen's disease 92; *see also Mycobacterium*
Hantavirus 27
hares 27
heirloom species 105
helminths viii, 1, 3, 5, 7, 17–18, 88, 105–9
hemorrhagic fever 27–30
Hendra virus 4–5
Hepatitis A 37, 48
Hepatovirus 36
Herpes B *see* herpes viruses
Herpesviridae 23–5
herpes viruses: Herpes B 24; human herpes viruses 23–6
HIV vii, 4, 21, 39, 40–1, 88; HIV-1 15, 40–2, 51; HIV-2 16, 40–2, 51; *see also* HIV-AIDS; SIV
HIV-AIDS 24, 39, 65, 94; *see also* AIDS
HMPV 37–8, 48
hominids 9, 22
hominins 9, 22
Homo erectus vii
horses 4–5, 23, 32, 54, 69, 71, 90
host: accidental 3, 7, 31, 68; amplifying 3–4, 14, 20; competence 7, 11, 13–14, 20; dead-end 3, 7, 20, 31–2, 42; definitive/primary 3, 7, 65; host-parasite relationship viii, 3, 12, 14; immunocompromised 86; intermediate/secondary 3, 7; range 13, 55, 57, 67. 109; specificity 57–8, 67, 86; *see also* reservoir

host-parasite relationship *see* host
host switching 13, 22, 41, 66, 68, 84, 109–10
howler monkeys 10, 18, 28, 32–3, 57, 72; *see also Alouatta*
HPIV 1–4, 35–6, 47–8; *see also Respirovirus*; *Rubulavirus*
HRSV 37–8, 48
HTLV 39–40; *see also* PTLV; STLV
human African trypanosomiasis 68–70; *see also Trypanosoma brucei*
human-associated bacteria 18; *see also* bacteria
human immunodeficiency virus *see* HIV
human metapneumovirus *see* HMPV
human parinfluenza virus *see* HPIV
human respiratory syncytial virus *see* HRSV
human T-lymphotropic virus *see* HTLV
hunting vii, 5, 7, 9–10, 12, 14–15, 19, 39–40, 42, 83, 95, 110; *see also* bushmeat
hyenas 29
Hylobates species 56, 59, 65, 90–1, 94, 97; *H. pileatus* 49; *see also* gibbons
hyraxes 71

immunocompetence 14
impalas 69
impetigo 98
Indri indri 18, 81, 96, 102–3; *see also* lemur; prosimians
Industrial revolution 12
Infectious Diseases in Primates (book) 9
insecticide 8
insects 8, 23, 57, 70, 88, 91, 94; *see also* fleas; lice; midges; mosquitoes; sandflies; tsetse fly
interepidemic 8; *see also* epidemic

jaguars 65
Japanese encephalitis 30–2, 46
jungle cycle *see* sylvatic cycle

kala azar *see* leishmaniasis cutaneous: visceral
kangaroos 84; *see also* marsupials
Kaposi's sarcoma 23–4
Karesh, W. 110
Klebsiella: *K. oxytoca* 87; *K. pneumonia* 86–7, 100; *Klebsiella* species 86–7, 100
Kyasanur Forest disease virus 30, 32–3, 46

laboratory exposure to infection, human *see* occupational exposure
laboratory exposure to infection, non-human primates *see* captive primates, exposure to parasites
Lagothrix: *L. cana* 73, 77; *L. lagotricha* 77, 91; *L. poeppigii* 77; *Lagothrix* species 67, 77, 80, 87, 91
landscape change 12–13
langur 33, 39, 59; *see also Semnopithecus*
lateral transmission *see* host switching
Lebombo virus 39
Leishmania: *L. amazonensis*; *L. brasiliensis* 72, 81; *L. chagasi* 72, 81; *L. infantum* 72, 81; *L. major* 72, 81; *L. mexicana* 72, 81; *L. shawi* 72, 81; *Leishmania* species 71–2
leishmaniasis cutaneous 71–2; muco-cutaneous 71–2; visceral 71–2
Lemur: *L. catta* 71, 101–2; *Lemur* species 56, 65, 89–90, 100–1
lemurs 9, 17, 87, 89–90, 92, 95, 97–8; *see also Eulemur*; *Indri*; *Lemur*; *Lepilemur*; *Microlemur*; *Prolemur*; *Propithecus*; *Varecia*
Lentivirus see HIV; SIV
Leontopithecus: *L. chrysomelas* 87, 100; *L. rosalia* 80; *Leontopithecus* species 55, 71–2, 80, 97; *see also* tamarins
Lepilemur 103; *see also* lemurs; prosimians
leprosy *see* Hansen's disease
Leptospira: *L. interrogans* 96–7, 102: *Leptospira* species 95–7, 102
lice 18, 84, 96
life history hypothesis 14
lions 65, 69
Listeria: *L. monocytogenes* 92; *Listeria* species 92, 101
Listeriaceae 101

livestock 7, 12, 17–18, 86, 91, 110; *see also* cattle; domesticated animals; goats; horses; pigs; sheep
Loa loa 106
logging 12
Lophocebus: *L. albigena* 35, 45, 47, 50–3, 62, 69, 79, 103; *L. aterrimus* 51; *Lophocebus* species 53, 56; *see also* mangabeys
lorises 9; *see also Nycticebus*; prosimians
Lutzomyia 71, 84; *see also* insects; sandfly
Lyme disease 96
Lymphocryptovirus see herpes viruses: human herpes viruses

Macaca: *M. cyclopis* 73; *M. fascicularis* 17, 24, 29, 31, 36, 45, 49, 51, 60, 62, 73, 93, 101, 106–7; *M. fuscata* 31; *M. hecki* 62; *M.* hybrid 62, 101; *M. maura* 62, 101; *M. mulatta* 24, 34, 36, 41, 47–9, 63, 88, 101; *M. nemestrina* 45–6, 51, 62, 73; *M. nigra* 62, 101; *M. nigrescens* 62; *M. ochreata* 62, 101; *M. radiata* 32, 36, 46–9; *M. seniculus* 55, 61–2; *M. sinica* 45, 64; *M.* species 56–60, 65, 70–1, 90–2, 94, 97; *M. tokeana* 62, 101; *see also* macaques
macaques 2, 17, 24–5, 27, 29, 31–2, 37–9, 41, 44, 56, 58–60, 69, 88, 93, 106, 110; *see also Macaca*
malaria vii, 2–3, 7–8, 16–17, 65–8, 72, 88; *see also Plasmodium*
mammals 14–15, 23, 43, 54, 56–7, 65, 85, 88, 91–2, 97; *see also* listings of individual animals
Mandrillus: *M. sphinx* 44–5, 47, 50, 52, 55, 61, 69; *M. leucophaeus* 29, 63
mangabeys *see Cercocebus*; *Lophocebus*
Mansonella streptocerca 106
Marburg virus 14, 28, 30; *see also Ebolavirus*
marmoset 10, 16, 24, 28, 33, 35; *see also Callibella*; *Callithrix*; *Cebuella*; *Mico*
marsupials 28, 86
Mastadenovirus 21, 25
Mayaro 28, 43, 52–3
measles 35–6, 47
Mico 55, 71; *see also Callithrix (Mico) argentata*; marmoset
Microcebus rufus 62; *see also* lemurs
microcephaly vii, 35
midges 28; *Culicoides paraensis* 28; *see also* insects
mining 12
Miopithecus: *M. ogouensis* 50, 102; *Miopithecus* species 70; *M. talapoin* 79
mites 3; *see also* arthropoids
mode(s) of transmission viii, 1, 5–8, 56
mollusks 23
mononucleosis 23
mosquitoes 3, 7–8, 17, 20, 28, 30–4, 39, 43–4, 53–4, 56, 109; *see also Aedes*; *Anopheles*; *Coquillettidia*; *Culex*; *Culiseta*; *Haemagogus*
MRSA (methicillin-resistant *S. aureus*) *see Staphylococcus aureus*
mumps 35–6, 48; *see also Rubulavirus*
Mycobacteriaceae 92–4, 101–2
Mycobacterium: *M. africanum* 93; *M. asiaticum* 94, 102; *M. avium* 94, 102; *M. bovis* 93, 102; *M. leprae* 92–3; *M. microti* 93; *M. tuberculosis* 93–4, 101–2

nagana 69; *see also Trypanosoma*
Nairovirus 27
nematodes 18, 105
Neolithic Age 12
Neotropics 2, 14, 16, 33, 35, 67
New World monkeys 8, 10–11, 18, 21, 24, 27, 21, 33, 35–6, 38, 40, 42, 53, 55–60, 65–7, 70–2, 87, 89–91, 94–5, 97, 108; *see also* genera of *Alouatta*; *Aotus*; *Ateles*; *Brachyteles*; *Cacajao*; *Callibella*; *Callithrix*; *Callimico*; *Cebuella*; *Cebus*; *Chiropotes*; *Lagothrix*; *Leontopithecus*; *Mico*; *Pithecia*; *Saguinus*; *Saimiri*; *Sapajus*
Ngari virus 27–8
niche, ecological 8, 10, 13, 109–10
Nomascus 59; *see also* gibbons
nosocomial infection 28, 87, 91, 97
Nunn, C. 2–3, 9
Nycticebus 59; *see also* lorises

occupational exposure 6, 24, 30, 42, 53; in laboratories 6, 24, 30, 42, 53; in research centers 6, 24, 42; in zoos 6, 42
Old World monkeys 18, 21, 24, 27–9, 31, 42, 57, 65, 67, 59, 71, 72, 87, 94–5, 97, 108; *see also* genera of *Cercocebus*; *Cercopithecus*; *Chlorocebus*; *Colobus*; *Erythrocebus*; *Lophocebus*; *Macaca*; *Mandrillus*; *Miopithecus*; *Papio*; *Presbytis*; *Procolobus*; *Semnopithecus*
Onchocerca volvulus 106
Onchoceridae 105–6
one health 110–11
O'nyong-nyong virus 43–4, 52–3
orangutans 24, 30–1, 35–8, 54, 59, 69, 87, 94, 97–8; *see also Pongo*
Orbivirus 38–9
Oropouche virus 27–8, 45
Oroya fever 84; *see also Bartonella*
Orthobunyavirus 27
Orthoreovirus 38
Orungo virus 39, 48
overwintering 8
owl monkey 2, 33, 40, 72; *see also Aotus*

Paleolithic Age 12
pandemic vii, 4, 41–2, 90, 109, 111; *see also* epidemic
Pan paniscus 19, 25–6, 40, 50–1, 68, 73, 78; *see also* bonobos
Pan troglodytes 12, 19, 25–6, 36, 41–2, 45, 48–9, 51, 53, 55–6, 61–4, 68, 71, 73–4, 78–9, 83, 92–4, 96, 99–100, 103–4, 108; *see also* chimpanzees
Papio: *P. anubis* 29, 50, 53, 58, 61–3, 72, 79, 81, 93, 95, 102–3, 107; *P. cynocephalus* 50, 58, 61, 69, 81, 95, 103; *P. hamadryas* 18, 61, 64, 107; *P. papio* 61, 95–6, 103, 108; *Papio* species 10, 47–9, 53, 55–6, 60, 63, 71, 85–6, 91–2, 94, 96–7, 99–104, 107–8; *P. ursinus* 26, 48, 50, 52, 60–1, 64, 83, 89, 93, 99–102, 107–8; *see also* baboons
Papionines 58
Papovaviriadae 25, 27; *see also* SV40 virus
Paramyxoviridae 35–6
parasite defined 2–3
pathogen, defined 2–3
Perodicticus potto 78–9
pet-keeping 2, 5–7, 14–16, 24, 35, 56, 58, 65, 87, 93–4, 96, 110
Phlebotomus 71; *see also* sandflies
Phlebovirus 27
Picorniviridae 36–7, 48
pigs 22, 31, 55, 69, 85, 90–1, 98; *see also* suids; swine
Piliocolubus: *P. badius* 50, 79, 103; *P. tephrosceles* 18, 50, 63–4; *P. tholloni* 50; *see also* colobus monkeys
pinta 96; *see also Treponema*
Pithecia: *P. irrorata* 77, 80; *P. monachus* 77; *Pithecia* species 24, 33, 53, 55–6, 67, 72, 77; *P. pithecia* 46, 52, 73, 77; *see also* sakis
plague 90
Plasmodium: *P. brasilianum* 67, 74–8; *P. cynomolgi* 67–8; *P. falciparum* 65–7, 73; *P. knowlesi* vii, 16–17, 65, 67–8, 73, 109; *P. malariae* 8, 65–8, 74–8; *P. ovale* 65–6, 68, 78; *P. simium* 8, 67, 74
Plasmodium species 3, 65–8, 73–8; *P. reichenowi* 66; *P. vivax* 65–8, 70, 73–4; *see also* malaria
Pneumoviridae 37–8, 48
polio 19, 25, 27, 36–7
poliomyelitis 32
poliovirus 25, 36
Polyomavirus 25
pongid, defined 9
Pongo pygmaeus 26, 45–9, 53, 55, 61, 100, 102
Pongo species 56, 65, 90, 94, 103–4
Pongo spp. *see* orangutan
Presbytis: *P. cristata* 49; *P. femoralis* 62; *P. melalophos* 73, 106–7; *Presbytis* species 56
Primate T-lymphotropic virus *see* PTLV
Procolobus: *P. badius* 47; *Procolobus rufomitratus* 18
Prolemur simus 62

Propithecus: *P. diadema* 64; *P. verreauxi* 64, 83, 99, 103
prosimians 9, 42, 44, 55–7, 59, 65, 69–71, 83, 89–91, 95–6
Prosimii 9
Prosthenorchis elegans 18
Proteus: *P. mirabilis* 88; *P. penneri* 88; *Proteus* species 86, 88, 100; *P. stuartii* 88
protozoa viii, 1–3, 7, 17
Pseudomonadaceae 94–5, 102
Pseudomonas aeruginosa 94–5, 102
PTLV 39–40; *see also* HTLV; STLV

Q fever 86; *see also Coxiella*

rabbits 86, 90
railways 12
RBC Duffy negativity 66
Reemtsma, K. 6
Reoviridae 38–9, 48–9
Reovirus 39, 49
reptiles 23, 32, 56–7, 65, 91
reservoir 3–5, 7, 11, 13–14, 28–30, 35, 39, 41, 53, 55, 67, 69, 71–2, 84, 89–90, 93, 106, 109, 111; *see also* host
Respirovirus 35–6, 47; *see also* HPIV
Retroviridae 39–43, 49
rhinoceros 27
Rhodnium prolixus 70
rice cultivation 16
Rift Valley Fever virus 27
river blindness 106
r/K selection 13–14
road construction 12–13, 16, 109
rodents 17, 27, 32, 71, 84, 86, 90–1, 93
roseola virus 24
Ross river virus 43
Rousettus aegyptiacus 30; *see also* bats
rubeola *see* measles
Rubivirus 43
Rubulavirus 35–6, 48; *see also* HPIV; mumps
Rotavirus 38, 49
roundworms *see* nematodes

Saguinus: *S. fuscicollis* 18, 36, 80; *S. geoffroyi* 46, 72, 77, 80–1, 99–100, 102; *S. labiatus* 80; *S. midas* 47, 52, 64, 74, 77, 102; *S. mystax* 62; *S. nigricollis* 80; *S. oedipus* 36; *Saguinus* species 33, 53, 55, 60, 67, 71–2, 80, 89–91, 94, 97; *see also* tamarin
Saimiri: *S. boliviensis* 71, 77, 80; *S. oerstedi* 63; *S. sciureus* 36, 52, 62, 64, 73, 78, 80, 100; *Saimiri* species 53, 55–7, 60, 67, 73, 77, 87, 90–1; *S. ustus* 78, 80; *see also* squirrel monkeys
sakis 33, 72; *see also Chiropotes*; *Pithecia* spp.
Salmonella: *S. bongor* 88; *S. enterica* 17, 88, 100; *Salmonella* species 86, 88–9, 100
samplers 4
sanctuaries, primate 29, 68, 98, 104
sandflies 71, 84; *see also* insects; *Lutzomyia*; *Phlebotomus*
Sapajus: *S. apella* 62, 64, 72, 78, 80–1; *S. libidinosus* 16, 35, 47; *Sapajus* species 56, 72, 74; *see also* capuchins
Sarcocystis: *S. kortei* 60; *S. nesbitti* 60; *Sarcocystis* species 60, 64; *S. suihominis* 60
Schistomatidae 106–8
Schistosoma: *S. haematobium* 107–8; *S. japonicum* 107–8; *S. mansoni* 107–8; *S. mattheei* 108; *Schistosoma* species 106–8
schistosomiasis 1, 105–8
Seadornavirus 38
Semliki Forest virus 43–4, 52–4
Semnopithecus: *S. entellus* 33, 46–9; *S. priam* 62; *Semnopithecus* species 59; *see also* langurs
sexual transmission 4–5, 30, 34, 40, 71
sex workers 4
sheep 39, 84, 90–3
Shigella: *S. boydii* 89, 100; *S. dystenteriae* 89, 101; *S. flexneri* 89, 101; *S. sonnei* 89, 101; *Shigella* species 17, 86, 89–90
shingles 23; *see also* herpes viruses: human herpes viruses
sickle-cell trait 66

simian foamy virus 39, 42–3
simian immunodeficiency virus *see* SIV
simian T-lymphotropic virus *see* STLV
simian varicella virus 24
simian virus 40 *see* SV40
Sindbis virus 43, 53–4
SIV vii, 39, 40–2, 51; SIVcpz 41–2, 51; SIVgor 41, 51; SIVsmm 16, 41–2, 51; *see also* HIV
sloths 28, 71
snails 106
spider monkeys 32–3, 40, 57, 89–90; *see also Ateles*
spillback 4, 31, 44
spillover 4–5, 7–8, 12, 16, 44, 53, 69
Spirochaetaceae 95–7
spreader 4
Spumavirus 39, 42–3
squirrel monkey 2, 10, 65, 72; *see also Saimiri*
squirrels 32, 71, 84
Staphylococcaceae 97–8, 103–4
Staphylococcus aureus 18, 97–8, 103–4; *Staphylococcus* species 97–8, 103
St. Louis encephalitis 31–2, 46
STLV 39–40, 49–51; *see also* HTLV; PTLV
Streptococcaceae 98, 104
Streptococcus species 98, 104
Streptocococcus: *Streptococcus* D 92; *S. pneumoniae* 98, 104; *S. pyogenes* 98, 104; *S. suis* 98
suids 69; *see also* pigs; swine
surveillance 9–11
SV40 25, 27
swine 22–3, 94, 98, 109; *see also* pigs; suids
Sykes monkey 72; *see also Cercopithecus*
sylvatic cycle 7–8, 28, 31, 33, 35, 44; *see also* urban cycle

tamarin 10, 18, 33, 60, 87, 94, 96–7; *see also Leontopithecus*; *Saguinus*
tapeworms *see* cestodes
tarsiers 9
ticks 3, 32, 72, 96
tigers 65
Togaviridae 43–4, 51–4
torque teno virus 22
Toxoplasma gondii 60, 64–5
Trachypithecus: *T. cristatus* 36, 106–7; *T. obscurus* 106–7; *Trachypithecus* species 59; *T. vetulus* 62
transfusion, blood 4, 22, 34, 68, 70–1
trematodes 105–6
Treponema: *T. carateum* 96; *Treponema pallidum* 95–6, 102–3; *Treponema* species 95–6
Triatoma infestans 70
trypanocidal factor 69
Trypanosoma: *T. brucei brucei* 68–9; *T. brucei* complex 68, 71–2; *T. brucei gambiense* 68–9; *T. brucei non-gamibiense* 79; *T. brucei rhodesiense* 68–9; *T. cruzi* 2, 70, 79–80; *see also* American trypanosomiasis; human African trypanosomiasis
tsetse fly *see Glossina*
turkeys 57; *see also* birds

UNA virus 52–3
urban cycle 7–8, 28, 31, 33; *see also* sylvatic cycle
urbanization 4

Varecia species 56, 103
varicella-zoster virus *see* chicken pox; herpes viruses: human herpes viruses; shingles
vector-borne parasites viii, 1, 3, 5, 7–13, 16–17, 27, 30–4, 39, 44, 54, 65–72, 84, 90, 105–6, 109
vectors: bridge vectors 8, 54
vertical transmission 5, 41, 43, 65, 68, 70, 71
Vibrio cholorae 17
viral chatter 11
virulence 3–4
viruses: category viii, 1, 3, 7, 19, 109; *see also* specific viruses

warfare 19
water-borne 5–7, 17, 22, 55–9, 65, 70, 83, 85–6, 88–90, 94, 97, 108–9
water buffalo 27

West Nile virus 13, 32, 46
World Health Organization 1, 6
Wuchereria bancrofti 105–6

xenotransplanation 6

yaws 95–6; *see also Treponema pallidum*
yellow fever 7–8, 30, 33–4, 43–4, 46–7, 109
Yersinia: *Y. enterocolitica* 90–1; *Y. pestis* 90; *Y. pseudotuberculosis* 90–1, 101; *Yersina* species 17, 86, 90–1

zebras 69
Zika virus vii, 4, 7, 16, 28, 30, 34–5, 47, 109–10
zoo exposure to parasites, human *see occupational exposure*
zoo exposure to parasites, non-human primates *see* captive primates, exposure to parasites
zoonosis defined 1–2

For Product Safety Concerns and Information please contact our EU
representative GPSR@taylorandfrancis.com Taylor & Francis Verlag GmbH,
Kaufingerstraße 24, 80331 München, Germany

Printed and bound by CPI Group (UK) Ltd, Croydon, CR0 4YY
11/04/2025
01844009-0017